To
Sam, Dan the Man, and Captain Christopher

Studies in
Writing & Rhetoric

IN 1980, THE CONFERENCE ON COLLEGE COMPOSITION AND COM-
munication perceived a need for providing publishing opportunities
for monographs that were too lengthy for publication in its journal
and too short for the typical publication of scholarly books by the
National Council of Teachers of English. A series called Studies in
Writing and Rhetoric was conceived, and a Publication Committee
established.

Monographs to be considered for publication may be speculative,
theoretical, historical, or analytical studies; research reports; or
other works contributing to a better understanding of writing, including interdisciplinary studies or studies in disciplines related to
composing. The SWR series will exclude textbooks, unrevised dis-
sertations, book-length manuscripts, course syllabi, lesson plans,
and collections of previously published material.

Any teacher-writer interested in submitting a work for publication in this series should send either a prospectus and sample manuscript or a full manuscript to the NCTE Coordinator of Professional
Publications, 1111 Kenyon Road, Urbana, IL 61801. Accompanied
by sample manuscript, a prospectus should contain a rationale, a
definition of readership within the CCCC constituency, comparison
with related publications, an annotated table of contents, an estimate of length in double-spaced 8½ × 11 sheets, and the date by
which full manuscript can be expected. Manuscripts should be in
the range of 100 to 170 typed manuscript pages.

The works that have been published in this series serve as models
for future SWR monographs.

NCTE Coordinator of Professional Publications

Rhetoric and Reality
Writing Instruction in American Colleges, 1900–1985

James A. Berlin

WITH A FOREWORD BY DONALD C. STEWART

Published for the Conference on College
Composition and Communication

SOUTHERN ILLINOIS UNIVERSITY PRESS
Carbondale and Edwardsville

Production of works in this series has been partly funded by the Conference on College Composition and Communication of the National Council of Teachers of English.

Printed in the United States of America
Edited by Marilyn R. Davis
Designed by Design for Publishing, Inc., Bob Nance
Production supervised by Natalia Nadraga

90 89 88 87   4 3 2 1

Library of Congress Cataloging-in-Publication Data

Berlin, James A.
  Rhetoric and reality.

  (Studies in writing & rhetoric)
  "Published for the Conference on College
Composition and Communication."
  Bibliography: p.
  Includes index.
  1. English language—Rhetoric—Study and teaching—
United States—History. I. Conference on College
Composition and Communication (U.S.) II. Title.
III. Series.
PE1405.U6B473 1987   808'.042'071173   86-20428
ISBN 0-8093-1360-X

Contents

Foreword
Donald C. Stewart

BECAUSE I BELIEVE THAT IGNORANCE OF THE HISTORY OF OUR profession, particularly ignorance of the history of writing instruction, is the single greatest deficiency in the majority of this nation's English teachers, and because I believe that we have just come through a remarkable period in which we have reexamined and re-evaluated many old assumptions about the teaching of writing and have thus arrived at a moment of temporary intellectual exhaustion, poised to retreat and retrench once again, James Berlin's *Rhetoric and Reality: Writing Instruction in American Colleges, 1900–1985* arrives at a most opportune time.

In this work, an extension of his earlier monograph, *Writing Instruction in Nineteenth-Century American Colleges,* Berlin identifies three epistemological categories—objective, subjective, and transactional—that have dominated rhetorical theory and practice in the twentieth century. "I have chosen epistemology rather than ideology as the basis for my taxonomy," he says, ". . . because it allows for a closer focus on the rhetorical properties—as distinct from the economic, social, or political properties—of the systems considered." But he does not neglect ideology and in so doing challenges his readers to examine not only the epistemology that informs but the ideology that is served by what they do, day by day, in the composition classroom. For example, composition teaching which places greatest emphasis on copyreading skills and limited concepts of usage and organization, whether or not one wishes to call it current-traditional (recent bantering about the validity of the terms, "current-traditional," should not draw our attention away from the fact that whatever one wishes to call it, it is a pedagogy which is deeply rooted still in the American high school and college classroom), is grounded in a positivist epistemology which assumes that reality is located in an empirically verifiable material world which it is the duty of a writer to represent as accurately as possible. Furthermore, this kind of composition teaching has been popular because it serves an upwardly mobile managerial class in our society.

In addition to current traditional rhetoric, Berlin finds three other objective rhetorics—behaviorist, semanticist, and linguistic—appearing in this century. As one would expect, Korzybski, Hayakawa, Fries, Chomsky, Skinner, and Zoellner all receive attention in this section. I might add that his analysis of Zoellner's controversial *College English* monograph (January 1969) is the first really intelligent assessment of that work and its place in twentieth century composition theory and practice that I have seen.

His second category, subjective theories, which "locate truth either within the individual or within a realm that is accessible only through the individual's internal apprehension," have their roots in Platonic idealism modified somewhat by Emerson and Thoreau in the nineteenth century and encouraged by twentieth-century depth psychology. The best-known recent advocates of the subjective approach are D. Gordon Rohman and Albert O. Wlecke whose work with prewriting represented a sharp and distinctive break away from current-traditional rhetoric.

Berlin defines the third of his categories, "transactional theories," as those which "are based on an epistemology that sees truth as arising out of the interaction of the elements of the rhetorical situation." Included in this group are classical, cognitive, and epistemic rhetorics, the last of which is clearly most congenial to him.

The organization of the book is straightforward. After his overview of the entire work, Berlin summarizes the nineteenth century background and then takes up the various rhetorical theories he defines, in twenty-year blocks from 1900 to 1960, and in the fifteen-year period from 1960 to 1975. He concludes with some generalizations about developments from 1975 to 1985.

I find it difficult to express fully my admiration for the work that James Berlin has done. The scope of this project is huge and the author's coverage stunning. He has had to examine an enormous mass of pedagogical material and, assisted by intellectual histories of our century, generalize about it in meaningful and significant ways.

The sheer effort of assimilating this material occasionally leads the author into composing the "box," as Winston Weathers calls it, but it may well be that the organizational box is the only vehicle in this situation enabling both writer and reader to keep some sense of direction in the entire study.

For several reasons, pedagogical, philosophical, and professional, this is a hugely significant book. Professor Berlin establishes at the outset the legitimacy of rhetoric and composition as a field of study and the absurdity of demeaning it as essentially remedial work. (The knowledgeable reader remembers, with no small degree of irony, the fact that one hundred years ago the classicists demeaned modern languages and literature as the accomplishments of educated gentlemen, not as legitimate fields of study in a university, and said, in effect, that work in these areas should be taken care of in the high schools.) Furthermore, Berlin notes that rhetoric (the production of discourse) and poetics (the interpretation of it) have historically been linked and that both are pluralistic terms. "Rhetoric" has really meant "rhetorics," both over its long history and at particular moments in that history. And its variety, as great as that of poetics, has come from the fact that different rhetorics are grounded in different epistemologies and ideologies.

In essence, Berlin has drawn a map of the territory we call English, particularly the teaching of writing, in the twentieth century. Not everyone will agree with all the details of his map—I do not even agree with all of them myself—but those disagreements are superficial and must not obscure the significance of what he has done. He has told us who we are and why we think the way we do about the field of English.

Parochialism in our field will undoubtedly persist, but because of this book, it can no longer be excused. The literary critic, the bibliographer, the literary historian, and the editor who continue to insist that the primary business of the English department is the examination and interpretation of literary texts; the composition teacher who is committed to a particular "method" without any awareness of the historical and intellectual slot that method occupies; these must henceforth be regarded as anachronisms, impeding the work of an English department with a broad and deep perspective on its past and a comprehensive view of its structure and mission in the years to come.

Acknowledgments

I WOULD LIKE TO THANK THE UNIVERSITY RESEARCH COUNCIL
of the University of Cincinnati for a summer grant and Fred Milne,
my department head, for arranging a term leave—both of which
contributed greatly to my completing this manuscript. The National
Endowment for the Humanities generously provided a year with
Richard Young at Carnegie-Mellon University and a summer with
Sheldon Rothblatt at the University of California, Berkeley. I am
also grateful to the English department of the University of Texas at
Austin for inviting me to be a visiting professor during the time this
manuscript was being completed. Lucy Schultz, my associate director of freshman English at Cincinnati, has also been generous in assuming more than her share of the workload during my absences.

I want to thank a number of people who introduced me to rhetoric
and in one way or another have contributed to my study of it:
Sharon Bassett, Lisa Ede, David Fractenberg, Bob Inkster, Charles
Kneupper, Victor Vitanza, Sam Watson, Vickie Winkler, and the late
Bill Nelson, a leader whom we all miss. A number of people read
and criticized this monograph along the way: Lester Faigley, Locke
Carter, John Fracasso, Kay Halasek, David Harvey, Mara Holt, Fred
Kemp, Greg Lyons, and Rick Penticoff. I thank them for their sug-
gestions and absolve them of any responsibility for the final text.

I am also grateful to Paul O'Dea of the National Council of Teachers of English, to Kenney Withers of Southern Illinois University
Press, and to NCTE's Publications Committee for Studies in Writing
and Rhetoric for their support and encouragement throughout.

Finally, I want to thank my family—Sam, my wife, for deciding to be a potter, a vocation that has made her willing to travel, and Dan and Christopher, our sons, who have tolerated numerous disruptions in their lives as their father pursued his unholy quests. You have given me much more than I have deserved.

Rhetoric and Reality

1

An Overview

LITERACY HAS ALWAYS AND EVERYWHERE BEEN THE CENTER of the educational enterprise. No matter what else it expects of its schools, a culture insists that students learn to read, write, and speak in the officially sanctioned manner. It is for this reason that rhetoric, the production of spoken and written texts, and poetic, the interpretation of texts, have been the indispensable foundation of schooling, regardless of the age or intellectual level of the student. In this study, I will examine the forms that rhetorical instruction in writing has taken in the twentieth-century college classroom. In so doing, however, I will also be glancing at the corresponding developments in poetic. Considering both will be necessary for two reasons. Writing and reading have from the start been lodged in the same department in the modern university. More important, as Tzvetan Todorov, Kenneth Burke, and Charles Sears Baldwin have demonstrated, rhetoric and poetic historically have enjoyed a dialectical relationship, the one's functions being defined and determined by the other's. I will thus be concerned with the way in which writing instruction has been shaped by instruction in literature and, correspondingly, the ways in which approaches to literary interpretation have been affected by methods of teaching the production of rhetorical texts. My main focus, however, will be on rhetoric.

My reading of the rhetorical history of this period tends to vindicate the position of writing instruction in the college curriculum—particularly the freshman course, a primary concern of this study. While such vindication is superfluous for anyone knowledgeable about the history of rhetoric or the history of education—the two always having been closely related—I am aware that many in English studies are unfamiliar with this background, especially since historical considerations have been for quite some time out of favor in literature classrooms. Even if we forget for the moment that Aristotle, Cicero, Quintilian, and Augustine all considered rhetoric to be the center of learning and were themselves specialists in the teaching of rhetoric, a glance at the Anglo-American experience in university education demonstrates closer to home that rhetoric has continually been an essential feature of college training. In the nineteenth century, for example, instruction in speaking and writing was a principal feature of the college curriculum in America, and until about 1850 the dominant texts used were three imports from British universities—the works of George Campbell, Hugh Blair, and Richard Whately. Campbell wrote his *Philosophy of Rhetoric* (1776) while he served as professor of divinity and principal of Marischal College, Aberdeen. The work, a theoretical treatise, was designed to establish the philosophical ground for the discipline that served as the core of the curriculum. Blair was Regius Professor of Rhetoric and Belles Lettres at the University of Edinburgh when he presented classroom lectures that were collected in *Lectures on Rhetoric and Belles Lettres* (1783), a volume that went through 130 editions by 1911. And Whately's *Elements of Rhetoric* (1828), written while he was principal of St. Alban's Hall, Oxford, was intended for his divinity students—among whom was John Henry Newman.

This brief sketch underscores the fact that writing instruction was an integral part of the British and American college systems at a time when only the well-endowed and the well-prepared were in attendance. Instruction in rhetoric was in no way considered remedial, designed only for those who should have mastered it in the lower schools. It was instead regarded as a necessary concern of the college curriculum. To have suggested to Campbell, Blair, Whately, or their American counterparts—Samuel Newman or Henry Day, for example—that instruction in rhetoric was the exclusive duty of the lower schools would have been as outrageous as suggesting to the chair of any English department today that students have learned in high school all that they need to know about interpreting literary texts, and that they might better spend their college days pursuing other courses of study. Most college teachers today, within and without the English department, would agree that students need additional experience in interpreting literary texts, both to improve their ability to read with understanding and to inform their personal, social, and professional lives. This history is intended to demonstrate that writing instruction is no less essential for college students. As beginning students encounter an overwhelming array of new ideas and new ways of thinking, the rhetorical training they bring with them inevitably proves—regardless of their intelligence or training—unequal to the task of dealing with their new intellectual experience. It is for this reason that the freshman writing course in college has remained a part of the curriculum throughout the century, despite the calls from a small minority for its abolition and the broadly publicized removals of it as a requirement—removals that are almost invariably followed by a quiet reinstatement in one form or another. Rhetoric has been a permanent and central part of the college curriculum throughout the twentieth century, just as it had been for the previous three centuries in American and British universities.

A few preliminary theoretical matters must now be considered. My studies in the history of rhetoric—both the standard surveys of George Kennedy, James Murphy, Edward P. J. Corbett, and the like, and my own examination of primary materials—have convinced me that rhetoric is no more a monolithic field than is poetic. In other words, the term *rhetoric* refers to a diverse discipline that historically has included a variety of incompatible systems. While one particular rhetorical theory may predominate at any historical moment, none remains dominant over time. Each major system is destined to be replaced eventually. Thus, we ought not to talk about *rhetoric* but, as Paolo Valesio has recently suggested, of *rhetorics*, seeing the field as providing a variety equal to that of poetic. This diachronic diversity in rhetoric is matched by a synchronic one. At any historical moment, it is common to discover a number of different rhetorics, each competing for attention and claiming to be the one, true system. The difference in these rhetorics is not—as I have shown in *Writing Instruction in Nineteenth-Century American Colleges*—a matter of the superficial emphasis of one or another feature of the rhetorical act. The difference has to do with epistemology—with assumptions about the very nature of the known, the knower, and the discourse community involved in considering the known. A brief consideration of this matter will be useful.

In opening this discussion, I emphasized that literacy involves a particular variety of rhetoric—a way of speaking and writing within the confines of specific social sanctions. This is possible because every rhetorical system is based on epistemological assumptions about the nature of reality, the nature of the knower, and the rules governing the discovery and communication of the known. These matters, of course, converge with the elements of the rhetorical triangle: reality, interlocutor, audience, and language. A particular rhetoric thus instructs students about the nature of genuine knowledge, or truth—sometimes, for example, located in the material world, sometimes in a private perception of a spiritual realm, sometimes in group acquiescence, sometimes in language itself, sometimes in one or another dialectical permutation of these elements. The nature of truth will in turn determine the roles of the interlocutor (the writer or speaker) and the audience in discovering and communicating it. It is important to keep in mind that as the conception of the real alters—as a society or class or group moves from, say, a positivistic to a phenomenological orientation—the roles of interlocutor, audience, and language itself undergo a corresponding alteration. Furthermore, because societies are constantly changing it is common to find more than one rhetoric at any single moment—a simple result of there commonly being more than one epistemology competing for attention at any given time.

The transformations that occur in a society's rhetorics are also related to larger social and political developments. In taking into account this relationship, we are in an area of thought commonly designated as ideology. Here the term will be used in its most descriptive and neutral sense, in the manner, for example, of the literary critic Sacvan Bercovitch, the anthropologist Clifford Geertz, or the Neo-Marxist political theorist Göran Therborn—all three seeking in different ways to rid the term of its doctrinaire associations. Ideology will simply refer to the pluralistic conceptions of social and political arrangements that are present in a society at any given time. These conceptions are based on discursive (verbal) and non-discursive (nonverbal) formations designating the shape of social and political structures, the nature and role of the individual within these structures, and the distribution of power in society. It is not difficult to see the close relationship between these elements and the elements of the rhetorical context—the individual interlocutor, material reality, the audience, and language. The plurality of competing rhetorics is always related to the plurality of competing ideologies. Ordinarily, one particular rhetoric is dominant—the rhetoric embodying the ideology of a powerful group or class—but the exclusion of all other rhetorics is never completely achieved, not even in a totalitarian state where the effort to do so is common. In a democracy, those whose power is based on a particular notion of rhetoric (for example, a rhetoric maintaining that only certified experts may speak or write, or only those who have attained a certain level of financial success) will likewise restrict challenges to their conception of rhetoric because such challenges constitute a threat to their continued claim to eminence. They too are intolerant of alternative rhetorics. A democracy, however, ordinarily provides political and social supports for open discussion, allowing for the free play of possibilities in the rhetorics that appear—although these possibilities are obviously never unlimited.

In examining the variety of rhetorics that have appeared in the English departments of American colleges in the twentieth century, I will be looking simultaneously at several patterns. I will be concerned with the rhetorical theories that have appeared, as well as with the epistemological and ideological elements to which they are related. But I want also to examine the concrete classroom practices to which these theories have led. I will thus be as concerned with what the authors of articles and textbooks say they are attempting as with their pedagogical strategies for achieving their aims. Changes in rhetorical theory and practice will be related to changes in the notion of literacy, as indicated by developments in the college curriculum. The curriculum, in turn, is always responsive to the changing economic, social, and political conditions in a society. Obviously, the kind of graduates colleges prepare have a great deal to do with the conditions in the society for which they are preparing them. This study will demonstrate that the college writing course, a requirement for graduation for most students throughout the century, responds quickly to changes in American society as a whole, with literacy (as variously defined by the college curriculum over the years) serving as the intermediary between the two—between the writing course and larger social developments. Finally, I would hope that the study of the dynamics of change in writing classes during the present century will serve as a guide in charting the course of composition instruction in the future.

Theories of Rhetoric

I would like now to consider in outline the major rhetorical theories found during the century. My reasons for doing so here are numerous. It will be helpful to have an overview of the approaches that will later be discussed in greater detail. This history, moreover, will be less concerned with theoretical matters than with offering a chronicle of events. But there is an even more compelling justification for considering theoretical matters here. As I will show, writing instruction during the century has suffered from the failure of both its supporters and its detractors to conceive of alternatives to the positivistic rhetoric that has dominated the teaching field until just recently. Rhetoric for most English professors has meant one theory and one theory only, and the fact that past and present have provided alternative models has gone largely unnoticed. I will consider the reasons for this obtuseness in the next chapter. For now, I offer the following as an introduction to the rich diversity of thought on rhetoric that has appeared in this century despite an environment that has often been unfriendly to innovation.

In considering the rhetorical theories of the period, I have chosen epistemology rather than ideology as the basis for my taxonomy, doing so because it allows for a closer focus on the rhetorical properties—as distinct from the economic, social, or political properties—of the systems considered. (Ideology, however, as already noted, is always present by imbrication.) I have accordingly divided these theories into three epistemological categories: the objective, the subjective, and the transactional. Objective theories locate reality in the external world, in the material objects of experience. Subjective theories place truth within the subject, to be discovered through an act of internal apprehension. And transactional theories locate reality at the point of interaction of subject and object, with audience and language as mediating agencies. It should be noted that none of the categories is monolithic; each offers a diversity of rhetorical theories. I should also add that this taxonomy is not meant to be taken as exhaustive of the entire field of rhetoric, but is simply an attempt to make manageable the discussion of the major rhetorics I have encountered in examining this period. In discussing the separate categories, I will focus on the ways in which the elements of the rhetorical situation are defined and related to each other—that is, on the ways in which each theory conceives the nature of the real, the interlocutor, the audience, and the function of language. This emphasis is not for mere convenience, however. As I have already indicated, in teaching writing we are providing students with guidance in seeing and structuring their experience, with a set of tacit rules about distinguishing truth from falsity, reality from illusion. A way of seeing, after all, is a way of not seeing, and as we instruct students in attending to particular orders of evidence—sense impression, for example, in the injunction to "be concrete"—we are simultaneously discouraging them from seeing other orders of evidence—in the present example, the evidence of private vision or of social arrangements. Our decision, then, about the kind of rhetoric we are to call upon in teaching writing has important implications for the behavior of our students—behavior that includes the personal, social, and political. As the present study will show, there have been teachers in every decade of this century who fortunately have been fully aware of the consequences of their teaching in the larger experience of their students, writing instructors whose methods deserve close attention.

Objective Theories

Objective rhetorics are based on a positivistic epistemology, asserting that the real is located in the material world. From this perspective, only that which is empirically verifiable or which can be grounded in empirically verifiable phenomena is real. The business of the writer is to record this reality exactly as it has been experienced so that it can be reproduced in the reader. Language here is a sign system, a simple transcribing device for recording that which exists apart from the verbal. The dominant form of this approach in the twentieth century has been what is called current-traditional rhetoric. I have traced the development of this rhetoric in my *Writing Instruction in Nineteenth-Century American Colleges*, and C. H. Knoblauch and Lil Brannon in *Rhetorical Traditions and the Teaching of Writing* have devoted a chapter to its classroom procedures. Here I would like briefly to describe its epistemology and its classroom concerns in order to demonstrate the features of an objective rhetoric. I will also indicate three other varieties of this genre that appeared later in the century.

For current-traditional rhetoric, reality is located in the material world. Based on Scottish Common Sense Realism, the most influential philosophy in America during the nineteenth century, this position argues that the mind is equipped with faculties that enable it to perceive the external object directly through the medium of sense impression. Truth is determined through the inductive method—through collecting sense data and arriving at generalizations. The role of the observer is to be as "objective" as possible, necessitating the abandonment of social, psychological, and historical preconceptions that might interfere with the response of the faculties to the external world. The responsibility of the observer, then, is to engage in an innocent reaction to sense impression, examining it without allowing any distortion to occur. Once the truth is determined through observation, the next task is to find the language to describe one's discoveries. Truth, located first in nature and then in the response of the faculties to nature, exists prior to language. Language is regarded at worst as a distorting medium that alters the original perception, and at best as a transparent device that captures the original experience so that it might be reproduced in the faculties of one's audience. The audience is likewise outside of the meaning-making act. It is also assumed to be as objective as the writer, so that the language presented can stimulate in the reader the experience that the writer originally had.

It is important to note that the source of current-traditional rhetoric is to be found in the work of Campbell, Blair, and Whately, as well as in their nineteenth-century American imitators. In the former it is saved from being purely mechanistic by concern for the role of emotion in providing motivation for the pursuit of the ethical in persuasive discourse. In the hands of A. S. Hill and Barrett Wendell of Harvard and John F. Genung of Amherst in the late nineteenth century, however, this rhetoric abandoned concern for the ethical as it became completely positivistic in intent. In this approach, truth in written discourse is conceived exclusively in empirical and rational terms, with emotion and persuasion relegated to oral discourse. The writing class is to focus on discourse that deals with the rational faculties: description and narration to be concerned with sense impression and imagination (the image-making faculty), exposition with "setting forth" the generalized ideas derived from sense impression and understanding, and argument with understanding leading to conviction. This rhetoric is subservient to the ends of science and is no longer concerned with the probabilistic nature of value in the legal, political, and social spheres. As I will demonstrate in the next chapter, the fact that current-traditional rhetoric appeared in response to the new scientific curriculum of the modern American university had a great deal to do with this positivistic cast. For now, it should be noted that this rhetoric makes the patterns of arrangement and superficial correctness the main ends of writing instruction. Invention, the focus of Aristotelian rhetoric, need not be taught since the business of the writer is to record careful observations or the reports of fellow observers (in the research paper, for example). In the world of current-traditional rhetoric, all truths are regarded as certain, readily available to the correct method of investigation. Even the probabilistic realms of ethics and politics are regarded as ultimately amenable to the scientific method, as the university-sponsored approaches of the social and behavioral sciences attempt to demonstrate.

Current-traditional rhetoric thus teaches the modes of discourse, with a special emphasis on exposition and its forms—analysis, classification, cause-effect, and so forth. However, it also pays special attention to language, doing so for important reasons. Since language is arbitrary and enters into meaning only after the truth is discovered, the writer must take pains that language not distort what is to be communicated. Language must thus be precise. Since it is to reproduce in the reader the experience of the original observer, it must also possess energy and vivacity. Finally, since language is to demonstrate the individual's qualifications as a reputable observer worthy of attention, it must conform to certain standards of usage, thereby demonstrating the appropriate class affiliation.

Current-traditional rhetoric has been the most pervasive of objective rhetorics in the last hundred years and, in fact, the dominant rhetoric overall. For the majority of English teachers, it has been a compelling paradigm, making it impossible for them to conceive of the discipline in any other way. There have been three other varieties of objective rhetoric, however, that have attracted a following: behaviorist, semanticist, and linguistic rhetorics.

The use of behavioral psychology in writing instruction appeared in its most detailed and best-known form in Robert Zoellner's 1969 *College English* article entitled "Talk-Write: A Behavioral Pedagogy for Composition." Zoellner attempted to apply the principles of

B. F. Skinner's psychology of learning to writing instruction, arguing that teaching and learning ought to be conceived of as observable, empirically verifiable behavior. According to this view, writing can be taught as a variety of operant conditioning in which the student is given reinforcement when appropriate writing behavior is demonstrated. The complexity of Zoellner's approach and its effects on writing instruction will be considered in a later chapter. Here it is important only to note that the epistemology underlying this approach is identical to that of current-traditional rhetoric.

Semanticist rhetoric received its initial statement in the General Semantics theory of Alfred Korzybski, but was developed and popularized by S. I. Hayakawa. Arising in the thirties when the United States was concerned about the threat posed by Germany, General Semantics was first offered as a device for propaganda analysis. During the ensuing war and afterward, it came to be seen as a useful approach to the teaching of reading and writing. Semanticist rhetoric focuses on the distortions that are introduced in communication through the misuse of language. It is important to note, however, that this rhetoric assumes an objective reality, a fixed and incontestable notion of truth that language attempts to capture in order that it be transferred to the mind of another. In this system language has nothing to do with the discovery of meaning; its function is to serve as a transparent medium of communication, with the principles of General Semantics serving as a guide to avoiding distortion. Semanticist rhetoric was also highly influential in the communications course—the course that combined instruction in reading, writing, speaking, and listening, occupying a large place in the general education movement in the thirties, forties, and fifties.

Finally, the appearance of structural linguistics in the English department in the fifties and sixties at first promised to create a new rhetoric based on the scientific study of language. The composition class, it was thought, would have its own subject matter, the structure of language, and with it an effective method for teaching writing. This faith persisted among many—although there were plenty of detractors from the start—until the challenge of transformational grammar took over the field in language study, making many distrustful of the hope for a new rhetoric growing out of linguistics. Structural linguistics was even more limited than semantics in its

claim to explain the problems that arise in communication. However, it shared the same epistemology, a conviction that the empirical study of the structure of language would serve as a model for
the empirical investigation that is at the heart of rhetoric. In other
words, structural linguistics implied a positivistic view of reality and
was thus another type of objective rhetoric.

Perhaps the best way to characterize the nature of truth in objective rhetorics is to recall Descartes's discussion of rhetoric in his
Discourse on Method: "Every time that two men speaking of one
and the same thing put forth opposite judgments, it is certain that
one of them is wrong; and, what is more, neither knows the truth,
for if one of them had a clear and distinct opinion, he would eventually force others to agree" (qtd. in Florescu 195–96). Truth is prior
to language, is clearly and distinctly available to the person who
views it in the proper spirit, and is ultimately communicable in clear
and distinct terms. Disagreement has always to do with faulty observation, faulty language, or both, and never is due to the problematic
and contingent nature of truth.

Subjective Theories

Subjective theories of rhetoric locate truth either within the individual or within a realm that is accessible only through the individual's internal apprehension, apart from the empirically verifiable
sensory world. The most obvious historical precedents for this approach to rhetoric are in Plato and, more recently, in one of the
strands of Emerson's thought on rhetoric (Berlin, *Writing Instruction*, ch. 5). Thoreau also is often called upon by the proponents of
this approach. Their influence was the strongest in the rhetoric of
liberal culture, an aristocratic and elitist rhetoric that appeared in
certain Eastern colleges during the first two decades of this century.
The most immediate sources of subjective theories for college writing courses during the twenties and thirties are found in the depth
psychology of Freud's American disciples. These theories were further encouraged by the rise of aesthetic expressionism and by the
experiments in childhood education conducted by the proponents
of progressive education. In the English department, subjective
rhetorics were also supported by schools of literary criticism based
on Crocean idealism and, later, depth psychology. In more recent

time—the sixties and seventies—subjective rhetorics were influenced by cognitive psychology, by the post-Freudian psychology of such figures as Carl Rogers and Abraham Maslow, and by English department interpretations of romanticism as found, for example, in M. H. Abrams.

Rhetorics that are grounded in philosophical idealism commonly present a subjectivist stance. The most frequently cited example is in Plato. Truth here transcends the mutable material world, being located in an unchanging realm of ideas. This supersensory realm can be discovered by the individual through private vision. Ordinarily, however, it cannot be expressed. Truth can thus be known but not shared, not communicated. The business of rhetoric in such a scheme is to correct error as one speaker engages in a dialogue with another, each sharing a dialectical interchange in which mistaken notions are exposed. This purging of the false then prepares them to perceive the true through an individual act of visionary perception (Cushman).

This view of rhetoric makes the speaker a Jeremiah, a harsh critic who reveals to us our wickedness. There is another interpretation of the rhetoric of Plato, however, that allows for a more comprehensive conception of rhetoric (Richard Weaver). Here the basic epistemology is the same: truth transcends the material realm, is attainable through a solitary vision, and resists expression. In this interpretation, though, the possibilities of rhetoric are expanded by calling on a different conception of language. While ordinary language refers to the material world and thus cannot express the realm of ultimate truth, it is possible through the use of original metaphor to suggest the supersensory. Thus, the speaker or writer can offer positive knowledge as well as correct error. It is important to add, however, that truth can be passed on from one individual to another only in a limited sense. Truth must still be discovered by the individual in a private act. The suggestions of the permanently valid that are offered by the gifted speaker or writer must be confirmed in and through the individual's personal experience. Thus, an interlocutor can suggest truths already discovered by her auditor or she can suggest truths not yet discovered. In the case of the latter, the truths can be accepted as authentic only if and when they are confirmed through the auditor's personal experience, through her own private confirmation in an act of intuition. This phenomenon accounts for the visionary, the individual whose prophetic words go unheeded until the truth is finally confirmed by the perceptions of others.

This conception of rhetoric creates special difficulties for the teacher. Since truth must finally be discovered or, at the least, confirmed through a private act of intuition, the teacher cannot communicate truth. Indeed, the teacher cannot even instruct the student in the principles of writing, since writing is inextricably intertwined with the discovery of truth. The student can discover truth, but truth cannot be taught; the student can learn to write, but writing cannot be taught. The only strategy left, then, is to provide an environment in which the individual can learn what cannot be taught. This environment must include provisions for encouraging the expression of private versions of experience couched in original metaphors, metaphors which show by their freshness and uniqueness that they are not simply imitative reports of the vision of others.

Before outlining this approach in the twentieth-century college classroom, I would like to examine how this rhetoric of philosophical idealism is encouraged by the findings of modern depth psychology. While Freud claimed the status of science for psychology, the way his thought was adapted by Americans for the classroom transformed it into an echo of the optimistic strands of American romanticism (Cremin, 210). According to this reading of Freud, truth is discovered through looking within in a private act of intuition which each person must make alone. The expression of this private vision is never direct, never discursive, but always suggested through metaphor. This is the realm of the dream world of displacement and condensation. The roles of the psychiatrist and the subjectivist writing teacher have important similarities. The Freudian therapist is nondirective, encouraging the individual to arrive at an understanding of the unconscious forces working themselves out in behavior. The therapist can never cure the patient by explaining to him his difficulties, even though the therapist may thoroughly understand them. The situation of the writing teacher is similar in that she is unable to tell the student the truth or the way to express it. Her task is to provide an environment in which individual students are allowed the freedom to arrive at their own versions of truth. One final similarity ought to be mentioned. While Freud himself looked upon the repression of certain unconscious desires as appropriate, normal, and necessary—dangerous only when its excessiveness caused psychic harm—many Americans have interpreted Freud to mean that unconscious desire, like the Platonic realm of ideal truth, is inherently good. Attempts at repression are thus interpreted as dangerous to normal, healthy development and destructive of authenticity and self-realization (Cremin 207–11; Hoffman, ch. 3).

The pedagogy encouraged by this rhetorical theory revolves around three central activities, each designed to teach the unteachable by fostering a learning environment that encourages private vision. These activities are the search for original metaphor, the keeping of a journal, and participation in peer editorial groups. Since the unconscious manifests itself through such strategies as condensation and displacement, it is never accessible except through tropical language. Furthermore, it is only through the unique metaphor that the individual can express her unique vision. As a result, metaphor is encouraged in these classes, sometimes through exercises in analogy or in defining terms metaphorically (happiness is . . .). The keeping of a journal is important because it encourages the individual to record her observations of the world in her own unique way. Studying these observations, however, is designed not to promote learning about the external world, but to get the student to see the way she perceives and structures her experience. In other words, these observations allow the individual to study the extent to which her response to experience is unique or imitative, doing so in order to cultivate an original, creative perspective. This perspective at once enhances the quality of life and leads to the private perception of ultimate truths, truths which the conventions of society prevent us from realizing. Finally, peer group editing is used so that students may discover what is inauthentic in their writing. The editors obviously cannot tell the student how to arrive at truth or how to express it. They serve instead as friendly critics, pointing out when the writer has been inauthentic (bureaucratic voice, clichéd language, and the like), trying in this way to lead the writer to authenticity in voice and vision. However, they are never to serve as an audience whom the writer attempts to please or accommodate. The writer's only concern is to be true to her personal vision, regardless of the reservations of others.

Transactional Theories

Transactional rhetoric is based on an epistemology that sees truth as arising out of the interaction of the elements of the rhetorical situation: an interaction of subject and object or of subject and audience or even of all the elements—subject, object, audience, and language—operating simultaneously. The three major forms of transactional rhetoric in the twentieth-century writing class have been the classical, the cognitive, and the epistemic. The classical, seen early in the century in the work of Baldwin, underwent a renaissance in the fifties and sixties. The cognitive did not appear until the sixties and seventies, when it emerged in the work of such figures as Janet Emig, Janice Lauer, and Frank D'Angelo. The epistemic got a start in the speculation of Fred Newton Scott in the first two decades of the century, reappeared in attenuated form in the thirties, and then came into its own in the sixties and seventies—in, for example, the work of Richard Ohmann, Ann Berthoff, and the team of Richard Young, Alton Becker, and Kenneth Pike. Because of the variety of transactional rhetorics, it is difficult to discuss them succinctly, their theory and classroom practices being so broad. Here I will briefly outline only the general features of each major type.

The most common form of transactional rhetoric is the classical. Truth is here located in a social construct involving the interaction of interlocutor and audience (or discourse community). Science and logic are outside the rhetorical realm since both are concerned with the indisputable, with certainties that do not ordinarily lead to disagreement. The truths of rhetoric, on the other hand, are by their very nature uncertain, open to debate, contingent, probable. They deal not just with the empirical or rational analysis of experience, but with the emotional, aesthetic, and ethical—in other words, with the total range of human behavior. Arriving at truths regarding these matters, despite the difficulties, is central to the existence of individuals and society. These truths, after all, concern the basic ethical and political decisions that affect the safety of all; they concern the distribution of power in legislation, the courts, and social groups. In arriving at decisions about these matters, science and logic can be helpful, but ultimately choices are made on the basis of public discourse—individuals working together within a community of discourse trying to decide what will be in the best interests of the group and the individual. The crucial feature of these transactional activities is that new knowledge, new truths, emerge from the interaction. The rhetorical act discovers meaning in its proper realm, just as the scientific act discovers meaning in its own sphere.

Cognitive approaches to rhetoric grew out of the psychological studies of such figures as Jerome Bruner and Jean Piaget. The epistemology of these rhetorics assumes a correspondence between the structures of the mind and the structures of nature. The mind, furthermore, passes through a series of stages in achieving maturity. The work of the writing teacher, then, is to understand these basic cognitive structures and the way they develop in order to provide experiences for students that encourage normal development and prevent structural distortions. The teacher intervenes in the composing process of students in order to ensure that their cognitive structures are functioning normally, thus enhancing their ability to arrive at truth in examining the external world. The emphasis in this classroom is on the individual, but the individual is conceived of as inherently transactional, arriving at truth through engaging the surrounding material and social environment.

Epistemic rhetoric posits a transaction that involves all elements of the rhetorical situation: interlocutor, audience, material reality, and language. The most significant difference is that language enters into this transaction and is present in every instance of its manifestation. The reason for this is that interlocutor, audience, and material world are all regarded as verbal constructs. Classical transactional rhetoric conceives of realms of human behavior in which language is not significant—the areas of science and logic—and the same can be said for the cognitive position. These theories, furthermore, regard language as being representative of nonsymbolic activities and divide even the social into the nonverbal and the verbal, the latter serving as mere signs for the former. In epistemic rhetoric there is never a division between experience and language, whether the experience involves the subject, the subject and other subjects, or the subject and the material world. All experiences, even the scientific and logical, are grounded in language, and language determines their content and structure. And just as language structures our response to social and political issues, language structures our response to the material world. Rhetoric thus becomes implicated in all human behavior. All truths arise out of dialectic, out of the interaction of individuals within discourse communities. Truth is never simply "out there" in the material world or the social realm, or simply "in here" in a private and personal world. It emerges only as the three—the material, the social, and the personal—interact, and the agent of mediation is language.

Before closing this chapter, I would like to include one more statement about my method. Robert Connors has recently found fault with my *Writing Instruction in Nineteenth-Century American Colleges* for its failure to be impersonal and "objective," charging it with filtering events "through powerful terministic screens" ("Review" 247, 249). His assumption here and in much of his own historical research is that it is possible to locate a neutral space, a position from which one can act as an unbiased observer in order to record a transcendental object, the historical thing-in-itself. Those who write history from this vantage point, he claims, are objective and scholarly, providing research especially developed for specialists, research which is, at its best, definitive—meaning, presumably, that its authoritativeness brings discussion to a close. Those who do not share this neutral vantage point are subjective and biased, have "an axe to grind," and offer what is, at most, "popular history" (247).

This distinction is simply untenable. As Karl Popper has argued in *The Open Society and Its Enemies*, in writing history "a point of view is inevitable; and the naive attempt to avoid it can only lead to self-deception, and to the uncritical application of an unconscious point of view" (261). Furthermore, there are the lessons learned from Kenneth Burke's work—especially his discussion in *Language as Symbolic Action* of the ineluctability of "terministic screens"— the lessons of recent Marxist theory and of French and American poststructuralist cultural critics, the lessons from the contributions of American Neo-Pragmatists—particularly Richard Rorty—and, most important here, the lessons garnered from the poststructuralist historiography of Hayden White and Michel Foucault—all strongly arguing that it is impossible to perceive any object *except* through a terministic screen. It is thus incumbent upon the historian to make every effort to be aware of the nature of her point of view and its interpretive strategies, and to be candid about them with her reader. This has been my purpose in much of this introductory chapter. I might also add—although by now it is probably not necessary—that I have been especially influenced by Burke in my understanding of rhetoric. In my historical method I have found suggestive the work of White, most notably his discussion of the relationship between modes of emplotment, modes of explanation, and modes of ideological implication. Also valuable to me has been Foucault's discussion of the relationship between knowledge and power in discourse communities, and of the role of discursive and nondiscursive practices in shaping consciousness within these communities. I should add, however, that I cannot claim to be a disciple of any one of the three.

In this history I have tried to include all major and most minor developments in the teaching of writing in American colleges between 1900 and 1985. I have been concerned with both rhetorical theory and actual classroom practice and accordingly have examined hundreds of articles in scholarly journals on literature, writing, and education, and numerous theoretical treatises and textbooks—attempting throughout to follow rigorous scholarly procedures. I have not, however, written the results of my research exclusively for specialists, and especially not for the kind of specialist who makes endless distinctions without considering their significance for the lives of those who must observe them. Douglas Ehninger long ago called for the end to the mere recording of the facts of rhetorical history and the beginning of the interpretation of these facts. I have prepared my interpretation for that large group of people who teach writing to college students—a group ranging from tenured full professors to overworked and underpaid nontenurable faculty—intending to share with them the richness of their heritage and its central place in the life of our society. I do not claim to be definitive. A great deal more needs to be said about this period, and I hope others will be encouraged by this study to do so—just as I have been encouraged and aided by John Michael Wozniak's *English Composition in Eastern Colleges, 1850–1940* and John Heyda's doctoral dissertation, *Captive Audiences: Composition Pedagogy, the Liberal Arts Curriculum, and the Rise of Mass Higher Education.*

The next chapter will provide some background on the formation of the English department and the place that rhetoric and poetic have since occupied relative to each other. The chapters that follow will pursue a chronological development: chapters 3, 4, and 5 cover twenty-year periods beginning with 1900, and chapters 6 and 7 consider the years between 1960 and 1975. Chapter 8 offers a tentative statement about the last ten years. The developments of this period, however, have been so numerous, varied, and recent that I offer only a few speculative comments about their significance.

2

The Nineteenth-Century Background

THE ENGLISH DEPARTMENT WAS A CREATION OF THE NEW
American university during the last quarter of the nineteenth century. Its prototype appeared at Harvard, the leader of the time
in curricular reform. Its initial purpose, contrary to what William
Riley Parker has argued, was to provide instruction in writing. After
all, the writing course had been firmly established as the staple of
the curriculum in the last century—a requirement for all students
during the sophomore, junior, and senior years. Although the rhetoric course originally included speaking as its major component, by
the third quarter of the century its main concern was writing instruction (Halloran; Berlin, *Writing Instruction*). The study of literature in the vernacular, on the other hand, was a rare phenomenon, occurring at only a few schools, and even there considered a
second-class undertaking (Rudolph, *Curriculum* 140). Charles William Eliot, Harvard's president from 1869 to 1909, had in fact considered writing so central to the new elective curriculum he was shaping
that in 1874 the freshman English course at Harvard was established, by 1894 was the only requirement except for a modern language, and by 1897 was the only required course in the curriculum,
consisting of a two-semester sequence. By the last date, however,
the study of English (but not as yet American) literature had become
the main concern of the department, and the place of a writing
course in the college curriculum had already been challenged at the
first meeting of the Modern Language Society (Hart). How in this
short time could writing—the core of the nineteenth-century curriculum in the sophomore, junior, and senior years—have been reduced to a single year's offering, and English literature—a study that

had no place in the old curriculum—have become the main interest of the department? In this chapter I would like to offer a brief explanation for this development and then go on to consider the relation of rhetoric and poetic in the early English department and after.

The devalorizing of the writing course in the curriculum was the result of the convergence of a remarkably complex set of forces. Raymond Williams has offered a compelling description of the larger economic, political, and social developments that led to the enthronement of the poetic text and the denigration of the rhetorical during the eighteenth and nineteenth centuries. Here I would like to focus on how these larger developments manifested themselves in the English departments of American colleges.

The "new" university had arisen to provide an agency for certifying the members of the new professions, professions that an expanding economy had created (Wiebe). These college graduates constituted a new middle class, a body claiming and receiving economic privilege and political power on the basis of its certified, professional status. The old university had been elitist and had prepared students of means and status for the three major professions: law, medicine, and the church. The new university encouraged a meritocracy, opening its doors to anyone who could meet the entrance requirements (a growing number, due to the new free high schools), offering upward mobility through certification in such professions as agriculture, engineering, journalism, social work, education, and a host of other new professional pursuits.

Members of the newly established English department were themselves a part of this quest for a certifiable, professional designation. They too were struggling to define a specialized discipline, one akin to those of their counterparts in the new science departments, in order to lay claim to the privilege and status accorded other new professions, and to serve as the certifying agency for admission to this select group (Bledstein). But why was rhetoric not made the basis of this new certifying procedure?

The old college teachers in language—the rhetoric teachers and the teachers of Latin, Hebrew, and Greek—had been devoted to undergraduate teaching, and to undergraduate teaching only. They had, furthermore, been overworked and poorly paid. The new composition teacher was not much better off. In keeping with the scientific and practical orientation of the new undergraduate curriculum, writing was taught as a practical activity, using—as John F. Genung of Amherst explained—the "laboratory method" (10). This simply meant extensive writing—in some schools, as we will see later, a daily theme. The correcting of papers could become a monumental task. At the University of Michigan in 1894, for example, four teachers and two graduate assistants were responsible for 1,198 students. The situation at Harvard was little better, with twenty teachers handling 2,000 writing students. Furthermore, to have suggested that the new English department might also provide instruction in historical rhetoric—in, for example, the works of Aristotle, Cicero, Quintilian, or Augustine—would have meant becoming identified with the old classical curriculum that was then being discredited everywhere. The language of learning in the new university was to be English, not Greek or Latin. This bias against classical rhetoric in fact became a standard feature of the English department—with the single exception of Charles Sears Baldwin's work—that continued until the 1950s.

In order to distinguish the new English department professor from the old rhetoric teacher or the new composition teacher, a new discipline had to be formulated, a discipline based on English as the language of learning and literature as the specialized province of study. This was a radically new development since, as Laurence Veysey has pointed out, "not even the classics were taught from a literary standpoint in the mid-nineteenth century" (*Emergence of the American University* 182). English was indeed the new language of scientific learning, but the study of literature in the vernacular was counter to the history of higher education in both England and America. As mentioned earlier, Williams offers the best explanation of the global forces at work in the shift. The most crucial local event in this curricular innovation was probably the establishment of Johns Hopkins University in 1876, the first American university whose main mission was graduate education. Based on the model of the German research university, Johns Hopkins signaled the shift in American higher education from an exclusive concern with undergraduate education to an excessive, if not exclusive, concern for graduate education and research. Johns Hopkins, like its German counterparts, included the study of literature in the vernacular, granting its first doctorate in literature in 1878. Of equal importance, it attempted in 1876 to hire Francis James Child—Boylston

Professor of Rhetoric and Oratory at Harvard, editor of Spenser and a well-known edition of English and Scottish popular ballads, and author of philological studies of Gawain and Chaucer. (The canon of the new English department was at first based on works that could rival the classics in age and difficulty.) In order to keep Child, Eliot freed him from all responsibilities for freshman composition—the first such exemption to be granted (Rudolph, *Curriculum* 130). Harvard had its first specialist in literature who was without responsibility for teaching freshmen. Although this arrangement was not common until the twentieth century—Child and George Lyman Kittredge being the only Harvard faculty so treated until then (Self 130)—the precedent had been established and literature was on its way to becoming the dominant concern of the new English department.

The establishment of literature as the basis of the new discipline does not, however, alone explain how a course that had required three years of upper-division work in the nineteenth century was at first relegated to the freshman year, and then by many English department members declared to be a job that should be accomplished in the high school. The most important motive continued to be dissociation from the penury and labor of the old curriculum, but justification for the claim was found in a new area. In 1874, Eliot introduced a test of the student's ability to write in English as a part of the Harvard entrance requirement. This was another radical departure that proved to be very significant, since this new writing requirement was the first step in replacing the classical languages and the curriculum based on them. Since the language of learning at the new university was to be English, it seemed appropriate that entering students be tested in this language (Kitzhaber, "Rhetoric" 56–59). Furthermore, the test in English ensured that the new open university would not become too open, allowing the new immigrants, for example, to earn degrees in science or mathematics without demonstrating by their use of language that they belonged in the middle class. However, establishing the entrance test in composition suggested that the ability to write was something the college student ought to bring with him from his preparatory school, a place which was more and more likely to be one of the new public high schools that were now appearing everywhere. And Eliot probably had this in mind, thereby hoping to cut costs in the English department. The fact that no freshman class had ever been able to write in the manner thought appropriate for college work and that additional writing instruction had always been deemed necessary for college students seems not to have been noticed by either Eliot or the staff of his English department. A look at the sample essays from the entrance exam of 1894—published by the Harvard Board of Overseers in indignation at the errors it found—reveals that the best students in the country attending the best university of its time had difficulties in writing. Rather than conclude that perhaps it was expecting too much of these students and their preparatory schools, however, the Board of Overseers excoriated the teachers who had prepared these students and demanded that something be done (Kitzhaber, "Rhetoric" 71–79). This vilification of high school English teachers has since become a common practice as college English teachers have tried to shift the entire responsibility for writing instruction—a responsibility that throughout Anglo-American history has been shared by the college—to the lower schools.

The fall from grace of the college rhetoric course was thus the result of the convergence of a number of elements. The attempt to improve the status of English department members, the establishment of the study of English literature in the college curriculum, the shift in the language of learning in college, the new entrance exams in English, and even the establishment of the new public high school— all played a part in changing the nature of writing instruction in colleges. The notion that rhetoric might be a fit study for the new graduate school—a commonplace today—quickly became so alien that a survey conducted at the turn of the century found that nearly half of the college teachers responding could not imagine what might be considered in such courses (Mead, "Graduate Study of Rhetoric"). As Frederick Rudolph has commented, by 1900, "English language and literature had replaced the classics as the backbone of the humanities" (*Curriculum* 140). Eliot meanwhile was surprised to discover that English, and not one of the new scientific disciplines, was the most popular major among undergraduates (Morison 347).

It is one thing to say that a course of study that required three years in the old college should now be relegated to the high school; it is another thing to do it. Indeed, no amount of protestation on the part of college teachers since has succeeded in bringing about this shift in responsibility. No group of entering students—not Harvard's or Columbia's or Michigan's or Stanford's—has ever been able to manage the rhetorical tasks required in college without the college providing instruction in writing. As a result, the English department has been forced to continue to teach writing to freshmen even as some of its members simultaneously disavow its responsibility for doing so. This protest is always loudest, of course, when enrollment is high, and is conspicuously muted during periods when low enrollment makes the freshman writing course a safeguard against unemployment. The English department has, moreover, commonly used the power and income gained by performing this "service" to reward those pursuing the "real" business of the department—the study of literature. And while this pattern does not hold for every college and university, it was until just recently the dominant one at large public institutions—the schools which are responsible for educating the majority of college students in the country.

Rhetoric and Poetic in the English Department

I would now like to consider the nature of the rhetorical and poetic theory that marked the early English department. I wish to demonstrate that the two were at first thoroughly compatible, being grounded in a common epistemology. In time, however, this relationship changed—unfortunately, much to the detriment of freshman English—as rhetoric became petrified in a positivistic configuration while poetic continued to develop and grow. Interestingly enough, however, the two continued to shape each other, although in unexpected and singular ways.

A few preliminary remarks about the nature of the rhetoric-poetic relationship are in order, remarks based on a longer discussion already in print (Berlin, "Rhetoric and Poetics"). I find compelling the arguments of Baldwin in *Ancient Rhetoric and Poetic* and Tzvetan Todorov in *Theories of the Symbol* which demonstrate that rhetoric and poetic have historically enjoyed a dialectical relationship, the two serving as binary opposites, each giving the other significance by contrast. A given rhetoric thus always implies a corresponding poetic and a poetic a corresponding rhetoric. Most important, the members of a particular contrasting pair have historically shared a common epistemology, a common notion of the nature of the real and how it is known. Their distinguishing feature—and here I am relying on Kenneth Burke's "Rhetoric, Poetics, and Philosophy" as well as on Todorov—is that rhetoric is concerned with symbolic action in the material world, with practical consequences as an end, while poetic is concerned with symbolic action for itself, with contemplation of the text for its own sake. The norm for the relationship can be seen most clearly in Aristotle's creation of a treatise on rhetoric and a treatise on poetic, the one concerned with action, the other with contemplation, but both grounded in a common epistemology.

The early English department maintained this normal pattern for the rhetoric-poetic relationship. In the ensuing years, however, the two disciplines diverged so far that the contrastive feature of a given rhetoric-poetic configuration is now likely to be the very element which historically the two invariably shared—the concept of epistemology.

The rhetoric that appeared in the English department in the late nineteenth century has come to be called current-traditional rhetoric. Grounded in a positivistic epistemology, it provided a counterpart to the scientific logic that distinguished the methodology of the courses in the new elective university from those in the old college, with its required curriculum based on classical studies. In chapter 1 I described this rhetoric's most important features. The scholastic world view—the view that sees deduction as the only method for arriving at truth—is replaced in current-traditional rhetoric by the Newtonian, inductive scheme. According to this view, nature is an orderly mechanism and the key to unlocking its meaning is sense impression. The mind is made up of a set of faculties that correspond perfectly to the data of sense, enabling the individual to use the inductive method in arriving at the immediate perception of self-evident truths—truths that are always external to the individual, located in an exterior object. The task of the writer in this scheme is to reproduce in the mind of the reader the particular experience as it took place in the mind of the writer. Thus, language is a sign system that transcribes nonverbal sense experience so that the effects of this sense experience can be reproduced in the reader. The work of the writing teacher is to teach the transcription process, providing instruction in arrangement and style—arrangement so that the order of experience is correctly recorded, and style so that clarity is achieved and class affiliation established.

The approach to literary criticism in the new English department that appeared contemporaneously with this rhetoric was perfectly compatible with it, displaying a common epistemology and tacitly observing the action-contemplation distinction in defining its province. This literary criticism was trying to be as scientific as the new university that had given it birth. Its approach emphasized philological and historical analysis, conceived in empirical terms. Thus, the influence of Herbert Spencer's Darwinian approach (which also supported middle-class economic views) was widespread in academic literary criticism. John Fiske at Harvard, for example, explained that his criticism of the Homeric poems used "the science of comparative mythology" and the "science of philology, as based upon established laws of phonetic change" (qtd. in Rathbun and Clark 92). Fiske's Harvard colleague and friend, Thomas Sargent Perry, worked along related lines, heralding science for showing literature the necessity of observing the laws of nature. Similarly, the positivistic methodology and evolutionary theory of Hippolyte Taine influenced the literary histories of Moses Coit Tyler of Cornell and then Michigan, Fred Lewis Pattee of Pennsylvania State College, and William B. Cairns of Wisconsin. Finally, in 1900 Barrett Wendell himself displayed the influence of Taine in his *Literary History of America*. Thus, at the turn of the century, American academics' dominant approach to literary scholarship and their dominant method of writing instruction shared a common epistemology.

The philological and historical approaches to the study of literature were soon questioned and were eventually overthrown. Current-traditional rhetoric, on the other hand, despite the numerous challenges to it that form the substance of this study, continued to be a force in most English departments and survives even today. One reason for this staying power is that the freshman course has been proffered as a concession on the part of the English department to the scientific and meritocratic interests of the university, interests represented by professional schools and many career-minded students. I would like to explore another reason, however, one less obvious but perhaps ultimately more powerful.

During the short history of the English department, current-traditional rhetoric has remained dominant while academic literary criticism has changed and developed because successive schools of literary criticism have found it necessary to point to a positivistic rhetoric in order to establish their own distinguishing and superior characteristics. To demonstrate the unique and privileged nature of poetic texts, it has been necessary to insist on a contrasting set of devalorized texts, the kind of texts described in current-traditional rhetoric. By repeatedly characterizing poetic and rhetoric in this way, these academic approaches to literary criticism have ensured that current-traditional rhetorical instruction will remain in the college writing classroom. There is obviously also a power relationship implied in this arrangement. In tacitly supporting the impoverished notion of rhetoric found in the freshman writing course, academic literary critics have provided a constant reminder of their own claim to superiority and privilege, setting the range and versatility of their discipline against the barrenness of current-traditional rhetoric, the staple of the freshman course.

Successive schools of academic literary critics have insisted on distinctions between poetic and rhetoric that support this contrast. In 1910, Joel Spingarn at Columbia proposed the "New Criticism," an approach that denies to criticism all the extrinsic concerns of history and genre—specifically, theories of metaphor and simile from Greco-Roman rhetoric. Instead, the critic is to ask of the work of art: "What has the poet tried to do, and how has he fulfilled his intention? . . . What impression does his work make on me, and how can I best express this impression?" (18). Here the art object and the response of the critic to it are placed in a privileged realm. The critic is herself a creator: "That is to say, taste must reproduce the work of art within itself in order to understand and judge it; and at that moment aesthetic judgment becomes nothing more nor less than creative art itself" (34). The creativity available to artist and critic is set up against the criticism that relies on objective, verifiable criteria, the kind found in historical and philological study and current-traditional rhetoric. Similarly, the Greek-inspired New Humanism of Irving Babbitt at Harvard and his student Paul Elmore More, while opposing the expressionism of Spingarn, also saw in science the antithesis of art and literary criticism. In *Rousseau and Romanticism* (1919), for example, Babbitt attacked the mechanism of literary naturalism, and in *Literature and the American College* (1908) he wrote of the danger Spencer's views posed to education and literary criticism. The expressionist and the humanist were allied in their insistence on trusting inner laws of human nature that are more compelling than external laws of science.

In 1938, Cleanth Brooks and Robert Penn Warren published *Understanding Poetry: An Anthology for College Students,* presenting still another "new criticism." In their introduction, they too set up poetry in opposition to science: "Science gives us a certain kind of description of the world—a description which is within its own terms verifiable—and gives us a basis for more effective practical achievement. Science is, as Bertrand Russell has called it, 'power-knowledge.'" Poetry, on the other hand, satisfies a "non-practical interest," dealing with experience that "eludes the statements science can make" and appealing to "a basic and healthy human interest" (lv). Brooks and Warren are especially appropriate to this context since their composition textbook, *Modern Rhetoric,* demonstrated explicitly their relegation of rhetoric to the scientific (see Berlin and Inkster). It should also be noted that Brooks and Warren tried to claim for poetry a realm separate from rhetoric and superior to it, yet sharing with it a concern for a text existing independent of creator and reader. In their view the formal properties of the text take precedence in both rhetoric and poetic.

Finally, as Gerald Graff has noted, Northrop Frye in the sixties based his critical approach on a distinction between mythical and logical uses of language, seeing the first as poetic and the second as positivistic (182–83). Graff finds the same disjunction in the more recent work of Paul de Man, who, Graff explains, divides all discourse "into language that deconstructs itself by calling attention to its own fictiveness and undecidability and language that presumes a naive confidence in its ontological authority" (178). Once again, the division between poetic and scientific statements is insisted upon.

This thumbnail sketch shows that a number of powerful groups of academic literary critics have divided discourse into two separate and unequal categories: the privileged poetic statement and the impoverished rhetorical statement, the one art and the other "mere" science. R. S. Crane's description of the New Critics might be applied to a variety of literary critics who came before and after them. The New Critic, he wrote, "knows what the nature of 'poetic language' must be because he has begun by dividing all language into two opposing and incommensurable kinds—the language of 'logic' and the language of 'symbolism'—and then has deduced from this initial assumption that the 'symbolic' language of poetry must necessarily possess the contraries of all qualities commonly asserted of 'logical discourse'" (34). As a result, literary critics within the English department have appropriated as their domain all uses of language except for the narrowly referential and logical. What remains—a trivial and barren concern at best—is given to rhetoric, to the writing course. Thus, current-traditional rhetoric, with its positivistic epistemology and its emphasis on superficial matters of arrangement and style, continues to be the officially sanctioned rhetoric of the English department. Attempts to alter this notion of rhetoric—in the direction of an Aristotelian or Emersonian or Burkeian conception, for example—are usually seen as inappropriate encroachments into the realm of the literary critic. Of course, this system further consolidates the powers and privileges of academic life in the hands of those who deal with the valorized literary texts, while it relegates those who teach writing to an area of marginal value, dealing as they do with a limited and relatively unimportant variety of discourse. What is more discouraging, however, is that it impoverishes the rhetorical training for citizenship that our students receive—but more of this later.

Fortunately, this relegation of rhetoric to a narrowly scientific and rational discourse did not exhaust the field of rhetorical development in the English department. The following chapters will show that there have been numerous challenges to the dominance of current-traditional rhetoric. As I stated earlier, historically rhetoric and poetic have shared a common epistemology and have defined each other by contrast, resting on the action-contemplation distinction as their distinguishing characteristic. The appearance of a complementary rhetoric and poetic distinguished by differing epistemologies was a historical anomaly. The new rhetorics that have challenged the current-traditional approach fit the historical norm and have received a hearing because they share with one or another school of literary criticism a common epistemology. Thus, subjective rhetorics, for example, have been tolerated in the English department because they share with expressionistic literary theories as well as with New Criticism certain conceptions of writer, reality, audience, and language—making claims for rhetoric that were previously made exclusively for poetic. Similarly, transactional rhetorics have appeared in tandem with transactional literary approaches—Vernon Louis Parrington's and Granville Hicks's, for example. In short, richly diverse classroom rhetorics have appeared in the twentieth century as epistemological counterparts to theories of literary criticism, and noting these relationships will be a passing concern of the following chapters.

3

The Growth of the Discipline:
1900–1920

THE MOST IMPORTANT SINGLE EVENT MARKING ENGLISH STUD-
ies as secure in the college curriculum of the new university was
the establishment of the Modern Language Association in 1883. The
most important event for maintaining the discipline's commitment to
students was the appearance of the National Council of Teachers of
English in 1911. The MLA had by 1920 decided that its main interest was to be scholarship and scholarship only (Armstrong; Fisher).
It then publicly acknowledged what had been obvious to any atten-
tive member for at least fifteen years: teaching was no longer to be
a concern of the only professional association of college English
teachers in America. The NCTE attempted to respond to this deficiency, although it at first focused on the interests of high school
teachers. Its attention to college teaching, however, led to a college
edition of *English Journal* in 1928, a publication that became *College English* in 1939. The commitment of *English Journal* to the
undergraduate curriculum makes it the most reliable source of information on the thought guiding the teaching of English—both
literature and composition—in American colleges in the early years
of the century.

In this chapter, I would like to consider the formation of the
NCTE. I will also examine the three dominant approaches to writing instruction from 1900 to 1920 and the ideology of each that
NCTE journal articles and organization reports recorded and encouraged. Next I will look at the approaches to preparing college
teachers for instructing students in writing and literature, as well as

the kinds of undergraduate courses in writing offered during this period. Finally, I will turn to the effects of World War I on the discipline of English studies in the high school and college.

The NCTE

The National Council of Teachers of English was founded in protest against college domination of the high school English curriculum exercised through the agency of the Uniform Reading Lists (Applebee; Hook). The Uniform Lists consisted of titles of books on which students were tested for admission to college. In 1874 Harvard, under the presidency of Charles William Eliot, was the first to institute such a procedure, requiring "a short English composition, correct in spelling, punctuation, grammar, and expression, the subject to be taken from such works of standard authors as shall be announced from time to time" (qtd. in Wozniak 70). Very soon, other colleges began to require a similar essay. Unfortunately, the colleges refused to agree on the works to be included in their lists. Since high school English teachers were beginning to base their courses on these works in order to prepare their students for college, the lack of uniformity caused a problem. The demand for a single set of titles resulted in two regional lists in 1879 and 1893 and finally in the formation of the National Conference on Uniform Entrance Requirements in English (NCUER) in 1894, an organization that eventually included the North Central Association of Colleges and Secondary Schools and the College Entrance Examination Board among its subscribers. The NCUER provided high school English teachers with a list of works that included a number intended for "deep" study and a number for "wide" study.

The Uniform Lists gave the high school teacher a sense of security, but another problem soon emerged. The colleges were determining the high school English curriculum at a time when only a small percentage of high school students went on to college—only four percent of those from eighteen to twenty-one years old (Rudolph, *Curriculum* 155). Moreover, because of immigration patterns an increasing number of students were coming from homes in which English was not spoken. Many of the works recommended by the lists did not seem appropriate for these students, a complaint voiced especially by teachers in New York City. A protest movement developed, one that was encouraged by the example of the Michigan plan for college admissions, used by a number of Midwestern and Western states. Here state colleges accredited high schools that met a certain number of curricular standards, and accepted graduates of these schools without entrance exams. Educators in these states, led by Fred Newton Scott of the University of Michigan, wanted the lists abolished so that their English teachers did not need to be concerned about those of their students who wanted to go to Eastern schools for college work. Most high school English teachers in the East did not support abolishing the Uniform Lists, but they were interested in a greater variety of literary materials for study in the curriculum. The New York State English Teachers Association, on the other hand, was militantly opposed to the lists, and in 1911 it demanded their elimination, along with a revision of college entrance exams so that such tests would henceforth be based on abilities developed, not information acquired. The New York teachers took their protest to the National Education Association (NEA), asking that a formal protest be lodged with the College Entrance Examination Board, the leading administrator of the English exam. The NEA referred the matter to its English Round Table of the Secondary Division, a loosely formed, temporary committee in existence at the time. This group put together another committee consisting of Scott, James F. Hosic of Chicago Normal College, Edwin L. Miller of Detroit Central High School, and John M. Clapp of Lake Forest College. It was this group that finally, encouraged by the NEA, called the first meeting of what was to become the National Council of Teachers of English for December 1 and 2, 1911, in Chicago. The NCTE's fight against the Uniform Lists was successfully completed when in 1916 there appeared only a brief list for intensive study and no list at all for the comprehensive test in literature—and the brief list was itself dropped in 1931. This was to be the first of many similar victories for the NCTE.

Although the NCTE was formed around the issue of college domination of the English curriculum, it included among its early leaders a number of college teachers, most notably Scott—president of the MLA in 1907, president of the North Central Association of Colleges and Secondary Schools in 1913, president of the American Association of Teachers of Journalism in 1917, and first president of the

NCTE—and Hosic—founder, owner, and first editor (1912–21) of *English Journal*. It at first appears anomalous that two college English teachers should be so actively involved in a group that was stimulated by the protest of high school English teachers against their collegiate counterparts. As will later become apparent, however, the NCTE was from the start an agency for improving the teaching of English at all educational levels, even if its main focus initially was secondary school instruction. Moreover, college teachers such as Scott looked to *English Journal* as the most important forum for considering developments in college writing instruction.

The Major Schools

Three major approaches to the teaching of writing appeared between 1900 and 1920. The oldest was what is now known as current-traditional rhetoric. It was most conspicuously in force at Harvard and Columbia, but it also found a home in a number of the state universities—Illinois, Wisconsin, and Texas, for example. This rhetoric, positivistic and practical in spirit, was designed to provide the new middle-class professionals with the tools to avoid embarrassing themselves in print. In short, this was the rhetoric of the meritocracy. Its principal rival in the East was the rhetoric of liberal culture, advanced at such schools as Yale, Princeton, and Williams. This rhetoric was elitist and aristocratic, contending that the aims of writing instruction in the English department ought to be to encourage those few students who possessed genius. For the rest, courses in literature should provide lessons in taste, emphasizing appreciation, contemplation, and self-expression. Proponents of this rhetoric denied that writing courses had an important place in the college, arguing that geniuses were few and that writing instruction for the rest ought to be handled in high school. The result was not, however, the abandonment of writing instruction, but the use of a belletristic approach—courses in writing about literature. Finally, the third major approach to writing instruction emphasized writing as training for participation in the democratic process—a rhetoric of public discourse. This view, a part of the progressive education movement, was uniquely American. Its most conspicuous spokespersons were Scott at Michigan, Joseph Villiers Denney at Ohio

State, and Gertrude Buck, a former student of Scott's, at Vassar. At the college level, this democratic rhetoric was primarily a Midwestern phenomenon, but it was found in the West and Southwest as well. It was also extremely influential in the high schools of the period. This rhetoric was a well-articulated precursor of epistemic rhetoric.

Current-Traditional Rhetoric

As I have said repeatedly, current-traditional rhetoric has been the dominant form of college writing instruction in the twentieth century. Its original home was Harvard, and it represented a particular conception of literacy, a view shaped by the elective curriculum of Eliot. At the start of the century, American universities were divided into three groups: those emphasizing utility, those emphasizing liberal culture, and those emphasizing research and graduate study (Veysey, *Emergence of the American University*). Harvard, despite its growing graduate school, was devoted to the undergraduate program, to providing for the meritocracy of middle-class professionalism.

The fact that current-traditional rhetoric was a product of the new, elective university is crucial. This university, a uniquely American phenomenon at the time, was at once committed to the scientific method and to the creation of a professional meritocracy consisting of an emerging middle class (Veysey, *Emergence of the American University* 173; Bledstein 123–24). The old American college had been aristocratic in its clientele and classical in its curriculum. The new university invested its graduates with the authority of science and through this authority gave them an economically comfortable position in a new, prosperous middle-class culture. It is not surprising, then, that the rhetoric that A. S. Hill and Barrett Wendell forged at Harvard and that John F. Genung shaped at Amherst was designed to emulate the scientific method. As I have shown, their colleagues in literary criticism were doing the same. The result for writing instruction was unfortunate: creation of a rhetoric that denied the role of the writer, reader, and language in arriving at meaning, that instead placed truth in the external world, existing prior to the individual's perception of it.

This attempt to be scientific in rhetoric was based on the assumption that knowledge in all areas of human behavior could be readily discovered and validated through the scientific method. In other words, it was assumed that ethical and political questions, as well as aesthetic ones, could be as efficiently and decisively resolved as the scientific and technical questions of the late nineteenth century had been—and resolved in the same way. (Today we are not this confident even of the power of the scientific method to answer the questions of its own province.) The result of this naive faith was that the economical and political interests of the new professional middle class were perceived as being inherent features of the universe. Validation for the social and political arrangements that contributed to the welfare of the new meritocracy was thought to be rationally and empirically derived through an objective examination of the material world. Unable to conceive of observer, audience, or language as integral to the process of discovering knowledge, the members of the new middle class found the elements they brought to the external world within the external world itself. Since all truth was considered to be external to the individual, to be discovered through correct perception, the doctors or lawyers or engineers or business managers—having been certified as experts, as trained observers, in their disciplines—felt they were surely correct in discovering that economic and political arrangements that benefited them were indeed in the nature of things. And the fact that all of the members of this new class tended to agree—tended to discover the same truths—when they turned to decision-making in political and social matters only confirmed their sense of being objective and accurate. Thus, acting in the name of science, the new professionals used current-traditional rhetoric to justify their privileged status in society.

A look at the way current-traditional rhetoric was taught at Harvard at the turn of the century is instructive (Wozniak 125–27). Students used Hill's *Principles of Rhetoric* as their text. This work was divided into two parts, the first dealing with superficial correctness (barbarisms, solecisms, and improprieties) and the second with the forms of discourse. Students wrote a theme for each class day—a total of six per week—using uniform theme paper. The choice of subjects for four of these was limited to descriptions of surrounding scenes, while the other two required a translation from Latin, Greek, French, or German (ordinarily done on Saturdays) and a summary or comment upon the lecture of the period when all sections met together. All themes were read and corrected with the use of a set of abbreviated marks of correction. The emphasis in this method was on superficial correctness—spelling, punctuation, usage, syntax—and on paragraph structure. Students were often asked to rewrite themes with a view to correcting their errors. There was some variety—for example, an occasional imitation of an English writer. The forms of discourse emphasized were description, narration, and exposition, with argument omitted because it was considered too complex for the short essay. Students also wrote longer fortnightly themes, and these included all the forms of discourse—six expository themes in the first semester and two themes in each of the other forms in the second. In addition, the students were asked to do outside reading in English literature, were given examinations, and engaged in conferences with their teacher. The requirement of the daily theme was dropped shortly after the turn of the century, but the kind of writing attempted and the instruction in arrangement and style remained.

The freshman writing course early became the center of controversy. A criticism of it that appeared in *Century Magazine* prompted W. E. Mead (Wesleyan University) of the pedagogical section of the MLA to conduct a survey on its value (Mead, "Undergraduate Study of Composition"). The *Century* article had claimed that an experiment involving two groups of freshman students—one studying Shakespeare with no training in rhetoric or practice in writing and the other pursuing a course similar to Harvard's—indicated that there was no difference in the technical merits of the themes written by the two groups of students in the sophomore year. Mead's survey asked for comments on the questions raised by the experiment described, information about similar experiments, and comments on the possibility of conducting such an experiment in the future. In reporting the results, Mead explained that the responses constituted a representative sample of colleges and universities throughout the country, and although no evidence of this was given, there is no reason to doubt him.

Mead considered the questions regarding similar experiments first, reporting that while many had been planned, no results were available. He did indicate, however, that the experiment alluded to in the *Century* essay was probably one conducted at Harvard involving the comparison of Harvard's daily theme writing and Yale's literary approach to writing instruction. The results there, however, were just the opposite of those reported, with Harvard's students judged to be clearly superior. Indeed, most of Mead's respondents were skeptical of the results reported in *Century*, arguing that practice would be more valuable than reading in improving writing. Mead summarized the responses on the questions raised by the experiment:

> They generally emphasize the fact that composition is an art rather than a science, and therefore can be mastered only by practice; and this preferably under competent instruction. They point out important aspects of work in composition that may or may not co-exist along with technical correctness, such as unity of conception, logical development of a theme, proportion of parts. These and many other matters . . . are, they urge, the very things that trouble us most, even when we have read widely and carefully for years, and have given anxious thought to the task of expressing ourselves with clearness and precision. ("Undergraduate Study of Composition" xvii)

This survey on the relative merits of writing and reading in the teaching of composition pointed to a larger issue involving not only rhetorical instruction but the entire undergraduate curriculum. The debate between those who would teach writing through practice and those who would teach it through the reading of literature represented a conflict between those who saw literacy as utilitarian and those who saw it as self-fulfillment. The first group wanted colleges to provide students with the expertise that would enable them to serve society and to enjoy the professional success of the new middle class. The supporters of this stance tended to become closely allied with those who saw research as a major concern of colleges. The second group, the proponents of education as liberal culture, saw colleges as cultivating character by providing aesthetic and ethical experiences through the traditional humanistic studies (Veysey, *Emergence of the American University*, ch. 4). The result would be a kind of aristocrat who demonstrated his education through living a certain kind of life—rather than through doing, through serving society in one's chosen career. The aim of liberal culture was self-cultivation and self-refinement. The major institutions promoting the service ideal at this time were Harvard and Columbia in the

East and the large state universities in the Midwest and West. The ideal of liberal culture was dominant primarily along the Atlantic seaboard, with Yale and Princeton leading the way. The kind of rhetoric encouraged in this latter group will be discussed later in this chapter.

The conflict between these two positions was taken up again in a somewhat different form in another survey conducted by the pedagogical section of the MLA in the following year. Here the respondents were to choose between two conceptions of composition instruction—one described in a citation from an English reviewer and the other encapsulated in a passage from Genung. (This passage, incidentally, was not in fact representative of Genung's position.) Mead, again the reporter of the survey, summarized the two positions on teaching composition: "(a) the art of writing clearly and correctly about ordinary matters; (b) the production of literature" ("Conflicting Ideals" viii). The two represented the opposing views of the service ideal and the ideal of liberal culture in education. Harvard and Columbia held that if writing instruction were offered it ought to be open to everyone and ought to emphasize practical competence. Yale and Princeton held that if writing instruction were offered it ought to be creative writing and be reserved only for those who demonstrated genius. What is especially significant about Mead's survey—and again we have only his word for its being representative—is that it was inconclusive. The respondents fell into three camps: those who favored writing as preparation for practical living, those who favored writing as preparation for creating literature, and those who favored a combination of the two. Mead was forced to conclude, "There can be little doubt that conflicting ideals, both in aims and methods, are firmly held by many leading teachers of English throughout the country" ("Conflicting Ideals" xxii). Still, as Mead suggested and as this chapter will demonstrate, teaching composition as creative writing exclusively will always represent a minority position.

Current-traditional rhetoric frequently appeared at large state universities, which adapted Harvard's plan to a much different setting. The University of Illinois was in many ways typical of these efforts. In 1914 it enrolled 1,450 students in Rhetoric 1, organizing them into fifty-five sections taught by twenty-five instructors. Students were required to take two courses to satisfy the freshman English sequence. The first term consisted of exposition and the second of argumentation, narration, and description. The first term's aims were "to remove such traces of illiteracy as still remain, and at the same time to give some advanced instruction in the principles of composition which will enable the student to write unified and coherent, if not emphatic, exposition" (Tieje 590). Edwin Woolley's *Handbook of Composition* was used to get rid of "illiteracy." Teachers in the course met weekly to discuss standards and how to apply them in grading essays, but it is clear that the primary emphasis was on superficial correctness—on matters of form, grammar, and usage—even though "individual thinking," that is, dealing with "the subject in a new, or at least fresh, way," was encouraged (Tieje 592). In the second term, arguments were evaluated on the basis of the use of evidence and reasoning from premises to conclusions, structural fluency, and a tactful and forceful presentation. The emphasis here, however, was formal and rational, with no concern for invention or content. More important, "mechanical requirements" were such that a failing grade could be given for any *one* of the following violations: two misspelled words, one sentence with a "violent change of construction," one unclear sentence, one straggling sentence, one grammatical error, ignorance of the use of comma or semicolon, or monotony in diction or construction. Furthermore, one grade of E or F (grades given were A, B, C, D, E, F) on any theme prevented a student from earning a passing grade for the semester.

A similar system was in place at this time at a number of other large universities, most notably Wisconsin (Woolley, "Admission to Freshman English") and Texas (Thompson, "Notebook System"). In addition, the Universities of Illinois (Sutcliffe), Wisconsin (Woolley), and Chicago (Boynton) used placement tests—consisting of a writing sample and an objective test of grammar and usage—and conducted remedial "sub-freshman" English courses. In doing so they were again following the lead of Harvard and, this time, Pennsylvania as well (Wozniak 132).

Finally, the importance given current-traditional rhetoric in the new college curriculum can be seen in the statements of Charles Sears Baldwin of Columbia, whose college textbooks on writing were highly successful after 1902. Although Baldwin was an authority on ancient rhetoric, his composition texts displayed little of the influence of the dominant tradition of Aristotle, Cicero, and Quintilian. In his *College Composition* (1917), for example, he paid only passing attention to invention, defining rhetoric instead as primarily an art of "composition," meaning by this arrangement and style. This capitulation to current-traditional rhetoric was further demonstrated in Baldwin's use of the four modes of discourse, which he drew along classical lines only insofar as he divided them into the rhetorical—exposition and argument—and the poetic—description and narration. Baldwin regarded rhetoric as a managerial art—simply arranging what is discovered outside the rhetorical act—and he accordingly emphasized the inartistic proofs, the modes, and stylistic abstractions.

This is not to say, however, that Baldwin regarded college writing instruction as unimportant. On the contrary, he considered it the center of the curriculum. As a member of the MLA pedagogical section committee that had conducted the survey reported by Mead in 1902, he appended a comment on the results. He divided composition into the "logical" and the "artistic." The first "proceeds from proposition to proposition" while the second is "the sort whose progress is not measured by propositions" (Mead, "Undergraduate Study of Composition" xxiii). In the essay the two overlap, but the artistic or literary as an exclusive concern is a province for only a small minority of students. Courses in this area may be offered, but teaching is less important in these cases since the students enrolled in such courses ought to be the gifted few who do not rely on the instruction of others. The freshman writing course, however, is designed for all students because it provides what can and must be taught: the use of logical writing. This instruction must include argumentation, persuasion, and exposition for writing and speaking. Reading will of course contribute to this learning, but competence can be attained only by practice. The ability to use language logically "is one of the most valuable parts of a college education" since "rhetoric may then be made to serve in particular each course on which it depends for material and in general the great object of all the courses together" (xxiv). Baldwin concluded by asserting that rhetoric has thus come to serve for us the function that logic served for the ancients. It is our "organon," the organizing discipline of our educational system.

The Rhetoric of Liberal Culture

As indicated earlier, the rhetoric of liberal culture was aristocratic and humanistic, set up in intentional opposition to the democratic and practical tendencies of current-traditional rhetoric. This opposition was described in 1912 by Glenn E. Palmer of the University of Kansas in an article entitled "Culture and Efficiency through Composition." Palmer was responding in part to Thomas Lounsbury's attack on the compulsory composition course in the November 1911 issue of *Harper's Monthly Magazine*. Palmer explained that the differences between the two rhetorics were easily summarized. The Yale model held that if writing were to be taught in college it ought to be taught to the few who were gifted, and then in order to encourage the creation of art. The Harvard plan, on the other hand, insisted that writing instruction should be required for all and should simply cultivate "good language habits." Yale was concerned with providing all of its students "the inspiration of literature, recognizing that there can be no literary production without culture" but aiming toward the encouragement of a "few geniuses." Harvard stressed instead "painstaking drill in the writing of short themes" in order to "train a class of Philistines prepared for the everyday needs of democracy, by enforcing good language habits, and increasing expressiveness." In short, Palmer concluded, Yale and Harvard represented "the old distinction between culture and efficiency" (488).

Palmer wished the two camps to learn from each other and to arrive at a higher synthesis. Charles G. Osgood of Princeton disagreed with him in a 1915 essay entitled "No Set Requirement of English Composition in the Freshman Year." Osgood argued against requiring any writing course for anyone at any level of the curriculum, and he provided an alternative. For Osgood, the required course—and he certainly had Harvard's in mind—was only concerned with "visible correctness and propriety." But errors on the superficial level, he believed, were symptoms of a deeper disorder, a disorder in "the very springs of the student's nature and action and expression" (232). Teachers therefore had to go to the source of the symptoms, not treat the symptoms themselves. The way to do this was by teaching literature, thereby "making young men more sensitive, more observant, more just, more consistent, more spiritual." Osgood explained that the preceptorial method at Princeton was designed to do just this, directing small groups of students—"three to seven men"—in discussing literature, the teacher "becoming something of an artist" as he guided the development of his charges. The student was ready to write only after he had discussed his subject with his teacher—discussion that was to continue as the student wrote, since "more of the art of composition can be taught while the act of composing is going on." The purpose of all of this was "to reform the intellectual and spiritual health of the student." Some students would not respond to this method since it was "peculiarly adapted to the training of the *better* men," such men being the nation's greatest need at a time "of the worship of 'the Average'" (234–35). Finally, Osgood felt that any courses devoted exclusively to writing instruction should be held during the senior year, when students had arrived at intellectual and spiritual maturity.

The statements of Osgood were representative of the rhetoric of liberal culture and were echoed in the published positions of Hiram Corson and Lane Cooper at Cornell, William Lyon Phelps as well as Lounsbury at Yale, and Frank Aydelotte of Indiana (later president of Swarthmore and founder of the nation's first honors program). As mentioned earlier, this rhetoric emerged as part of a larger reaction to the scientific and professional concept of literacy encouraged at Harvard and at most large state universities. Grounded in a Brahminical romanticism, it found its home in departments of language, art, and philosophy in the new university. The rhetoric was based on an epistemology that grew out of philosophical idealism (Veysey, *Emergence of the American University*, ch. 4). It held that all material reality has a spiritual foundation and that the business of education was to enable students to see beyond the material to the ideal. The study of art was thought to be uniquely designed to do just this. As Corson, a professor of English, explained, the aim of an education in liberal culture was "to induce soul states or conditions, soul attitudes, to attune the inward forces to the idealized forms of nature and of human life produced by art, and not to make the head a cockloft for storing away the trumpery of barren knowledge" (qtd. in Veysey, *Emergence of the American University* 185). The purpose of education was to cultivate the individual so that he would be in touch with the permanent and the true. This involved encouragement of a wisely passive response to experience, rather than the aggressively active response of the new professional. The aim of this education was preeminently self-realization, the self arriving at its fulfillment through the perception of the spiritual qualities inherent in experience. Learning to see these qualities was considered to be the primary purpose of a literary education.

The rhetoric of liberal culture was aristocratic and openly distrustful of democracy. The perception of the ideal beyond the real was possible only through study and then was finally attained only by the gifted few. The colleges that embraced this educational stance were a very small but conspicuously vocal minority. They included those schools that were the last to abandon the prescribed classical curriculum of the Yale Report of 1828, a document reactionary even when first presented; among them were Yale, Princeton, Williams, Amherst, Bowdoin, and Hamilton (Rudolph, *Curriculum* 190). Liberal culture was an ideal based on a tacit social and moral code as well as on an aesthetic creed. Most proponents were Anglophiles who favored class distinctions and aspired to the status of an educated aristocracy of leadership and privilege, a right that was claimed on the basis of their spiritual vision—partly a matter of birth and partly a product of having attended the right schools. In making their claims, the supporters of liberal culture often called upon Matthew Arnold's definition of culture as the best that has been thought and said, supporting his contention that the proponents of culture will address and resolve moral and social problems by virtue of their sensitivity to the aesthetic.

The rhetoric of liberal culture defined writing as the embodiment of spiritual vision, a manifestation of the true significance of the material world. The writer, however, had first to arrive at this spiritual vision before attempting to record it; as we have seen, this was accomplished by years of literary study, by the close reading of predecessors who had attained this vision. The writing cultivated in this rhetoric thus valued the individual voice, the unique expression that indicated a gifted and original personality at work. Of course, this personality could not be allowed to violate the strictures of a certain notion of cultivation and class. Still, unique self-expression within these bounds was encouraged. There was also an insistence on organic form, on the inextricable relation of form and content. Indeed, it was considered to be this organic relationship that enabled the personality to express itself in its own unique way, finally making the text it produced intranslatable. As Veysey has explained, "Advocates of culture liked to believe in an ultimate and rather titillating mystery of things; therefore they did not want even to admit that the dimensions of their study might be neatly pinned down" (*Emergence of the American University* 185). And it was the business of the student-writer to strive to capture this "mystery of things" in prose, suggesting through a unique style the otherwise inexpressible.

The rhetoric of liberal culture had its literary antecedents in American Critical Idealism (sometimes called the "Genteel Tradition"), a system represented by the likes of James Russell Lowell and Charles Eliot Norton of Harvard, George Woodberry of Nebraska and then Columbia, and Brander Matthews of Columbia. It included as its successor the elitist New Humanism of Irving Babbitt at Columbia. The educational ideal of liberal culture did not survive as a major force, despite its outspoken proponents at some of the most prestigious schools in the nation. It is worth noting, though, that it kept alive in the university a notion of art and literary criticism that was for a time eclipsed by the scientistic historical and philological criticism of the early English department. It also maintained the academic tie with romantic thought—however Brahminical the version—and this had its effects on an egalitarian conception of expressionistic rhetoric that appeared in the twenties. It should not be forgotten, however, that the proponents of the rhetoric of liberal culture discouraged writing instruction even as they continued to provide it to students in freshman literature courses that required writing about literature. In other words, they were engaging in the very activity they decried in others, meanwhile denying that their students needed this instruction or that they were providing it.

A Transactional Rhetoric for a Democracy

A third variety of classroom rhetoric arose in America during this time. It had originated in the 1890s in the work of Scott, Denney, and Buck, but it was widely disseminated during the next two decades, especially in the high schools. This rhetoric was the most complete embodiment of John Dewey's notion of progressive education, reflecting his conviction that the aim of all education is to combine self-development, social harmony, and economic integration (Bowles and Gintis 20–22). (Scott had known Dewey at the University of Michigan and had even taught a course in aesthetics for him in the philosophy department.) Scott's rhetoric in fact represented a uniquely American development, a rhetoric for a modern democratic state. It was, in addition, an early approximation of an epistemic position.

Scott took all of his degrees at the University of Michigan and began teaching there in 1899. In 1903 he became head of the Department of Rhetoric and served in that capacity until his retirement in 1926. During his career he was at various times president of the MLA, the first and second president of the NCTE, president of the North Central Association of Colleges and Secondary Schools, and president of the American Association of Colleges and Secondary Schools. He wrote in collaboration with others fifteen books on composition, aesthetics, and literary criticism, and independently approximately one hundred articles on rhetoric, literary criticism, linguistics, and pedagogy. At Michigan he created the Department of Rhetoric, which eventually separated from the Department of English. It handled beginning writing courses as well as advanced courses in rhetoric, journalism, and literary criticism. His distinguished students included Sterling Andrus Leonard, Ruth Weeks, Karl Young, Avery Hopwood, Marjorie Nicolson, Fletcher Harris, and Charles Fries. After Scott's retirement, his Department of Rhetoric was rejoined with the English department and then was quietly and efficiently dismantled (Stewart, "Rediscovering Fred Newton Scott").

Scott's rhetoric was consciously formulated as an alternative to current-traditional rhetoric, especially to the latter's emphasis on the scientific and the practical in rhetorical discourse. Scott saw reality as a social construction, a communal creation emerging from the dialectical interplay of individuals. While this social reality is bound by the material, it is everywhere immersed in language. Reality is thus neither objective and external, as current-traditionalists believed, nor subjective and internal, as the proponents of liberal culture held. It is instead the result of the interaction between the experience of the external world and what the perceiver brings to this experience. The transactional relationship that defines reality also includes the social, the interaction of humans. The medium of contact between perceiver and perceived is language. Language is not, however, conceived of as a simple sign system in which symbol and referent are perfectly matched. It is instead constitutive of reality, language being the very condition that makes thought possible. Language does not exist apart from thought, and thought does not exist apart from language; they are one and the same. Reality is the product of the interplay of observer (writer or speaker), other observers (audience), the material world, and, implicated in each, language.

Scott's rhetoric was throughout intent on providing for public discourse in a democratic and heterogeneous society. In "English Composition as a Mode of Behavior," he insisted on the student's right to her own language, arguing that the student's desire to communicate is destroyed by the teacher's insistence on abstraction and correctness. To take away a student's language is to deny her experience, forcing her to talk and write about what she does not know. In "The Standard of American Speech" Scott had similarly argued for a multiplicity of dialects, maintaining that differences in dialect do not impede communication: "Whence the speech comes does not matter. . . . If it is the voice of high wisdom, of moderation, of human nature at its best, the words will take on that power and charm which is the test of a great national speech" (9). Language is experience; to deny the validity of a person's dialect is to deny the reality of that person's experience and, finally, the reality of the person herself.

Perhaps the most succinct statement of Scott's rhetoric is found in an essay entitled "Rhetoric Rediviva," first delivered at the MLA meeting of December 1909. Here Scott traced the roots of a modern rhetoric to Plato, arguing that the tradition which sees the Greek philosopher as antirhetorical is "one of the most curious perversities in the history of scholarship." Scott found the other great tradition, the Aristotelian, too narrowly concerned with persuasion, with winning the day—and here intended an oblique reference to current-traditional rhetoric and its practical orientation. According to Scott, Plato includes in his rhetoric "every use of speech, whether spoken or written; not only speeches, but history, fiction, laws, and even conversation." What is of permanent value in Platonic rhetoric, however, is found in two areas: its social orientation and its notion of organic form. Plato, Scott explained, "takes what we should now call the social or sociological point of view. The value of any piece of discourse, or mode of communication, is to be measured by its effect upon the welfare of the community." Against the extreme individualism and class bias of current-traditional rhetoric and the rhetoric of liberal culture, Scott posed a rhetoric of public service, a system distinguished by its ethical commitment to the public good: "Good discourse is that which by disseminating truth creates a healthy public opinion and thus effects, in Plato's words, 'a training and improvement in the souls of the citizens'" (415). The writer or speaker must thus be committed to truth conceived of as a social phenomenon, with implications for the entire community. Finally, Scott held that Plato, in his conception of organic structure—of the inextricable relation·of form and content—has given us the guiding principle for the production of discourse. Thus, in his expansion of subject matter, in his notion of the social function of discourse, and in his insistence on organic unity, Plato has provided a program for a modern theory of discourse. And while it must be admitted that Scott's interpretation of Plato, as well as of Aristotle, was certainly unique, flying in the face of the traditions called upon in most historical accounts, it nevertheless resulted in a rich body of rhetorical thought.

When we turn to Scott's textbooks on rhetoric, done in collaboration with others, we find him less innovative than might be expected. Still, despite his inclusion of such current-traditional concerns as the forms of discourse, the structure of the paragraph, and the matter of usage, Scott diminished the impact of these matters by his emphasis on the rhetorical context, a context that is always social and transactional in nature. Thus, in *Elementary English Composition*, Scott and Denney underscored the public and dialectical nature of composing: "The forces which urge young persons to express themselves with tongue or pen are partly individual, partly social—partly impulses from within, partly solicitations from without. Pupils compose most naturally and most successfully when the two forces are in equilibrium" (iii). Subject and audience are both involved in determining the rhetorical purpose. In this framework, even superficial correctness can be regarded differently: "Presented as a means of meeting definite social needs more or less effectively, of winning attention and consideration, the various devices of grammar and rhetoric make an appeal to self-interest which pupils can understand. " Students learn to avoid errors in correctness because they come to "appreciate the value of these things to themselves as members of society" (iv). This concern for the complete rhetorical context is also seen in Scott and Denney's design of composition assignments. In the third number of *Contributions to Rhetorical Theory*, edited by Scott, Denney described the principles the two used in devising writing topics:

> If our object is to train the power of seeing and expressing relations, of grasping in imagination the meaning and total significance of a number of details, the statement of the topics should, if possible, suggest a typical situation in real life. And if we wish to enlist the personal interest of the writer in his work, the statement of the topics should suggest a personal relationship to the situation, of the one who is to write. Moreover it should suggest a particular reader or set of readers who are to be brought into vital relationship with the situation. . . . The composition that suggests a problem or solution calls into activity all of the resources of the pupil. (173)

Here is seen the insistence on the dialectical interplay of all elements in arriving at decisions about meaning while composing. Scott and Denney offered students a complete rhetorical situation arising out of their experience, including the purpose of the writer, her role, and the audience to be addressed.

There were others who promoted a democratic rhetoric of public discourse between 1900 and 1920. The most important was Buck, one of Scott's students and a prolific source of textbooks and theoretical statements on rhetoric and poetic during her twenty-two years of teaching at Vassar College. Two recent essays have surveyed her accomplishments—one by Rebecca Burke and the other by Gerald Mulderig. Other members of this democratic group were George Pattee of Pennsylvania State, Katherine Stewart Worthington of Columbia, Samuel Chandler Earle of Tufts, Homer A. Watt of New York University, and Harold G. Merriam of Reed College. The last two are noteworthy for having emphasized teaching the entire "process" of writing rather than simply responding to the "product," a result probably attributable to Dewey's insistence on learning as a process. Sterling Andrus Leonard, who was another of Scott's students and a teacher at Wisconsin, had also during this time begun his campaign against the insistence on distorting the student's language and life to conform to the biases of a narrow class interest (see Myers, "Reality, Consensus, and Reform"; Brereton). While never dominant, this democratic rhetoric remained a force, especially in high schools, throughout the period and reemerged with considerable energy during the economically troubled thirties.

The Ideas Approach

A related transactional approach to writing that also grew out of progressive education's interest in connecting learning to social and political life was found in the "ideas course," also called the "thought course" or "content course." Its origin was attributed to Harrison Ross Steeves of Columbia, who described the course in a 1912 article. In this approach, the student wrote essays about the traditional issues of rhetoric—legal, political, and social questions of a controversial nature—after reading essays that considered them. This course signaled the beginnings of the anthologies on political and social issues as well as those on the purpose of a college education, the latter attempting to address the questions arising out of the student's immediate experience. These essay collections commonly were designed to involve the student in controversy by presenting more than one viewpoint on a given issue, as in *Representative Essays in Modern Thought: A Basis for Composition*, edited by Steeves and Frank Humphrey Ristine of Hamilton College, the first of many such collections.

The ideas approach was an attempt to restore to rhetoric its concern with the probable, with arguing opposites in the realm of political action, and Steeves was clearly aware of this. As he explained in his article, "Ideas in the College Writing Course," the benefit of such a course was that it regarded the college student as "one of the republic of thought." Rather than encouraging self-expression in essays about the student's personal experience, the teacher placed the student within an intellectual and social context: "What is he with relation to himself, and to society, and to all that has been and is defined in the name of God, and to that, for him, mystic culture, which he knows he has come to college to partake of?" (49–50). Steeves felt that the English department had concerned itself too narrowly with "the esthetic aspects of both literature and composition" (54). By becoming a separate discipline, English had "lost its relationship to the general domain of ideas and affairs, and concerned itself with itself—as, indeed, sister-subjects were doing in a day of intense specialization" (53). The ideas approach was thus put forth in the interests of both poetic and rhetoric, restoring to each its appropriate sphere. Steeves argued that combining literary study with composition is wrong because it "abuses literature by subjecting it to a purpose for which it does not exist, and, possibly, . . . upholds an unpractical and discouraging esthetic ideal in composition" (48). In contrast, the ideas course preserved the distinction between rhetoric as the domain of action and poetic as the domain of contemplation.

This approach was applauded and condemned from a variety of perspectives. Norman Foerster, a conservative proponent of New Humanism, praised it because it was especially useful for the exceptionally talented leader—the person he thought higher education ought to serve. He did, however, wish to limit its use since he agreed with the proponents of liberal culture that learning to write primarily involved self-cultivation and self-expression, both based on literary experience. Joseph M. Thomas of the University of Minnesota, a professor sympathetic to progressive education, had reservations about it. Thomas thought that students should write about their immediate personal experiences, not about ideas, and the reasons he gave have been repeated throughout the century in criticizing the ideas approach. The university is a place of experts, he explained, and the English teacher cannot possibly be an expert in all of the disciplines involved in complicated social and political problems. These issues must be left to authorities "in the theories of economics, politics, sociology, philosophy, and religion" ("Do Thought-Courses Produce Thinking?" 84). Therefore, any ideas course that is to be offered should be held in the senior year, after students have taken courses in these disciplines. Thomas did not carry his argument to its logical conclusion, a conclusion that others have increasingly put forth: since the expertise of members of the English department is in literary criticism, and since the university exists to provide expert instruction, writing courses should deal with matters the English faculty knows best—literary texts. Lost in departments where such arguments prevail, I would add, is the historical concern of rhetoric for practical action in areas of public concern affecting all citizens. Where this concern is lost, rhetoric becomes subsumed by poetic and becomes a reflective discipline rather than an active discipline.

The Efficiency Movement

During the first two decades of this century, education at every level underwent a transformation that was the result of an uncritical application of the principles of scientific management to all areas of human behavior. Raymond E. Callahan's *Education and the Cult of Efficiency* has documented this development. Objectives and accounting procedures characteristic of the business community began to appear in discussions of academic matters. This is seen most clearly in the first formal study undertaken by the NCTE, an investigation of the efficiency of college composition teaching. In the lead article of the first issue of *English Journal*, Edwin M. Hopkins of Kansas asked "Can Good Composition Teaching Be Done under Present Conditions?" and he answered with an unqualified "No." A subsequent study was conducted by a joint committee of the MLA and the NCTE (Wozniak 169–70). The committee found that writing teachers in high schools and colleges were overworked, and its report demonstrated the point vividly with hard numbers. It indicated that the average number of words written per week by a high school student was about 400, and for a college freshman about 650. A teacher could read and correct manuscripts at an average rate of 2,000 words per hour for high school students and 2,200 words per hour for college students. Because of the energy required in correcting student manuscripts, a teacher could not reasonably be expected to spend more than 2 hours per day or 10 hours per week on this task. "Much more than this," the report stated, "results sooner or later in the physical collapse of the teacher." The study revealed that, on the average, high school teachers had 130 pupils assigned to them and college teachers in freshman composition classes had 105. This teaching load would thus have required 26 hours of manuscript reading per week for high school teachers and 31 hours for college teachers—not including other teaching responsibilities. The report accordingly recommended that numbers of pupils, not numbers of teaching hours, be the standard of measuring work load. A single composition teacher should never have more than 50 writing students per term in high school or 35 in college. Furthermore, the report continued, English composition in college should be taught by the best teachers in the department, not the newest, and teachers should never teach composition exclusively. Finally, it would be better to use theme readers rather than leave themes unread, but this would not be very "efficient."

A similar attempt to introduce efficiency into the teaching of composition was the use of quantitative evaluation scales, such as those devised by Edward L. Thorndike and Milo Burdette Hillegas of Columbia. Used primarily in high schools, these consisted of a series of passages arranged according to a scale of graduated value. In evaluating a student's writing, the teacher was to compare the student sample with those presented in the scale to find the one it most closely matched. The student would then receive the score of the sample closest to her own. The samples used were pieces written by students that had been given their numerical scores by a large number of English teachers. Elaborate statistical procedures were used to ensure reliability and validity. While the tests enjoyed currency for a time, many English teachers opposed them because they encouraged mechanistic, formulaic behavior in teacher and student and because they were commonly proposed for use in evaluating teaching effectiveness (Fred Newton Scott, "Our Problems").

Graduate Education in Rhetoric

In 1900, the MLA pedagogical section undertook a survey asking if rhetoric was a proper study for graduate work; if so, what constituted its scope and leading problems; and if not, what the reasons were for excluding it (Mead, "Graduate Study of Rhetoric"). Sixty-seven of one hundred circulars were returned, almost all of them from the North. The notable feature of the responses is that, while a majority favored such study, a sizable minority could not imagine what would be considered in graduate rhetoric courses. Clearly the effort to rid English departments of the vestiges of their roots in rhetoric had been so effective that the whole twenty-five-hundred-year history of the discipline no longer existed for a large number of

English department members. To many faculty, the freshman writing course had come to stand for all of the possibilities of rhetoric. Still, graduate study in rhetoric did exist during this period. The most extensive program was offered at the University of Michigan under the direction of Scott. As Albert R. Kitzhaber has noted, between 1904 and 1930 Scott's Department of Rhetoric granted 140 master's degrees and 23 doctorates. During the same period, the Department of English at Michigan granted 24 doctorates (*Rhetoric in American Colleges* 119). Other schools provided graduate courses in rhetoric to prepare their students for composition teaching, the most conspicuous of which was Chester Noyes Greenough's course at Harvard. Calls were also made—most notably by Denney, by Thomas, and by Raymond Alden of Illinois—for graduate courses to prepare students for careers as teachers of rhetoric and literature. A useful survey of the ways in which college English teachers were being prepared, entitled "Report of the Committee on the Preparation of College Teachers of English" and published in *English Journal* in 1916, did indicate the almost exclusive focus on British literature and the relative neglect of American literature and rhetoric at this time. Still, as Alden pointed out in 1913, the use of graduate students as "temporary faculty"—the beginning of the graduate assistantship—provided practical training in composition instruction.

Undergraduate Writing Courses

The required year-long writing course was nearly ubiquitous during this period, the only notable exception being Princeton, where literature was the exclusive focus of the freshman course. As William Morton Payne's 1895 survey of twenty "representative" universities makes clear, electives in writing beginning with the sophomore year were also the rule. By 1920, these one-term electives had been greatly expanded; they included "sophomore writing" and, beyond that, "advanced writing"; special courses in each of the four forms of discourse—narration, description, exposition, and argumentation; courses in the theory of rhetoric; courses in verse writing and playwriting; and courses in journalism. These offerings, it should be noted, were available at the oldest and most prestigious universities as well as at the new state schools. Yale and Wesleyan, for example, offered a course in short-story writing, and Harvard and Mount Holyoke offered one in playwriting. Columbia, Union, Mount Holyoke, Brown, Bucknell, Hobart, Middlebury, and New York University gave courses in rhetorical theory. Mount Holyoke even offered an undergraduate major in rhetoric. A course in teaching rhetoric was provided at Yale, Brown, Colby, and Mount Holyoke. Courses in journalism and newspaper writing were offered at Pennsylvania, Bucknell, and Washington and Jefferson. Instruction in business writing and writing for engineers was found at New York University and Lafayette (for a history of the latter, see Connors, "The Rise of Technical Writing"). And, as mentioned earlier, Harvard and Pennsylvania offered course in remedial writing (Wozniak 122–34). In the Midwest, Michigan was the leader with a program that included all of these areas. As these examples indicate, writing courses increased in number and variety from 1900 to 1920, an especially interesting development since literature courses were during the same period coming to dominate the department.

The Great War

One effect of World War I was to complete a development that had been taking shape since late in the nineteenth century: English studies became the center of public school education in the United States. An Arnoldian view of the value of cultural education had begun in the East, demonstrated in the work of Horace Scudder in the 1870s and 1880s. Scudder had pointed to the ethical value of literature as an alternative to the religion-based education no longer possible in America (Applebee 24). The war showed the power of basing education on the study of language and literature as public school teachers throughout the country made their subject "a way to instill a sense of national heritage and to encourage patriotism" (Applebee 68). The acceptance of American literature in the high school and college curriculum can be traced directly to this concern for encouraging loyalty in time of war. College English departments further benefited from the upward valuation of their discipline as money became available after the war for travel, research, and such projects as dictionaries (Armstrong, Manly). The concern for the English language and its study as the common bond of the nation also increased with the appearance of immigrants and the children of immigrants in the schools after the war. But the fervor for English studies would not have been nearly as intense had it not been for the national threat posed from abroad. English courses—from elementary school to university—were seen as central to the effort to make the world safe for democracy and America safe for Americans.

4

The Influence of Progressive
Education: 1920–1940

THE YEARS BETWEEN 1920 AND 1940 ENCOMPASSED THE BEST
and the worst of the American experience. The dramatic increase in
prosperity of the twenties was followed by the worst depression in
modern history. Despite the economic catastrophe—indeed, partly
because of it—college enrollments continued to grow steadily during the period, undergoing a decline only between 1932 and 1934.
In the 1919–20 school year, enrollments totaled 597,880. By 1929
this number had increased to 1,100,737, and by 1939 to 1,494,203.
The varieties of writing instruction in use during these years corresponded in a curious way to developments in the economy. Although current-traditional rhetoric continued to be the most common approach in the college classroom, it was rivaled during the
prosperous twenties by the appearance of a subjective rhetoric that
celebrated the individual. This rhetoric persisted through the thirties but was itself challenged by transactional approaches that emphasized the social nature of human experience. The single most
significant force behind these new rhetorics, however, was that of
progressive education, at this time making a strong impression in
the public schools and influencing activities in the college classroom.

It is difficult to define progressive education. Lawrence Cremin's
description is probably the most useful: "the educational phase of
American Progressivism writ large" (viii). Progressive education
was an extension of political progressivism, the optimistic faith in
the possibility that all institutions could be reshaped to better serve
society, making it healthier, more prosperous, and happier. The pro-

ponents of this effort aspired to disinterestedness, although they ultimately served middle-class political concerns. Progressive education attempted to emulate this larger political movement by
applying science to the education of young people, even as it simultaneously insisted on the inevitability of students' individual differences. It was likewise concerned with the school serving the
well-being of society, especially in ensuring the continuance of a
democratic state that would make opportunities available to all
without compromising excellence. The complexity of this program
led progressive education to distinctive and, at times, contradictory
turns between 1920 and 1940 that must here be taken into account.

Progressive education wished to apply the findings of science to
human behavior. This meant that the social and behavioral sciences
were strongly endorsed and constantly consulted as guides to understanding students. The findings of psychologists and sociologists
were immediately applied to the school, shaping the curriculum and
school policy in a number of ways. The shift from a subject-centered
to a child-centered school was implemented by calling upon such
psychologists as G. Stanley Hall, William James, and Edward L.
Thorndike. Meanwhile, the sociological treatises of Lester Frank
Ward, Albion Small, and George S. Counts were affecting the way
the behavior of groups was perceived. At the center of these two
divergent approaches to human behavior—the one focusing on the
individual, the other on the group—was John Dewey, the student of
Hegel who was attempting to accomplish a dialectical synthesis.
Most educators were not in fact followers of Dewey in this effort—
or, stated more accurately, they called upon Dewey only for that
part of his thought which supported their own partial views. Thus,
the respect for science led not only to a commitment to individual
differences, but to a faith in Thorndike's contention that any feature
of human behavior could be quantified, measured, and controlled.
The application of the empirical method to the study of writing behavior was widespread, and attempts were even made to apply it to
literary study. It resulted in the use of intelligence tests and
grammar-usage tests and organizational tests to determine one's
place in the college composition program—a program now concerned with providing for the individual differences of students. It
led to attempts to develop objective scales to measure the value of
student essays. And it produced survey after survey of classroom

practices and composition programs, each attempting to find the "solution" to the "composition problem."

There was another area in which progressive education had a strong impact on composition instruction. As mentioned earlier, progressivism contained within it two opposed conceptions of education—one psychological and individualistic and the other social and communal—which Dewey attempted to reconcile. The influences of these two orientations correspond approximately to a historical sequence. As Cremin and Clarence Karier have indicated, before World War I the emphasis of the progressives was on social reform, on bringing the school closer to serving the needs of society. After the war, there was a shift to a child-centered pedagogy—more specifically, to an interest in depth psychology and the creative arts, both intended to foster the development of the individual without regard for social or practical ends. The focus of this effort was the cultivation of the aesthetic capabilities of the student in the interest of bringing about health and sanity. Within this context, all writing came to be seen as inherently creative. After the economic collapse of 1929, the social reformism that had been the main concern of progressives before the war again became dominant. Many educators now saw writing as a social act with public consequences, and new instructional approaches were introduced compatible with this view. In examining writing instruction during these two decades, one finds the two orientations everywhere, the difference between the twenties and thirties being one of markedly contrasting emphasis.

In this chapter, I would like first to consider the effects of the passion for quantification on the teaching of writing (a practice reinforced by the drive for efficiency mentioned in the last chapter), looking at key surveys of composition programs. This discussion will also provide an overview of the general developments in the administration of writing programs from 1920 to 1940. I will next consider the writing programs themselves, examining in some detail the ways they were conducted. Finally, the chapter will turn to the approaches to composition instruction found during these two decades.

The Surveys

In 1926, H. Robinson Shipherd published a survey of required freshman composition courses at 75 colleges and universities in the United States. Of the schools included, 47% were Eastern, 24% Southern, 21% Midwestern, and 8% Western. Coeducational institutions constituted 53% of the sample, 32% were for women only, and 14% were for men only. (Where percentages do not total 100, the investigators have rounded off numbers.) In enrollment, 44% had fewer than 1,000 students, 33% had more than 2,000, and the remaining 23% fell in between. Of the total, 26% were state universities.

The patterns Shipherd discovered are remarkably familiar. The average section size was 27.6 students, with 22% of the sections having more than 30 students and 22% having fewer than 25. The average number of class meetings was three per week. On the average, students completed four pages of writing per week, or just under two short themes, and were also required to write two longer themes per semester. Reflecting the interest in providing for individual differences, conferences were required for all students in 82% of the schools. Conferences were held two or three times per semester at 35% of those schools, fortnightly at 18%, monthly at 18%, and weekly at 6%. Shipherd was dismayed to discover that only 25% of his respondents required rewriting, despite the testimony of professional writers to its necessity.

Shipherd discovered other features of the freshman composition course that surprised him. As a Harvard Ph.D. and student of LeBaron Briggs, he considered the "conventional arrangement" of the course to be exposition and argument during the first semester and description and narration during the second. He discovered, however, that only 28% of the schools used this sequence and that 38% omitted argumentation. He also discovered a wide use of literature in the freshman writing course, with 55% of the schools requiring one thousand or more pages of reading per semester—a practice that Shipherd saw as "relatively young." This reflected, of course, the growth of literature offerings in the English department, the use of faculty whose only training had been in literature, and the success of those who advocated the ideal of liberal culture (the last a reflection of the Eastern bias in Shipherd's sample). It also represented the desire of many English departments to make literature their sole concern. The use of literature was likewise apparent in a decrease in the reliance on rhetoric textbooks and handbooks. While all departments used "pure literature" to some extent, only 56% used a rhetoric textbook and only 53% used a handbook (*Fine Art of Writing* 323–30).

A more extensive study was conducted by Warner Taylor of the University of Wisconsin in 1927 and 1928. Taylor's findings were based on 225 institutions across the nation, with a combined enrollment of more than 100,000 freshmen. He also took great pains to arrive at a more representative sample, and he accordingly reported somewhat different, although not greatly inconsistent, findings. (He found, for example, that Eastern colleges diverged from the norm for other parts of the country, a fact he traced to the higher standards and the better students of these schools.)

Taylor discovered that Eastern schools were using a rhetoric textbook less and less, with only 40% of those in the survey still doing so. This compared to a usage rate of 73% in the Midwest, 60% in the South, and 65% in the West. Handbooks and collections of essays were used more frequently, but again the usage rate was lowest in the East. Handbooks were used by 96% of Midwestern schools, 90% of Southern schools, and 87% of Western schools, but only 58% of Eastern schools. Similarly, essay collections were used by 84% of Midwestern schools, 88% of Southern schools, and 87% of Western schools, but only 67% of Eastern schools (still, of course, a substantial number). These essay collections, unlike those of the ideas approach of the previous decade, tended to rely on contemporary essays, frequently from very recent periodicals. Their purpose, Taylor explained, was to provide "essays that offer challenges to the student mind, that start his thinking apparatus" (8). Taylor discovered that combined use of all three texts—rhetoric, handbook, and essay collection— was again least common in the East (20%), but even in other regions constituted less than 50% of the total: Midwest, 42%; South, 38%; and West, 43%.

Taylor also examined a category he labeled the "traditional conformity" freshman composition course. This year-long course was required for all first-year students. It used a rhetoric text, a handbook, and an essay collection; it emphasized the study of rhetoric rather than literature; and it consisted of three hour-long weekly recitations. Once again, he found that the less exclusive the admissions procedures of the school, the more likely its freshman composition course was to correspond to this pattern. Of the state universities, 27% had courses that fit the traditional conformity model. Of the private schools, 7% of those in the East, 37% of those in the Midwest, 31% of those in the South, and 41% of those in the West had this type of composition course.

When Taylor turned to the matter of literature in the freshman course, his findings were a bit confusing. They seemed to indicate that Eastern and Southern schools more often combined rhetoric and literature (the latter studied for its own sake and not as stimulus for thought or to provide models), whereas Midwestern and Western schools tended to restrict the course primarily to the study of rhetoric (73% of these schools followed this practice, as compared to only 39% of the schools in the East and South).

Taylor's information on the modes of discourse being emphasized in the freshman class supported and elaborated upon Shipherd's findings. He discovered that both argumentation and narration were on the decline. Most schools seemed to favor exposition as the focus of the course, with description serving as a part of exposition—trends that were predictable given the theoretical developments of the nineteenth century (Berlin, *Writing Instruction;* Connors, "Rhetoric of Explanation").

Taylor's examination of staffing patterns in the freshman English class yielded remarkable findings. Throughout the nation the course was taught largely by instructors and graduate students, with only the Eastern and Western schools staffing the course with less than 50% of this rank. The Midwest averaged only 17% of the professorial staff in the course and the South 38%, compared to 52% in the West and 58% in the East. Taylor also indicated parenthetically that Wisconsin, Ohio State, Minnesota, and Iowa averaged only 6.7% of the professorial staff in freshman English, most of these classes being taught by graduate students. Taylor discovered a corresponding reliance on graduate students throughout his sample of large schools: nationwide, 47% of the large institutions used graduate students as teachers and readers, whereas only 18% of the small schools did. By region, graduate students were relied on at 48% of the large Midwestern schools, 43% of the Southern schools, 59% of the Western schools, and 37% of the Eastern schools. Clearly, at the larger universities the graduate student had become a significant force in the freshman English course.

Taylor also compiled data on teaching loads, teacher-student relationships, and course requirements. He found that, among the 90 insitutions that provided solid data, the average number of students for which an instructor was responsible was 93 for three sections. As for the individual attention these teachers gave to their students, 66% of the schools surveyed customarily scheduled two to three conferences of fifteen to twenty minutes' duration per term. The average number of words per week required of students was 470, with the most commonly appearing number being 500.

Finally, one of the newest features of the freshman composition program revealed by the survey was the use of placement tests and the grouping of students according to ability. Taylor found that most schools used standard placement tests, a grammar test and theme writing, or a combination of the two. He learned that many schools also followed the Wisconsin pattern in including both advanced sections and "sub-freshman" composition sections, the latter carrying no credit. Of the total sample, 26% of the schools provided both advanced and remedial courses, 14% offered the remedial but not the advanced, 11% offered the advanced but not the remedial, 15% classified the students in other ways, and 35% did not classify them at all. Taylor also noted that only 9% of all schools included provisions for waiving freshman composition altogether.

Taylor summarized the trends that he had identified in the survey. Placement tests were multiplying and ability sectioning was becoming widespread. At the same time, rhetoric textbooks were being abandoned while literature was increasingly being introduced into the course. Finally, English clinics were being established— places where students who had completed the freshman composition requirement could go for assistance with their college writing assignments.

The surveys of Shipherd and Taylor identified trends in freshman composition that eventually became permanent features of the course. This can be seen in a study undertaken in 1940 and published in *College English* in 1942 under the heading "National Council of Teachers of English College Section." This survey covered 292 institutions: 132 liberal arts colleges, 103 universities, 21 engineering colleges, and 36 teachers colleges. It found that 80% of these schools required freshman composition. There were more frequent exemptions of able students, however: 49 of the institutions waived the requirement for this group of students, and 37 waived part of it. The composition course varied from two to twelve semester hours, with 79% of the schools requiring six hours over a one-year period. The median enrollment was 25 students, except for the teachers colleges, where it was 30. Ability sectioning was used at 67% of the schools, and the most common section levels were fast, average, and slow (the last sometimes being a noncredit course). The conference, on the other hand, was on the decline; only 61 schools reported requiring conferences and only 125 in all reported using them in any form. The median writing load consisted of twelve shorter themes and one longer theme. The writing "laboratory," the counterpart of the earlier English clinic, existed at 34 schools, providing assistance in course work and at some schools even being offered as a course itself. A number of schools also reported offering remedial work for upperclassmen with 37% providing systematic instruction.

The Writing Program and Current-Traditional Rhetoric

I would now like to turn to a consideration of the organized freshman writing programs that appeared from 1920 to 1940. Since all of these were structured according to the principles of current-traditional rhetoric, the discussion will move from developments in these programs to developments in this variety of rhetoric.

Organized freshman composition programs headed by directors and providing for elaborate administrative procedures for dealing with students were commonplace in the twenties and thirties. These most often appeared in Midwestern and Western state universities, but occasionally were found at private universities—at Harvard and Bradley, for example. Their minimal essentials were a placement test, grouping students by ability, and some sort of procedure for verifying the success of the program, such as exit tests or follow-up programs for students who later displayed shortcomings. Syracuse University in the early twenties displayed a typical freshman program. Its twelve hundred freshman students were given a placement test called a "Minimum Essentials Test" that consisted of a grammar section and a writing sample (Whitney, "Ability Grouping at Syracuse"). The samples were read by the most experienced faculty members. On the basis of the combined grammar and writing scores, the students were divided into three groups: the top 12½% into group A, the bottom 25% into Group C, and the remaining 62½% into Group B. (Students could be reclassified on the basis of their performance during the first month of class.) Group A students completed the English requirement in one semester, Group B in two, and Group C in three. Since the composition requirement for all students was nine hours, Groups A and B were given additional credit for the work they did. There was thus no "sub-freshman" English since all courses carried credit.

The content of the Syracuse courses was representative of an emerging pattern. English A was a course in writing about literature; it required fifteen weekly themes of two pages and a long review of a novel. English B was a course in expository writing that included a weekly out-of-class theme, a weekly in-class theme, and a research paper of two thousand words on a subject selected from an approved list (the paper was written after a unit in using the library). The first half of this course covered note-taking, bibliography preparation, research for writing a long paper, the composition as a whole (sources of material, purpose, arrangement, outlines, and manuscript form), and the paragraph (kinds, uses, and methods of development). No rhetoric textbook was used in the course; the instructor lectured in its place. The second half of the course covered the study of language—its history, the dictionary, style—and the correct form of social and business correspondence. All themes were written and corrected, with errors indicated by the correction symbols of the *Century Handbook*. Students were expected to correct the errors in each theme returned and to keep the themes in a folder to be examined by the teacher during one of the three scheduled conferences. An elaborate grading procedure was provided, with 25% of the grade decided by the research paper, 25% by the out-of-class theme, 25% by the in-class theme, and 25% by the final exam. The English C course dealt with sentence analysis and sentence structure. Grammar was reviewed, and a grade of at least 90% in spelling was required for passing the course. Students wrote no themes. Class work—done only twice weekly—consisted of instruction and drills in correctness.

The Syracuse plan tried to ensure uniform subject matter and uniform grading standards in all courses, although it did make allowances for "the personality of the instructor" (Whitney, "Ability Grouping at Syracuse" 487). The final examination in each course was also meant as a check of performance for teacher as well as student. Those students who failed the final exam were allowed to take it once more before being told to repeat the course. Teachers were required to submit their final grades to the departmental committee on grading, a committee that had the authority to "recommend such changes as . . . necessary for a reasonable distribution of grades for the whole group" (488). The grade distribution set up as the model consisted of 25% A's and B's, 50% C's, and 25% D's, E's, and F's (D was a passing grade), although perfect compliance was not mandatory.

Syracuse published another essay on its program four years later, in 1928, and it is instructive to see the changes made that attempted to move it even further in the direction of a scientific precision in placement and grading (Whitney, "Ability Grouping Plus"). The placement theme had been omitted due to the "subjective elements" caused by nervous students. To provide "more objective measures," a vocabulary test was used. The department now was "convinced that there is a direct relation between vocabulary test scores and specific aptitude for writing" (562). The literature course (Group A) had been assigned to the "best and most experienced instructors" and its emphasis was on the survey of the types of contemporary literature, not on writing, although writing about literature was undertaken. The forms of discourse in the Group B course had been abandoned and longer monthly themes had been added, but the course remained essentially the same. The Group C course was unchanged, but the department was now able to report that statistics on grade distribution indicated that the failure rate overall had declined, and that "Group C students do increasingly better work as they progress, never equalling their more fortunate companions, but constantly improving on their own records" (564).

Despite its forbidding emulation of a technological model, Syracuse's effort was an attempt to provide for the needs and abilities of students and to increase the chances of success for those who might otherwise fail. Theirs was an effort to democratize college, making it available to a new group of students, even students whose parents had not benefited from higher education. And in undertaking this effort, Syracuse and schools like it were simply emulating the example of Harvard.

During the twenties Harvard had instituted an "anticipatory examination" for the purpose of exempting some students from the freshman writing requirement. Later it exempted from the required English A-1 course (a year-long sequence) only those who had received a grade of 75% or better on the College Entrance Examination Board English section. Students who received a C or better during the first term were allowed to choose their second-term section from "Types of Literature," "Narration and Description," "Argumentation," and "Exposition." This system, however, did not provide enough "individual attention" ("English A-1 at Harvard" 388), and by 1932 it was decided to use a tutorial method. During the first term, students met weekly with their regular sections and also met bimonthly for one-half hour in individual conference with their instructors. During the second term, those students who had received a grade of A, B, or C+ for the first term were grouped together by fours for conferences. Those who had received a grade of C, D, or E continued the individual conferences. While this was, on the face of it, a move in the direction of the avowedly elitist preceptorial method of Princeton, the required course continued to be organized around writing, not literature, although literature was a part of the course. Students wrote approximately four papers a week with occasional longer themes and were required to read in *Prose Masterpieces* (an essay collection) and from a selected literary list, the latter assignment being five hundred pages each month.

The rigorously organized programs at Syracuse and Harvard were mirrored in varying degrees in the Midwest at Illinois, Purdue, Wisconsin, and Minnesota; in the West at UCLA; in the South at West Virginia, North Carolina, and North Carolina State; and in the East at Cornell. All of these, however, offered interesting variations on the pattern.

Bernard L. Jefferson, chair of the freshman rhetoric course at Illinois, described a program for three thousand students at his school that in 1930 was very close to that at Syracuse, although it included twelve sections of a sub-freshman course that offered no credit (Jefferson, "Our First Semester"). In 1935, however, Illinois began using a proficiency exam at the end of its first-term course that required the student to complete an objective test, summarize a long passage of prose, and write an essay on an assigned subject (Jefferson, Glenn, and Gettman, "Freshman Writing"). The evaluation of the essay was partly influenced by a new test in organizational ability developed by John Stalnaker at the University of Chicago. At Purdue, J. H. McKee was especially zealous in a similar use of objective tests and statistical procedures designed to justify his freshman composition program to the world. At Wisconsin, the noncredit remedial course was reintroduced in 1938 after having been dropped in 1931, but the basic program remained the same throughout, following the Illinois and Syracuse pattern. And at the University of Minnesota, Alvin C. Eurich called for the abolition of freshman English based on a comparison of the objective grammar-usage test scores of those who were exempt from the course and those who took it. Nonetheless, Minnesota continued its placement testing and its advanced, regular, and sub-freshman sections of freshman English (Eurich).

In other parts of the country, similar programs were flourishing. In 1938 Arthur Palmer Hudson, chair of freshman composition at the University of North Carolina, described the three-tiered system at that institution, with 11% of the students in the advanced course, 64% in the regular course, and 25% in the remedial section. His purpose for doing so, however, was to deplore the large number in the remedial course and to call for reform at the high school level. In 1935 North Carolina State had a similar three-tiered system, but it had found success in abandoning the handbook and rhetoric text for its A and B sections, relying instead on extensive reading and writing. Still, the grouping scheme and the study of grammar in the remedial section remained (Clark). In the West, an instructor at UCLA reported that by 1938 the school had run a successful sub-freshman course for a second year (Ringnalda). Finally, in the East, Cornell was offering two tracks of freshman writing and insisting on the value of literature for the advanced group because it provided training in the "science of reading and writing" (Tenney 365).

It is obvious that these current-traditional programs were including those features of progressive education that were compatible with their positivistic epistemology. Objective tests were strongly emphasized in placing students and in evaluating student performance. The use of ability grouping and of the student-teacher conference was, furthermore, a clear response to progressive education's concern for individual differences. It is important to note that all of these features were compatible with the scientistic orientation of the course offerings. These freshman composition classes remained focused on problems of arrangement and style, with the content of discourse relegated to activity outside the composing process.

Current-traditional rhetoric did undergo a number of changes during this period, even though none of them were substantive. One new addition to the classroom was the use of the research paper. Requiring students to engage in library research was a predictable outcome of a course taught by teachers whose major source of professional rewards was the accumulation of research publications. Furthermore, the research paper represented the insistence in current-traditional rhetoric on finding meaning outside the composing act, with writing itself serving as a simple transcription process. The first article in *English Journal* to discuss the teaching of the research paper appeared in 1930 (Chalfant), but use of the research paper was commonly mentioned in program descriptions in the twenties. Textbooks that included discussion of the research paper began to appear in significant numbers in 1931. After this, no year of *English Journal* passed without a number of articles on approaches to teaching the research essay. It should also be noted that the widespread use of this assignment was influenced by the improvements in library collections during the twenties, as well as by new ways of indexing these materials for easy access—the periodical guides, for example.

Another important development in the current-traditional class was in the kind of rhetoric textbooks and readers appearing at the time. In response to progressive education's emphasis on life experience—as found, for example, in the NCTE-sponsored *An Experience Curriculum in English* (1935)—textbooks began to replace the modes of discourse with the "types" approach. A notable example was *Writing by Types: A Manual of Composition*, by Albert C. Baugh, Paul C. Kitchen, and Matthew W. Black. This text contained discussions and illustrations of the critical essay, the feature article, the editorial, the after-dinner speech, and other practical writing tasks.

Still another significant development was the appearance of the college omnibus. Warren Bower, a teacher at New York University and a former associate editor of *Scribner's Magazine*, reported in 1938 that sales of rhetoric texts in the East and Midwest had almost ceased. Teachers were instead using a grammar handbook and one of several omnibus volumes, each a collection of essays, poems, short stories, plays, and (usually) a short novel. These collections had originated during the worst part of the Depression and were being touted by publishers as a way to save students money. Their effect, Bower explained, had been to make of freshman composition a course in reading rather than writing: "More and more emphasis has fallen on reading as a desirable end in itself, with an implied faith that if only a student will read enough good prose he will also be able to write it—the 'go thou and do likewise' theory of teaching" (848). This shift from rhetoric to literature as the basis of study in the writing course (Bower contended it had become a course in literary genres) had already been noted by Warner Taylor ten years earlier; given the literary training of all writing teachers, its appearance was inevitable. There was another force at work, however.

Liberal Culture

It has already been noted that those educators who supported current-traditional rhetoric looked upon the college as the training ground for a middle-class, professionally certified meritocracy. In their view, writing courses were to provide students with the skills necessary to write effectively within their professions; literature courses were to put students in touch with the civilizing influences of culture, thereby providing a basis for ethical behavior. As Bernard Jefferson explained, literature helped the student acquire a humane social sense that led to high ideals of citizenship ("English Literature").

The proponents of liberal culture, on the other hand, looked upon the university as the preparatory school for an elite, aristocratic group of individualists. Rather than being trained in the ways of a profession, students were to be immersed in the traditional learning of literature, language, and art. For the proponents of liberal culture, the purpose of the English teacher was to cultivate the exceptional students, the geniuses, and, at the most, to tolerate all others. It is no coincidence that Yale and Princeton, the last holdouts against the replacement of the traditional classical course of study by the new elective system, were the primary centers of this notion of education. And although Eastern colleges continued to be the home of this approach, it began to spread throughout the nation as graduates of Eastern schools were given teaching positions in other parts of the country. For example, George Shelton Hubbell, a Princeton Ph.D. at the University of California, deplored the mediocrity of his students and doubted that he could make them "good citizens." He was further concerned that "even the aristocratic tendency of lectures to leave all the good things with able students is counteracted by the democratic cheapness of filling the ears of five hundred at one sitting" (826).

Two outspoken proponents of liberal culture who argued against teaching rhetoric, insisting that writing is taught through cultivating the individual in literary study, where Charles G. Osgood of Princeton and Oscar James Campbell of Michigan and later Columbia. In addition, a dramatic attempt to compensate for the loss of the aristocratic ideal of liberal culture in the meritocratic university was the inauguration of the honors program. Started at Swarthmore by President Frank Aydelotte, a former English professor at Indiana, its purpose was to provide for the elite and to avoid the worst consequences of the democratization of opportunity in higher education (Rudolph, *Curriculum* 230–31; Phillip Hicks; Spiller).

The proponents of liberal culture, for all their aristocratic airs, performed a valuable service for the university. Their continued opposition to the narrow specialization of the professional curricula kept the liberal arts a vital force in higher education. While their ideal was sometimes extreme—at times implying that the true end of education should be a Paterian retirement from active life—it was perhaps occasionally necessary given the fervor of their opponents for the practical. Those English department members who advocated a rhetoric based on the ideal of liberal culture also played an important part in the development of a new rhetoric—a part they would not, however, point to with satisfaction.

Expressionistic Rhetoric

The ideal of liberal culture indirectly encouraged the development of expressionistic rhetoric through its philosophical idealism and its emphasis on the cultivation of the self, both derived from its ties to a Brahminical romanticism. We saw in the last chapter that Osgood in 1915 had pointed to the inability to write as a spiritual malady. In a 1922 essay he sounded the same note, asserting, "Clearness, force, correctness—these three—come not by process treatment, but only out of 'the abysmal depths of personality'." Citing Plato's *Phaedrus,* Osgood argued that good writing arises from the "energies of the spirit." Although the good teacher can reach these energies, "he or she cannot tell how, any more than Burns can tell us how to write an immortal song" (162). Writing involves the self and is an art. Learning and teaching it can be accomplished but not explained. Of course, the best approach is through literature, "literature employed as the revealer of nature and of life, literature as a personal matter, of the ear, the eye, the mind, the spirit" (164). Once again, Osgood was emphasizing the personal and private nature of knowledge and of composing. If we democratize his statements, holding that what is true for the composing of geniuses—of Burns or Plato—is true for all individuals (as did, for example, Emerson), we are in the realm of expressionistic rhetoric.

Liberal culture helped create a climate in which expressionistic rhetoric could develop, but the sources of expressionism are far from a nineteenth-century mandarin romanticism. The origin of this rhetoric can instead be found in the postwar, Freudian-inspired, expressionistic notions of childhood education that the progressives attempted to propagate. As Cremin explained, the earlier radicalism of "the artists and literati who flocked to the Greenwich Villages of New York, Chicago, and San Francisco" before World War I had been abandoned. In its place was established "a polyglot system of ideas that combined the doctrine of self-expression, liberty, and psychological adjustment into a confident, iconoclastic individualism that fought the constraints of Babbitry and the discipline of social reform as well" (201). This tendency in turn "developed its own characteristic pedagogical argument: the notion that each individual has uniquely creative potentialities and that a school in which children are encouraged freely to develop their potentialities is the best guarantee of a larger society truly devoted to human worth and excellence" (202). In the experimental schools of Caroline Pratt, Hughes Mearns and Satis Coleman, and Lucy Sprague Mitchell and Willy Levin was found an extension of the aesthetic expressionism of the music of Charles Ives, the dance of Isadora Duncan and Martha Graham, and the painting of Max Weber.

Expressionistic rhetoric was further encouraged by a popularized Freudianism. "Teachers were urged," Cremin explained, "to recognize the *unconscious* as the real source of motivation and behavior in themselves and their students. The essential task of education was seen as one of *sublimating* the child's *repressed* emotion into socially useful channels" (209). In practice, this too often became a permissiveness that located the basis of education in the abandonment of repression: "Preoccupation with repression became a denial of authority, preoccupation with the emotions, a denial of rationality" (210). The aim of education for both aesthetic expressionists and Freudians became individual transformation—not social change—as the key to both social and personal well-being. And for both groups art became the agency that brought about the transformation. Thus, an unlikely union of patrician romanticism, aesthetic expressionism, and a domesticated Freudianism brought about in American schools and colleges a view of writing as art that encouraged an expressionist rhetoric and a new emphasis on the value of creativity in the writing classroom.

For expressionistic rhetoric, we recall, writing—all writing—is art. This means that writing can be learned but not taught. The work of the teacher is to provide an environment in which students can learn what cannot be directly imparted in instruction. That which the writer is trying to express—the content of knowledge—is the product of a private and personal vision that cannot be expressed in normal, everyday language. This language, after all, refers to the public world of sensory data. Instead, the writer, like the patient underoing psychoanalysis, must learn to use metaphor in order to express this private realm. For the romantic poet, nature had meaning because it pointed metaphorically to a higher, spiritual reality. For the Freudian, nature has significance because it can be used to express in metaphor the truths of the unconscious, truths that come to us only in metaphor—through displacement or condensation, for example. The writing teacher must therefore encourage the student to call on metaphor, to seek in sensory experience materials that can be used in suggesting the truths of the unconscious—the private, personal, visionary world of ultimate truth. Through writing, the student is thus getting in touch with the source of all human experience and shaping a new and better self. The product of this creative process is organic, representing the merger of form and content. Each grows out of the other; to change one is to change both.

It is from expressionistic rhetoric in the twenties, and just before, that we get the first extensive discussions emphasizing the "process" of composing over the "product." In 1919, for example, Raymond Weaver of Columbia complained that the "process by which successful writers have brought their work to its final form has not been the interest of the pedagogue. Rather has he dissected the finished product—and from such analysis he has delivered to inarticulate students counsels of literary perfection" (63–64). Weaver felt that what was needed in teaching descriptive writing was a psychological approach in which the student must use all the senses in describing, "must catch the passing phenomenon in all its novelty and idiosyncracy; must dive bodily into the stream of sensation, momentarily escape from the inertia and momentum of practical life" (68–69). Writing is art, is divorced from the world of affairs, and the student must be persuaded that "Shakespearian gifts of intellect and imagination lie well hidden in some corner of his organism" (71). Weaver accordingly praised Vassar's course in descriptive writing because of its "emphasis on the creative side" and its effort "to enlarge, actually, the perceptive faculties" (74). Recognizing the literary nature of all writing, Vassar provided "analyses of the methods of great writers, together with constant survey of one another's work" (75). The editorial group, a commonplace of the expressionist classroom, was likewise encouraged. Weaver insisted that sensory details be used to suggest states of emotion, thereby achieving originality and—as he quoted from George Santayana—expressing the "qualities we may call tertiary, such as pain, fear, joy, malice, feebleness, expectancy" (78).

A similar approach to freshman composition was advocated in a number of essays appearing in the 1922 volume of *English Journal*. For example, Allan H. Gilbert of Trinity College, North Carolina, argued that "all honest writing—and no other sort is worth correcting—is the expression of the nature of the student." The teacher could not "make wholesale changes in the sentences of many students without pretty general substitutes of his own personality for theirs" (394). Indeed, Gilbert asserted that as far as writing ability was concerned, half of the students were equal to the instructor and some were clearly superior. He felt that students must write to please themselves, not the teacher, because "the teacher's power to bring about a change in the writing of students is limited by their minds, and only what springs from within them counts in making good writing." Each student should therefore be encouraged to develop her "own genius," the teacher meanwhile celebrating the diversity of the works produced since this would indicate that "pupils are developing their own natures" (396). Literature should be used for subject matter because, "as poetry is in contact with life, it is in contact with the experience of the student; hence everyone has an opportunity to use the fruits of his own observation" (399). From this perspective the work of art is simply a point of departure for students to record their own responses, not to attempt literary criticism. Gilbert used a workshop approach (called "laboratory work") that encouraged a nondirective method in the teacher: "In the laboratory work the teacher makes every effort to adjust himself to the individual student, considering that his duty is not to correct papers, but to bring the student to correct and improve them for himself" (403). The product displaying a small improvement that came from a student's own effort was to be preferred to the outstanding piece resulting from the teacher having recomposed a student's work: "The instructor is gadfly rather than dictator" (403).

Oakley Calvin Johnson of the University of Michigan argued in a 1928 *English Journal* essay that, since writing is an art, all writing teachers must themselves be writers. Freshman composition teachers are the counterparts of painters, poets, and musicians, and must not allow "practical" people to reduce them to theme correctors. The remedy is simple: "There must be less dogmatism, less pedantry, less arbitrary formalism, and more freedom, more up-to-dateness in language and in theme material, more emphasis on individuality." The student must, like artists in other areas, master tools and techniques, but the ultimate aim is to "express his personality" (413). There is something in all great artists that is beyond teaching, but much can still be taught in the freshman classroom, particularly the reports of artists on their learning of "the complete process" (414).

Adele Bildersee, associate professor of English at Hunter College of the City University of New York, published one of the most popular expressionist textbooks of the twenties and thirties. Entitled *Imaginative Writing*, the text was designed to deal with descriptive and narrative writing in discursive prose as well as in creative writing. It blurred the distinction between rhetoric and poetic, however, with both being considered as art. In her preface, Bildersee explained: "The aim of the book is to guide students in learning how to write. During twenty years, more or less, of experience, the teacher who writes the book has learned this: that the art of writing cannot be taught; it can only be learned. The part the teacher can play in this process is that of guide and adviser—collaborator, if need be" (ix). As a result, the subject matter of the book is not writing, but the student. The young writer, like the painter, can learn from the work accomplished by the masters—in Bildersee's text, almost always artists rather than rhetoricians—but even from them only a little can be gathered. At the basis of writing is a "mystery" that can never be simply formulated.

Bildersee did not mean to discourage the student with her commentary. She felt that while writing is indeed an art, it is one that all can learn. It is within the reach of every student, with the necessary caveat that the student be prepared to work. Her text thus incorporated excerpts in which writers discussed the pains involved in their composing, including both essayists, such as Lafcadio Hearn and Irvin S. Cobb, and artists, such as Amy Lowell, Keats, and Robert Louis Stevenson. And although Bildersee attempted to justify including pure sensory description for its own sake in a writing text, she explicitly called on Carlyle, Browning, and Shelley commenting on the ways in which sensory detail ought to be used metaphorically to suggest what lies beyond the material. The same emphasis on metaphor may be found in the chapter entitled "Feeling for Words," where she underscored the inherently metaphoric nature of language: "Indeed the greatest number of figures are those that we use quite unconsciously, without being aware that we have left prosaic literalness behind and that we are using figurative language" (85). It is this inherent metaphoric nature of language that the writer is to cultivate—striving, of course, for the fresh and original.

Proponents of expressionistic writing continued to appear in print in the late twenties and throughout the thirties. In 1928, Richard Reeve's "A Study in Dreams and Freshman Composition" recommended that students use their dreams as points of departure for writing personal experience essays. His application of psychoanalytical thought was innocent and simplistic, but it indicates the attempts being made to apply this mode of thought in the writing class. In 1930, Howard Francis Seeley's "Composition as a Liberating Activity" offered a more rigorous statement. Seeley, an education professor at Ohio State, saw writing as the use of language in order to create the self and believed students must be told that "originality means nothing more terrifying than being themselves in what they say and how they say it" (113). Writing itself will generate this original thought, he maintained, since imagination is shared by all. In a 1937 article, John C. McCloskey of the University of Oregon deplored the emphasis on the forms of discourse, arguing that this distorts "the actual process of writing" (125). His position was that writing is the "personal expression of ideas" (116), especially ideas that arise out of personal observation or reaction and that are couched in figures of speech. Finally, Edith Christina Johnson of Wellesley College, in a 1938 *English Journal* article, began by denying that the essay should be taught as self-expression, but soon after described it in these terms: "The essay, like poetry—it has been called the prose lyric—lifts the scales from the inner eye of mind and spirit as it awakens insight into truth revealed in familiar expression and scene" (762–63). She saw the essay as leading to "selfhood," "personal identity," and knowledge of the self, and providing "for the expression of thoughts, images, sudden visions of truth" (765) that are a part of everyone's experience.

Finally, J. McBride Dabbs in 1932 offered a full picture of the expressionistic writing class. He included the concept of organic form: "How we say a thing depends on what we have to say." He advised that students assume the attitude of the would-be artist, and he conducted his class as an extended editorial group, "reading, chiefly for inspiration, the writings of the class" (745). His students kept journals, "first, to give practice in writing; second, to remind [them] of the need of keeping alive to impressions and ideas; and, third, to serve as a storehouse for this material, some of which would later be developed and completed" (746). Writing in the class consisted of subjects and forms chosen by the students themselves—whether rhetorical or poetic—not discourse dictated by the teacher. And at the end of the course, each student submitted a portfolio consisting of the work completed—commonly a greater number of pages than when assignments were given, even though there "were no minimum or maximum requirements" (748). Students were evaluated on the quantity and quality of this work, but the real benefit of the course was "a more continuous sense of creation" (749).

The influence of expressionism in art and of Freudian psychology also encouraged the rise of creative writing courses in high schools and colleges. Alice Bidwell Wesenberg of Butler College commented in 1927 that the census of 1930 ought to include a tabulation of the poets in the nation since it seemed to her that everybody was writing poetry. She pointed to a number of reasons for this creative outburst. Foremost was "a changed attitude both toward poetry and toward the poetic faculty. Of poetry we think now as not more special than prose; the poetic faculty is now considered universal" (213). This breakdown of the distinction between rhetoric and poetic and the attendant democratization of the ability to create was, for Wesenberg, a part of the romanticism that led to expressionism and Freudianism and to the resultant flowering of creativity:

> It is the general—universal—desire for self-expression, a direct result of all our modern thinking, that is the fertile soil for all their seeds. . . . The young people now leaving the colleges have been encouraged since kindergarten days in creating; nothing at the family dinner table has been so interesting as the child's untrammeled talk. Repression has been taboo, expression canonized. . . . Blame Rousseau for it, or praise him; but remember he is largely responsible for the present flood of poetry in America. (215)

There was everywhere, Wesenberg added, an interest in poetry—in college classes offered, in the books available at corner bookstores, and in the periodical press, both popular and specialized.

Further evidence of this outburst of creative writing in the schools and colleges of the twenties and thirties is abundant. In 1929, *English Journal* devoted two separate editorials to the phenomenon, making a call in the second for articles on the subject. The review pages of this journal also frequently mentioned collections of the creative work of high school students, as well as collections of discussions by creative writers about their work. In addition, there were numerous articles on teaching creative writing in *English Journal*, including an engaging survey in 1931. Snow Longley Housh studied sixty-three college catalogs and received replies to questionnaires from a number of these schools. Unfortunately, although her sample was regionally representative, her statistical treatment is highly suspect. Still, her raw data are suggestive. She found that forty-one of the schools considered had "some form of creative writing as part of the curriculum" (672), but that all schools encouraged it as an extracurricular activity. Most creative writing courses provided for the selection of students on the basis of writing samples and stressed the development of critical standards rather than, as in the high school, personality enrichment. Indeed, a number of colleges—Amherst, Michigan, Columbia, Iowa, Northwestern, Smith—had hired famous poets. English departments, in Housh's opinion, were becoming like art departments, counting creative work as the equal of scholarship in awarding prizes. Finally, she found that colleges tended to go through predictable, evolutionary stages in arriving at creative writing courses. Schools first offered courses focusing on rhetorical principles, then combined rhetoric and composition, then offered composition alone, and, at last, developed distinctive creative writing courses.

One other development contributed to the flowering of expressionistic rhetoric and creative writing courses during this period. Throughout the twenties, attempts were made to replace the historical and philological method in academic literary criticism with an approach that emphasized the aesthetic qualities of the work of art. As we have seen, the best-known spokesperson for one branch of this reform movement was Joel Spingarn, who relied extensively on the work of Benedetto Croce. Spingarn opposed all existing academic approaches to literary criticism—classical and modern views of genre and figures, social approaches in the manner of Spencer and Taine, the moral approaches of the Genteel Tradition—and proposed in their stead "The New Criticism," the title of a lecture delivered at Columbia in 1910. He wished the critic to examine the work of art without preconceptions, looking to discover in it the author's intention and the degree to which this intention had been realized. This method demanded an act of creation on the part of the critic, a meeting of one creative spirit with another. In Spingarn's terms, "taste must reproduce the work of art within itself in order to understand and judge it; and at that moment aesthetic judgment becomes nothing more nor less than creative art itself" (34). Thus, criticism and creativity are both ultimately based on intuition since all truth is finally the result of an original and private vision, or the original and private verification of an act of original and private vision. Articles using Spingarn's approach in teaching literature appeared in professional journals throughout the twenties, providing a counterpart in poetic to the expressionistic rhetoric of the period (see Jones, Bennett, Gilman, Priestley, Solve).

Social Rhetoric

The tendency to view writing as a social activity, growing within a social context and carrying social consequences, increased after the onset of the Depression. In some ways this was a return to the social reform impulse found among the proponents of progressive education before World War I. There can be no mistaking in these approaches a return to collectivist alternatives to solving the nation's problems and an increasing opposition to individualism in both the economic and social realms. As Arthur N. Applebee has pointed out, policy statements by the American Historical Society, the Progressive Education Association, and the NCTE during the thirties all underscored a reawakened sense of communal responsibility both at home and internationally and a rejection of the ideal of extreme individualism (116).

The effects of this turn to the social and collective in the writing classroom were varied. At one extreme, the concern for the social implications of the composition class led to an exclusion of all writing tasks except those found at the time to be needed by adults. This very program for public schools was in fact recommended by an NCTE committee in 1926 after conducting a survey of the kind of writing most adults ordinarily undertook in their professional and private lives ("Report of the Committee on Place"). At its best, however, the recognition of the social nature of writing led to a fully blown rhetoric of public discourse, a transactional rhetoric that was close to an Aristotelian model. Here was an attempt to prepare students for a comprehensive response to varied rhetorical situations, involving a consideration of the writer's and audience's roles and the definition of issues and exigencies. This rhetoric appeared most fully articulated at the end of the thirties, but a number of noteworthy proposals led up to it.

Even before 1930, attempts had been made to shift the attention of the writing classroom away from expressionism on the one hand and current-traditional rhetoric on the other. Roy T. Thompson of the University of Southern California, while admitting that superficial correctness was more important than subject matter in freshman composition, argued that the course ought to prepare individuals for citizenship by asking them to write about political subjects. The purpose of doing so would be to train the individual to assume the responsibilities of citizenship in a democracy, "to stand alone in the sense that he can reach his own conclusions by processes of his own independent thinking" (578). E. C. Beck at Central State Teachers College in Michigan indicated a similar shift in emphasis. She assured the readers of *English Journal* that her experiment showing that individual conferences improved student performance would not result in the "loss of any social contacts, for the class recitation still retains the social situation" (596). And in a survey of 109 colleges published in 1929, Raymond P. Currier deplored the discovery that writing courses emphasized practical ability at the expense of "ethical, social, and philosophical attitudes" (848). He called for more courses dealing with these attitudes as well as a shift in writing classes toward closer attention to them. Finally, in "Social Ideals in Freshman English," Frank Earl Ward of Macalester College reported a current-traditional approach to writing instruction emphasizing arrangement and superficial correctness; yet at the same time he was trying to make the course serve the "social arts," emphasizing small-group work with teacher and peers in order to make freshman composition "a course in the art of social life" (297).

As the thirties brought its increasing store of human misery, the attention of composition teachers became more clearly focused on writing as a response to social contexts. H. W. Davis at Kansas State argued for writing as a social act in which the teacher must focus on "the writing process rather than the finished product" (802). According to her view, which was close to the epistemic, language is an activity that is a part of the entire range of the student's behavior.

The English teacher thus can play only a small role in the student's total development, but she must take this role seriously. The teacher's first duty is to be a writer herself, since only in this way can she come to understand the complexities of the writing process. This will also make the teacher realize an important fact: "'themes' or 'compositions' are rarely encountered in the world of literature, journalism, society, or business" (800); English department "themes" lack not only a compelling purpose but also the complex audience found in actual writing situations. In addition, Davis noted that college writing courses focused on correctness to the neglect of effectiveness, largely because the latter is the more difficult and the more important in learning to write and in evaluating performance. Writers, Davis insisted, "learn to write by writing—and correcting and revising" (802), and the teacher should feel free to use class time for this purpose.

Burges Johnson of Union College and Helene Hartley of Syracuse University received a large Carnegie Corporation grant during the thirties to conduct an extensive study of college writing. Johnson published pamphlets on the freshman course, creative writing courses, and journalism courses, and in 1936 he and Hartley reported the results of a research study they had conducted on the effects of three different approaches to teaching composition. The last offers a useful summary of the entire work of the two investigators. The methodology of this study is suspect, but its assumptions about rhetoric are worth considering.

Although Johnson and Hartley compared three approaches to teaching writing, only two were finally considered. The experimental approach used a seminar method based upon practices in creative writing and journalism courses. Student essays were drawn from personal experience, with early assignments being journalistic—requiring reporting and eventually editorializing—and with later assignments focusing on the informal essay. Also included were occasional short pieces of dramatic and literary criticism and brief fictional efforts. Reader interest and the use of authoritative citation when appropriate were considered important in these assignments. Most important was that students read all papers aloud to the entire class and were given immediate responses, with each student presenting one paper per week. No textbook or drill in mechanics was used, and the teacher did not lecture but acted instead as an additional respondent. The contrasting method was the current-traditional approach, which relied on the imitation of models, the forms of discourse, and the study of sentences, paragraphs, and larger structural units. A handbook was also used to help in marking errors in punctuation and grammar. After one year, this method was dropped from the experiment because of its obvious inferiority. Finally, a control group wrote about essays it had read, with classes focusing on using the reading to improve the thinking of the students, "on the theory that once the thoughts are clear, well organized and precise, the writing then will be clear, well organized and precise also" (20).

Not surprisingly, Johnson and Hartley concluded that the experimental method was superior to the control method when student essays were considered for "effectiveness," mechanical correctness, and "individuality of expression" (36), and when the results of an objective grammar and usage test and the responses of students to the two methods were compared. The researchers admitted, however, that no statistically significant differences between the two groups were found. Still, the study is important because it shows an attempt to break down the distinctions between different kinds of writing, especially the strictures separating creative writing, journalism, business and technical writing, and academic writing. Johnson and Hartley saw all of these as responses to particular rhetorical constraints and exigencies—rhetorical matters that should be considered in freshman composition. They also emphasized writing as a process of discovery, viewing writing not as transcription but as invention, the writer working out meaning in the process of writing. And they were interested in the relation of differing personality types and the composing process, sponsoring research by Floyd A. Allport, Lynette Walker, and Eleanor Lathers in this area. They even used a device called an oculophotometric instrument to measure eye movements of readers in an effort to arrive at a physiological measure of writing effectiveness. Johnson and Hartley were innovative and energetic examiners of the composing process who attempted to place writing within a larger context that included the physiological, the cognitive, and, especially, the social.

Another attempt to create a rhetoric of public discourse was undertaken by Herbert Ellsworth Childs of Oregon State Agricultural College, who wished to return a rhetoric of political and social action to the center of the curriculum. Disputing the view that freshman composition should be a course in technical fundamentals, he insisted that it "must provide the Freshman with an approach to his educational life." By this he meant that it ought to be a course in thinking about thinking, the student learning "why he should learn before he attempts learning itself" (232). Childs believed that the writing course should perform the duties it historically had served in the curriculum, introducing students "to the many-sided intellectual life," acting as a central, cohesive unit, "fixing together all the centrifugally inclined bodies of knowledge that constitute the typical curriculum in liberal arts and sciences." And it should do this by encouraging "the development of . . . students' opinions on scientific, religious, economic, and educational problems" (234), the traditional realms of rhetoric. Even technical and vocational students needed to understand that their specialties were related to "a social and industrial system based in the last analysis on a series of intellectual premises. Even the Tri-borough Bridge is intellectually related to the modern theory of the state" (235). In Childs's view, the freshman course offered "a mode of thinking, namely, the spirit of free inquiry" (256), and the teacher had to be aware of this if she were to fulfill her duty, participating "in the Freshman's whole education instead of the techniques of writing only" (237).

There were also a number of attempts in the thirties to build the freshman writing courses around addressing the social problems caused by the country's economic failure. Ralph L. Henry of Carleton College found that his students preferred a course based on "a process of stimulation growing out of vigorous class discussion of present-day controversial literature." Using essays, sometimes from current periodicals, Henry discovered that students' responses were "interested and intelligent" (395) and that by this process they produced writing superior to that elicited by the reading of literature. Karl W. Dykema of Ironwood Junior College in Michigan devoted an entire term to student essays on the topic of "multiplying functions of government in the domain of economy, health, safety, education, and cultural development" (763), focusing on the relevance of this issue to the local community. The most ambitious report of a course based on a rhetoric of public discourse was offered by Earl L. Vance of Florida State College for Women. Vance wished "to build the student's writing solidly on his life-background—its scene, people, ideology, social structure, and total character." The course centered for an entire semester on the student's writing about her hometown. Its procedure was to have the student present at the beginning of the course a plan for twelve short papers that would in sum present an accurate view of the community. The student was asked to emphasize in this plan "first, the individual characteristics of his particular town and, second, its paramount 'problems'," with the emphasis on being critical of "its shortcomings, its inherent conflicts, difficulties, possibilities, and danger spots" (319). Vance provided a set of questions for students to use in discovering the potential trouble areas in their hometown, focusing on geographical, economic, political, and social topics. These concerns ranged from "natural obstacles of climate, soils, water sources, and location" to "educational limitations, distorted moral values, unsound class distinctions" (321). As students dealt repeatedly with the same topic, their understanding grew, encouraging them to "revise and re-write and amplify their material." Most important, the composition course furthered the students' "educational progress" by relating writing to their studies in "history, economics, government, sociology, geography, religion, and ethics" (322). The writing course thus became the center of each student's "total education, experience, and self" (323).

Perhaps the most eloquent plea for a freshman course based on a rhetoric of public discourse was Warren Taylor's 1938 essay entitled "Rhetoric in a Democracy." His statement seems especially compelling when it is considered that he was one of the few instructors of professorial rank teaching the freshman course at Wisconsin, a school which at one point used teaching assistants for 80% of its freshman offerings. Taylor argued for the teaching of writing in a way that would serve the political role of the individual in a democratic state. He deplored the mechanical view of language found in two kinds of writing courses, the one emphasizing superficial correctness and the other focusing on wisdom as the exclusive province of the few. Taylor saw language as symbolic action carrying consequences in the material and social worlds. The student who is given this notion of language is offered genuine knowledge: "He knows that behind advertisement, editorial, newsreel, radio speech, article, or book there are motives which language may obscure or hide altogether. He knows what language in the process of expressing and comprehending motives, may do to them; and what motives, given form in language, may do to it" (853). Most important, Taylor was concerned that the uses of language in a democratic state be understood by teachers and students alike. Democratic conceptions of language and rhetoric establish an open community for free discourse, a community where the rights of the people to express themselves are protected. This makes knowledge available to all, whereas its opposite makes ignorance the normal state of the majority.

Taylor's concern was with defining a rhetoric that would provide for a democratic state. He was troubled that America lacked a conception of rhetoric to serve this end, and he wished to fill the need: "In this paper rhetoric is viewed as the art of making reasoned evaluations of public utterances, of discovering the worth of the means used to communicate instructive knowledge and to affect opinion. As such, it requires of its users a knowledge of the means by which lines of action designed to solve social problems may be presented to the people and of the ways in which they may respond to them" (854). Taylor insisted that this view of rhetoric should be at the heart of education, preparing individuals for their social responsibilities—responsibilities that must be fulfilled if they are to survive as free citizens. Universities must accordingly further three ends: "discovering truths, communicating truths, and, by training an enlightened citizenry, making it possible for political action to be brought in line with tested principles and not merely personal or party advantage." Universities not only must search for truth, they must come to understand its equitable dissemination, "the means of communicating knowledge that would enable the body politic to share the rewards of learning" (855).

Taylor felt that the classroom rhetorics of the time did not do this. He saw handbooks as useless: "Who we really are when we speak and to whom we speak when we speak and what we say when we speak and why we speak at all are factors not in the grouping of rules." Nor did the country need a rhetoric of "artifice and ostentation" (855) that would make the worst case appear the best. Significantly, Taylor did not want a rhetoric of persuasion, but called instead for a rhetoric of elucidation. As he explained, rhetoric considers "the ways in which ideas and misapprehensions take form in language and in action. The end of the use of the methods of rhetoric as a practical art of elucidation would be realized, not in results obtained, but in making unmistakably clear possible lines of action and their respective consequences. In a democracy, action should be the result of understanding, not of persuasion. Citizens should argue collectively on a course to be followed for the common good. If rhetoric marked all open roads clearly, the body politic, not rhetoric, could rightly be blamed for wrong choice" (856). There is a bit too much innocent faith in rational discourse in Taylor's argument and too little confidence in the power of dialogue in an open community to reveal the false and the inadvisable, but it clearly represents an enlightened conception of the role of a social rhetoric of public discourse in a democratic state. And for Taylor the keepers of this rhetoric were writing teachers: "Formulating the principles of a rhetoric for democracy and stating the criteria for the evaluation of the use of these principles in public utterances is rightly the job of composition teachers" (857). They must ensure that colleges produce students who can "realize the value of education in political action" (858). Rhetoric will then serve for us the same function as it did in ancient Greece: it will expose error, supply evidence, elucidate courses of action, and defend us from our enemies.

Taylor's statement offers a remarkably expanded role for the place of composition in the college curriculum. A number of factors in the thirties made for an environment in which such a statement was possible. The most pressing larger concerns were the Depression at home and the threat of fascism from abroad. More locally, the influence of progressive politics in defining the service mission of the University of Wisconsin was undoubtedly important. Still another important contribution to Taylor's position was the work of linguists who in the twenties and thirties were redefining the nature of language.

A number of landmark studies in current English usage implicitly supported the social basis of rhetorical discourse. The most important of these were Sterling Andrus Leonard's *The Doctrine of Correctness in English Usage, 1700–1800* (1929) and *Current English Usage* (1932), Robert C. Pooley's *Grammar and Usage in Textbooks on English* (1933), A. H. Marckwardt and Fred G. Walcott's *Facts about Current English Usage* (1938), and Charles Fries's *American English Grammar* (1940). While these individuals were committed to scientific and descriptive views of usage and grammar, their work insisted on the social basis of language and the need for English teachers to consider the importance of class and political contexts in teaching writing. The kind of view they encouraged can be seen in a 1937 essay by Walter Barnes, education professor at New York University, entitled "American Youth and Their Language."

Barnes began by setting forth his creed, "namely, that language is social activity" (283), meaning by this that it "is primarily a mode of social conduct, a type of group behavior" (285). It is not learned by studying thought processes (logical skills) or grammar and vocabulary (linguistics). It is learned by "adaptation to person; to time, place and circumstances" (286)—in other words, through using it in group activity. Language for "clear, calm reflection" and for "forceful, charming self-expression" is important, but for the most part the student's use of language and his learning of it "will depend upon his behavior as a member of a group, upon his agility and resilience, upon his adaptation to circumstances, his co-operativeness—in short, upon his social intelligence" (287). This means that the student must not subscribe to a single standard in the way language is used. Correctness or incorrectness in thought and usage is determined by the social context in which language is used, not by pre-determined and fixed standards: "Words are often not as useful as gestures or facial expression; style is a matter of attitude, voice, physical behavior; unity and coherence, so necessary in structural discourse, yield place to appropriateness and adjustment, naturalism and sincerity" (287). Language education must thus provide students with a wide repertoire of strategies for using language in a wide variety of social contexts. Students need to be prepared for the formal "Emily-Postish situation in life" (289) as well as for the informal demands of the colloquial, and the only way to accomplish this is for students to be allowed to try varied uses of language in the classroom.

Barnes's comments show a somewhat excessive reliance on the NCTE's *Experience Curriculum in English* (1935) in its tendency to base classroom activities on the actual social situations that students would later encounter. Still, Barnes simultaneously refused to restrict writing and speaking (the latter was also at the center of the Experience Curriculum) to formal patterns of arrangement and usage, as did the current-traditionalists, or to expressive uses, as did the expressionists. It is notable that he wished to include all three emphases so that students would learn to write and speak effectively in the entire range of discourse communities they would later encounter.

Finally, support for the social basis of rhetorical discourse also came from academic literary criticism. In the work of Vernon Louis Parrington is found a counterpart to Warren Taylor's reaction to the meritocratic rhetoric of the current-traditional approach and the individualism of expressionism. As Robert Weimann has commented: "The work of radical Jeffersonian democrat Vernon Louis Parrington, *Main Currents in American Thought* (1927–30), reflects both the triumph and the debacle of the progressive resolution of the crisis of bourgeois liberalism. This crisis led him to question the idea of the economic freedom of the individual and resulted in a break with the philosophy of individualism and the principle of laissez-faire" (106). The work of such Marxist critics as Granville Hicks—whose articles appeared frequently in the pages of *English Journal*—V. F. Calverton, and Bernard Smith also provided social approaches to literary criticism. And of course Kenneth Burke's method in *Counter-Statement* (1931) and *Attitudes toward History* (1937) provided a model for a social and dialectical approach to both rhetoric and poetic.

Conclusion

The thirties witnessed two notable calls for the abolishment of the required freshman writing course. In 1932, Alvin C. Eurich compared the objective test scores of students who had taken the freshman course with those who had not. Discovering no significant differences, he called for a type of writing-across-the-curriculum approach in which essays written in a content course would be evaluated for correctness by an English teacher. In 1939, Oscar James Campbell declared that the freshman writing course should be abolished because it was harmful to students and teacher. According to Campbell, students could not write because they had nothing to say, and the only solution was to fill this void. He recommended that this be done by a subject-matter teacher—a geology professor, for example—assigning essays in his or her area of expertise and evaluating them. In Campbell's view the present system had created a permanent underclass—an "academic proletariat" (181)—of composition teachers who were prevented from promotion and from teaching the area of their expertise: literature, the real business of the English department. He felt that English departments existed to provide the humanizing influence of literature, and composition was an "alien intruder" (183) that destroyed the faculty's credibility.

These two attacks on the freshman writing course represent two important rhetorical schools of the period—the skills approach of current-traditionalism and the humanistic approach of liberal culture. Eurich's and Campbell's pleas for abandoning the course were in vain. Most students could simply not be expected to meet the complex demands of the rhetorical situations presented in college without additional writing instruction. And this was true not only of the large, democratic state universities but also of the more exclusive schools of the Atlantic seaboard. Yale, for example, in the late twenties introduced a noncredit course called the "Awkward Squad" to provide remedial instruction for those students whose writing in the freshman literature course showed deficiencies (Towle), and a similar plan was installed at the same time at Columbia and Rutgers (Wozniak 185). In his report to the Board of Overseers in 1939, Harvard's President James B. Conant admitted, "From all sides, academic and nonacademic, we hear complaints of the inability of the average graduate to write either correctly or fluently" (qtd. in Wozniak 197). Conant's solution was "prescribed work" in the freshman composition class, and in this remedy he was followed by the vast majority of college presidents throughout the country.

5

The Communications Emphasis:
1940–1960

THE MOST SIGNIFICANT CURRICULAR DEVELOPMENT IN AMERI-
can colleges between 1940 and 1960 was the mushrooming of the
general education movement. This effort had first made an impact
after World War I as an attempt to provide a group of courses that
would compensate for the specialization encouraged by the new emphasis on training for the professions. It recommended that all students enroll in classes that provided a sense of cultural inheritance
and citizenship (Rudolph, *Curriculum* 237), such as the humanities
course offered at Reed, Chicago, and Columbia. Many schools also
provided broad courses in college adjustment and guidance, in the
methodology of learning, or in contemporary civilization. Most of
these efforts in general education fell to the fetish for specialization
among faculty as interdisciplinary courses were labeled as counter
to the spirit of specialized academic research. The push for general
education requirements again emerged just before World War II in
response to the Depression and the threats to democracy posed by
fascism from abroad. After the war, these programs increased dramatically, colleges again trying to combine the breadth of liberal
learning with professional specialization. Their motivation was to
safeguard the American way of life—the social stability provided by
the democratic method. This return to general education was led by
Harvard, which, in the words of Frederick Rudolph, "proposed to
democratize what had once been the education of a gentleman and
an aristocrat and make it the education essential to the responsibilities of every citizen" (*Curriculum* 259). A number of state insti-

tutions had preceded Harvard in this effort, but Harvard's endorsement of the concept led to its widespread appearance. While general education had always been an attempt to encompass the broad educational base of the curriculum of liberal culture, its appearance after the war included the commitment of progressive education to the individual student, to social values, and to democracy—even though, as shall be seen, sometimes one or another of these ends worked against or even excluded its partners.

The most conspicuous feature of most general education programs—with Harvard here serving as an exception—was the communications course. This course, commonly interdepartmental, combined writing instruction with lessons in speaking, in reading, and sometimes even in listening. Its appearance profoundly influenced the nature of college writing instruction during the years to come. In this chapter, I would like to trace the intellectual and social forces shaping the communications course, examine its typical manifestations, and consider its role in the formation of the Conference on College Composition and Communication (CCCC). I will then turn to the dominant concerns of the profession as manifested in the efforts of the fledgling CCCC, paying special attention to the relation of composition instruction to literature, linguistics, and rhetoric—all three areas being central to the organization's ongoing efforts.

The Communications Course

The most powerful intellectual force influencing the communications course was the General Semantics movement, founded in the thirties by Alfred Korzybski, a Polish-born mathematician and engineer. Korzybski was attempting to apply the techniques of scientific empiricism to the study of language. He was followed in this effort by such figures as Anatole Rapaport, a mathematical biologist; Stuart Chase, an economist; Wendell Johnson, professor of speech pathology and psychology; and Irving J. Lee, professor of speech. The most important disciple as far as communications courses were concerned was S. I. Hayakawa—author of *Language in Action* (1941), an attempt to apply General Semantics to the composition course, and of an expanded sequel entitled *Language in Thought and Action* (1949). Before World War II, General Semantics had been considered a valuable tool in the analysis of propaganda coming from fascist states abroad. After the war, it came to be regarded as useful in the teaching of language in speech and composition classes as well as in the communications course.

The major concepts of General Semantics that found their way into the communications course are discussed in Daniel Fogarty's *Roots for a New Rhetoric*. The first of these has to do with the "organism-as-a-whole" principle. This simply argues that in responding to a stimulus the individual organism acts as a whole—with feelings, thoughts, and physiological responses. This holistic response, moreover, can be evoked even by a partial stimulus—by a word rather than the thing itself, for example. This makes language and its structure important, since language alone can evoke responses without any actual physical stimulus being present. We must therefore study language and purify it so that it does not evoke inappropriate responses. We must also be careful about abstractions because these always include fewer details than the actual event. Since all words are abstractions, language can never represent wholly the thing-in-itself, but it can in its structure represent the relationship of things to each other. These structures in language and experience must be considered, a relatively easy task since Korzybski identifies only a few relations: cause and effect, spatial, geometrical, numerical, and qualitative and quantitative. Furthermore, we never know the objects of experience themselves but only the structural relations among them. Finally, in responding to experience, the individual should take care to count the physical as being more important than the symbolic, preferring always the inductions of sense data to the deductions of language.

Hayakawa called on these basic ideas of General Semantics, relying on three cognate concepts—the ladder of abstraction, consciousness of abstraction, and figures of speech—and on an epistemological statement about the relation of language to object. An abstraction ladder refers to a set of terms that become progressively general, moving farther and farther from sense experience, thus coming to include more objects and fewer details for each object. (An example is the progressive generalization from an actual cow, to the concept "cow," to livestock, to farm asset, to asset, to wealth.) We must constantly remain aware that we are abstracting in using language in order to avoid confusing levels of abstraction and our response to them. Hayakawa was also concerned with figures of speech, which provide us with new terms in language and which serve not simply as stylistic devices but as ways to express value. We must remember, however, that in language use there is always a distinction between symbol and thing, not only in metaphor but in purely descriptive statements. Consequently, Hayakawa was distrustful of definitions since these do not even describe things but only abstractions of things. He always preferred definition by concrete example because this device points to the object itself.

There is a great deal more that might be considered in the work of Korzybski and the early Hayakawa, but what has been offered is enough to suggest the positivistic nature of this school. In time, however, General Semantics came to be more complex as it moved from a positivistic to a phenomenological and transactional epistemology. In a 1954 essay entitled "Language as Communication: A Frame of Reference," Herbert Hackett argued that General Semantics had become the "middleman for the transmission of ideas from anthropology, sociology, psychology, biology, mathematics, and other disciplines" (293). The ideas he identified are the very ones that were strongly to influence the course of writing instruction in the fifties, sixties, and seventies, even after the parties making up the communications course returned to the departments from which they came. As such, they deserve consideration here.

In Hackett's view, the General Semanticists proved congenial to the emphasis of progressive education on the individual and on the total context of learning. They also agreed with its insistence on the social base of standards of usage and of learning in general. The semanticists derived from cultural anthropologists—from Jespersen, Malinowski, Sapir, Bloomfield, Whorf, Cassirer—a notion of language as a mode of social behavior and, more important still, an awareness of the ways in which language structures and defines reality. Hackett also mentioned the reliance of the semanticists on G. H. Mead in seeing the self as a social construction, and on Gestalt psychology and field theory in regarding language behavior as involving larger, interacting units, and not isolated molecules.

There are also two related social and political elements to consider in understanding the formation of the communications course, elements brought about by World War II. The first of these had to do with the number of veterans returning to school. In the 1939–40 school year, enrollment in American colleges and universities was 1,500,000. After shrinking to 800,000 in 1944–45, it jumped to 1,676,800 in 1945–46 and to a peak of 2,444,900 in 1949–50. The communications course was obviously an effective way to deal with the special problems of many of these students, including as it did the use of writing clinics. It also, of course, was a way to deal with the increased number of students, since the use of an interdepartmental staff could result in a more economical use of faculty. The other part the war played in encouraging the development of the communications course involved the courses the army had set up for recruits on college campuses as part of the Army Specialized Training Personnel (ASTP) effort. The ASTP program dealing with English emphasized the coordination of reading, writing, and speaking, and many of these courses were taught by college English teachers, who were available because of diminished wartime enrollments. After the war, the continuation of this coordinated course with returning veterans seemed a routine matter (see Buckley and Wiley; Malmstrom; Wykoff, "Army English").

The communications course appeared in a variety of settings. Sometimes it was housed in a general education program intended for students who would probably not continue in college beyond two years—as at Minnesota's General College, designed for the poorly prepared and those lacking confidence. More often it was a part of a separate General College for students in regular programs, as at Michigan State. And occasionally it was simply an informal arrangement of instructors from speech and English departments (as well as an occasional member of the education department) who combined forces—as found, for instance, at the University of Southern California in the late forties. The important common element in these variations was the commitment to teaching writing, speaking, reading, and, often, listening as a unified set of activities. By 1948, over two hundred colleges and universities had established these courses; more followed in the fifties. And before these courses declined, falling victim to academic specialization and departmental loyalty, they profoundly affected the nature of writing instruction.

While, as mentioned earlier, a number of communications courses appeared before World War II—most notably at Minnesota, Florida, Hiram, and Stephens—their position was not secure until after the war ended. I would now like to take a close look at two programs: the first at Iowa, representative of the more conservative variety, and the second at Denver, displaying some of the extreme possibilities of the basic plan.

The State University of Iowa began the course it called "Communication Skills" in 1945. The purpose of the course was to help students develop study skills for college success, to help them develop writing ability in "expository, argumentative, and critical techniques" (McGrath 18), and to lead them to recognize bad arguments and bias in discourse (especially propaganda). Students were given instruction in "reading, writing, speaking, and to a lesser extent, listening" as well as "a knowledge of the nature of words and their usage." And the emphasis was on teaching these things in a way that would enable students to continue to grow in these areas after the end of formal schooling. The course's objectives were clearly influenced by General Semantics. In the operating principle of the course, however, the influence of progressive education was also apparent: instruction was to be individualized, geared to "find out what the individual student needs and then [to] adjust his progress accordingly." The instruction in reading, writing, speaking, and listening was to be integrated, with all "studied as facets of a single process: communication" (19). It was also to be practical, providing lessons in "exposition, argument, and criticism—the everyday and practical modes" (20), not in belles lettres, the proper concern of literature and creative writing courses. Finally, the instruction was to be "skills-centered rather than content-centered" (19), meaning that it was not to be integrated with either literature or the social sciences but was to focus on "language and effective communication" (20).

These last two principles, emphasizing skills and the practical modes, were as closely related to current-traditional rhetoric as to progressive education and underscore the conservative bent of the Iowa program. There were other features of the program designed along these well-established lines. A battery of objective diagnostic tests was given, covering correctness and effectiveness of expression, reading ability, general vocabulary, something called "organizing, generalizing, and slanting" (22), and a few principles of "effective communication" and library use. The other component of the placement testing required that the student write an expository theme of at least 450 words in two hours and deliver an argumentative speech after an hour of preparation. Topics were assigned in both cases. Students were then grouped according to their performance, with 5% exempted from the communications course and the remaining 95% put in one of three tracks: a five-hour, one-semester accelerated course; a four-hour, two-semester main course; or a four-hour course in fundamentals to be followed later by the main course. Each of the first two courses emphasized either speech or writing, and students were assigned according to their weaknesses. The fundamentals course sought to instill confidence in the "deficient students." Students who were found to need more assistance than was provided by any of these courses were sent for additional help to one of three "clinics" in reading, speech, or writing.

The communication skills course at Iowa attempted a variety of goals and activities. The subject matter of essays and speeches was taken from the humanities, the social sciences, and the natural sciences so as to further integrate the curriculum. This program did not agree with "those who hold that the student should always be allowed to express what is within him without the inhibitions resulting from special demands upon form or content" (25), arguing that if the student could express what was in him, he would not be in the course. Classroom activities were also supplemented by biweekly lectures falling into four divisions: "(1) an introductory group of lectures on the nature of communication, (2) a group on college techniques (reading textbooks, listening to lectures, reciting and taking part in discussion, writing examinations, and using the library), (3) a group on language (words and their form, words and meanings, words and connotation, words and usage, the 'art of plain talk'), (4) a group on the mass media of communication (propaganda and advertising, the press and radio, motion pictures)" (25–26). There were also specific assignments for reading, speaking, and writing—the last including "at least 5,000 words distributed among five single-paragraph papers, three longer themes, one library paper, two class themes, two sets of examination-answer papers" (26). The units of study progressed from reading and discussion to preparing speeches and then to writing papers.

The faculty involved in the class were concerned with motivating students. They accordingly provided for special collections of books in the "skills library," a sixteen-page course magazine consisting of student essays published by students each semester, and a course radio program based on panel discussions featuring and produced by students. Other practices included exchanging instructors for special activities and inviting educational psychologists to faculty meetings to discuss pedagogical strategies. Pains were also taken to ensure the uniform evaluation of students and to determine the effectiveness of the program and its staff. The communication skills course did not form a separate department (as it did at Michigan State, for example), and teachers taking part also taught courses in their home departments. But there was minimal reliance on graduate students, and instructors were expected to be concerned with teaching. New faculty accordingly underwent training in evaluating student performance in speaking and writing during an orientation session, as well as during weekly meetings.

The general features of the communication skills course at Iowa were repeated in programs throughout the country. All tended to share the concern for integrating writing, speaking, reading, and listening, and to do so with special attention to the individual differences and needs of students. While Iowa's program was typical, it was also in some ways conservative, especially in its approach to writing instruction. Other programs included a greater use of linguistics and stressed the democratic and social purposes of communication. The University of Minnesota, for example, looked upon its communications program as placing "emphasis upon the linguistic process itself and upon the mass medium of communication in its effort to develop the student's general ability to communicate effectively as an adult citizen in a democratic society" (73). This stance was not surprising, since one strong impetus for general education courses had been a report by the President's Commission on Higher Education entitled *Higher Education for American Democracy* (1947), a report asserting the importance to democratic ideals of a common core of knowledge. Minnesota's program in social ideals, however, was on the whole moderate, as were most programs that shared this thrust—Florida's and Michigan State's, for example.

One general education program that was not moderate in any respect was the one found at the University of Denver. Although this program was an original member of the Cooperative Study in General Education sponsored by the American Council on Education from 1939 to 1944, it folded shortly after an essay by Levette

Davidson and Frederick Sorensen on its communications course appeared in *College English* in 1946. An examination of Denver's program, as described in this article, reveals the influence of General Semantics and, even more clearly, progressive education. More importantly, it shows the remarkable range of innovation that the communications course could engender as well as the unfortunate excesses that it could occasionally encourage.

It is not too much to say that Denver fell victim to the "life adjustment" emphasis in education that appeared after World War II. This development represented, in Arthur N. Applebee's terms, a distortion of the "traditional concern of progressive education with the continuing improvement of both the individual and society" (144). Paradoxically, it instead encouraged conformity and conservative values. Thus, for Denver, the skills of writing, speaking, reading, and listening were offered as tools for securing "the best possible adjustment of the individual in the complex field of human relations" (Davidson and Sorenson 83). Adjustment was one of the ruling objectives of the Denver program. Few students were exempted from the course, for example, because high scores on entrance tests indicated " oververbalized, intentionally oriented students" who were not "adequately adjusted in the field of human relations." As for students who had received high grades in speech in high school, they were "often egocentric extroverts" requiring "a great deal of additional training to undo the bad social habits . . . trained into them through competitive speech." Students with high grades in high school English, on the other hand, were commonly "egocentric introverts" who could prove to "need more help than the less 'superior' students" (84). Clearly a leveling process was going on at Denver.

The approach to reading, writing, and speaking instruction in the communications course was also influenced by psychological theory, with each area relegated to an appropriate "clinic" directed by its "clinician," a specialist in the subject area supervising a corps of graduate students who were also called clinicians. Student writing problems were interpreted and addressed in a remarkably unique way: "Work in the writing clinic is built upon the foundation of Rogerian nondirective counseling. It is felt that the student who considers himself a non-writer is blocked by fears similar to stage fright in the speaking situation. It is the task of the various clinics to find (if possible) the causes of the student's particular blockages and to help him to overcome them." Difficulties in writing were seen not as an indication of the failure of the high school to provide necessary skills (as a current-traditionalist would have argued) but as the result of psychic disorders. The solution, then, was to be found not in remediation alone but in remediation coupled with therapy—the writing teacher acting as a therapist. Thus, teachers at Denver, as mentioned above, were called "clinicians" and were usually graduate students in English or speech working for a master's degree. These clinicians first provided tutoring so that the student could gain immediate success, necessary because "failure in previous school or social situations is the usual cause of the fear which is a blockage to accomplishment, especially in the speech situation." According to this analysis, a weak student has commonly been stigmatized as a failure, "as 'poor' in spelling, writing, reading, speaking, and then he has to live up (or down) to his self-imposed, or otherwise imposed, standard." The clinician was supposed to go even further, however, in discovering the psychological blocks to learning how to communicate, being required "to collect and assemble as much biographical data as possible concerning the student, to find his needs and his hopes and fears." The clinician was seen as being ideally suited to this task "because, since he is also a student, he is on the same side of the fence as the student and because he does not give grades." The program also offered a guidance clinic and a full-time psychiatrist for students whose "problems" exceeded "the depth of the clinics" (84).

If in these measures the Denver communications program carried the progressive's concern for psychological health to its illogical extreme, it did attempt to implement the progressive's commitment to fostering social harmony and democratic modes of thought. Thus, the clinicians also provided remedial help for those who needed it, the hope being that this would discourage the notion that the university was solely dedicated to training an elite group of students. The communications course was also designed to emphasize cooperation rather than competitive thinking, working in this way toward a "world state" that would "avert the onset of another war and the consequent destruction of modern civilization as we know it." This emphasis on the social function of rhetoric was reflected in the structure of assignments. Essays and speeches were set within a rhetorical context, providing a purpose and an audience. And the speaking undertaken was primarily in "panels and co-operative discussion" (85) rather than formal speeches or debates, thus avoiding artificiality and the social separation of speaker and listener.

The writing course, a three-term sequence, was organized so that it reflected the strange mixture of life-adjustment, therapeutic, and social commitments of the total program. The first term was concerned with observing and reporting facts: "Preceding good communication must come good observing—fact first, then words." The second quarter focused on the research paper, an effort that involved the collecting, organizing, and presenting of facts. During the third quarter, the student discovered ways to arrive at interest and emphasis. While this description seems influenced by a current-traditional skills approach, it was in fact an attempt to combine a subjective rhetoric and a social rhetoric, working toward a dialectical interplay. The progress of the course was described in the following terms: "In the first quarter the student studies himself in his more limited environment; in the second he studies his relations to others in a wider environment (national-international); and in the third he studies that inquiry of the person-as-a-whole in his environment-as-a-whole which is called 'literature'" (85). This effort to achieve a dialectic between the individual and the social environment was probably not successful, but the content of the work in each quarter is worth considering, especially because of its departure from current-traditional rhetoric.

The first quarter's work was built around a long autobiography, the purpose of which was frankly therapeutic: "This is not the type of autobiography generally assigned in high school. It is analytical (almost psychoanalytical) and is based upon a long series of questions designed to reveal causes of speech or writing blockage or of social maladjustment." While the Denver program realized that this was a "dangerous business," it insisted that when used by the able teacher this kind of diagnosis contributed to "the highest type of education, designed to help the person adjust 'intellectually' and 'emotionally' to the kind of world and universe in which we live and will be living" (85). This autobiography was kept in a locked file, identified by number only, and read exclusively by the student's teacher and other appropriate clinicians. The reason for this confidentiality was understandable, given what the autobiography revealed about the stu-

dent: "We feel that, if the student will write out his emotional conflicts, his difficulties with mama-papa, or his so-called 'sins,' he will
help rid himself of the blockage of fear which comes from inward
festering. In the serious cases, we leave this aspect of the course to
the psychiatrist. And we do everything in our power to avoid treating anyone as neurotic or abnormal" (86). The second quarter of the
course was given over to the research paper. It also considered
grammar but, as in the first quarter, only insofar as the students
were provided what they needed to know. Little was said about this
quarter in the *College English* article. The third quarter's design,
however, was clear: the "main project" was "a piece of creative writing done by the student and presented in some appropriate way by
means of radio, stage, or publication" (86). Once again, the classroom activity followed the progressive's recommendation for an immediate purpose in a learning activity. Literature was produced
rather than studied—or, perhaps, was studied through the device of
creating it.

Unlike the teachers of many communications courses, those at
Denver were skeptical of tests, arguing that what they were trying
to teach had not yet elicited an appropriate test: "The growth of the
student, his adjustment to life and his determination, if necessary,
to adjust his environment as well as himself—these are what we are
most interested in; and we must be constantly on guard, in developing our testing program, not to slip into mere testing of skills" (86).
As a result, no formal testing procedures were introduced.

Three years after he and Davidson described the Denver program
in *College English,* Sorensen explained that flaws in its approach
eventually caused it "to blow up in various directions" ("Basic Communications Course" 325). However, the program is especially interesting to this history because it undertook a number of daring experiments in writing instruction and revealed some of the undeveloped
possibilities of the more conservative communications courses.
Thus, although the Denver experiment was abandoned soon after it
began to receive national attention, many of the commendable in-
novations it displayed continued to appear in other programs. For
example, Stephens College (Wiksell), the University of Florida
(Wise), and Michigan State College (McGrath) emphasized the social nature of communication, although they did so within a current-
traditional framework. The student-centered orientation of commu-

nications courses further nurtured psychological approaches to the teaching of writing among individual instructors. Charles I. Glicksburg of Brooklyn College, Robert L. Wright of Michigan State, and Ronald Cutler of the University of Florida—as well as the participants in a 1954 CCCC workshop entitled "The Freshman English Teacher as Counselor"—all argued that the composition instructor must consider the psychological integrity of students, treating them with respect and consideration. And the application of the Rogerian nondirective approach to the writing class eventually affected expressionistic rhetoric, as will be seen in a later chapter. Overall, the communications course—despite its occasional excesses and false turns—encouraged a fresh and worthy set of ideas in composition and finally made a substantial contribution to the development of writing instruction in colleges.

Communications courses received a great deal of attention in writing and speech journals during the forties and fifties, but they were never a dominant force in either English or speech departments. (At most schools, current-traditional rhetoric continued to be the central approach to composition instruction, and, as we have seen, was even a prominent element in some communications courses.) Their decline, moreover, was inevitable. Criticism of them began in the early fifties and continued throughout the decade (see Bowersox; Leggett, "What Are Colleges"; Arnold; Randall Stewart; Eble). Their fatal shortcoming in the end was the threat they posed to departmental autonomy and academic specialization. It is significant, for example, that the alternative to them commonly proffered by the English department was writing about literature. By the middle sixties, it was difficult to find communications courses at the major state universities, and even some of the smaller schools had abandoned them. But, as mentioned earlier, they kept alive a vital current of ideas, ideas that appeared in new forms in the sixties and seventies. Another important development that was indirectly encouraged by the communications course was the formation of the CCCC.

The CCCC

In 1947, a conference on college courses in communications was held in Chicago. Jointly sponsored by the Speech Association of

America and the NCTE, it was concerned with the course itself, its teachers, and its evaluation and administration. A number of participants hoped that this initial meeting would lead to more meetings to coordinate the efforts of speech and composition teachers. The hope was not fulfilled. In 1948, however, George S. Wykoff, director of English I at Purdue University, delivered a paper at the NCTE meeting on the importance of freshman composition to the college student. The discussion it generated was so long and intense that John Gerber of the University of Iowa proposed a spring meeting of a day or two to continue the talk about composition. The NCTE authorized the meeting for April 1 and 2, 1949, in Chicago, and five hundred people attended. Thus the Conference on College Composition and Communication was born—its name reflecting the interest of both teachers in composition programs and teachers in communications programs (Bird 33–35).

A number of elements contributed to the founding of a professional organization of composition teachers. During the Depression, almost all teachers in all English departments taught composition, with estimates as high as three-fourths of the total number then employed (French; Creek). The efforts to improve the status of freshman composition teachers had begun in the late thirties. Composition teaching had been regarded as apprenticeship work at most larger universities since World War I, a job that beginning teachers undertook until they had spent enough time in the profession to qualify for better things. Complaints about the burden of teaching freshman writing had been published in *English Journal* throughout the twenties, but had largely disappeared in the thirties, probably because composition courses were among the few still in demand. By the end of the thirties, however, enrollments in colleges were again increasing, and with the increase came a new sense of professional identity among all college English teachers, not just those teaching writing. One obvious result was the establishment of *College English* in 1939, replacing the college edition of *English Journal*. Another was the appearance of articles that called for establishing new directions for the study of both literature *and* composition. In 1939, for example, *English Journal* included articles on the future of literary study by James H. Hanford and Bennett Weaver of Michigan, Kenneth Myrick of Tufts, and Percy D. Shelly of Pennsylvania. Two essays by Wykoff, published in *College English* in 1939 and 1940, simultaneously argued for making college composition teaching a respectable professional alternative, rather than keeping it an apprenticeship program for literature teachers. Essays by Arthur M. Coon in 1943 and 1947 joined Wykoff's in calling for better teaching conditions for composition teachers.

The sense of professional identity indicated by the establishment of the CCCC had thus been crystallizing for some time. The increase in students just before the beginning of World War II and then again after it with the influx of veterans had created the need for teachers at the undergraduate level. The communications approach gave composition courses a new identity, placing them in a special program that carried with it a commitment to democracy and to the welfare of students who had just suffered the horrors of war. Even though these communications programs were often devices to use scarce faculty more economically, they did elevate freshman composition—as well as speech—in the university power structure. And with the establishment of the CCCC and its journal, *College Composition and Communication,* teachers of freshman composition took a giant step toward qualifying for full membership in the English department, with the attendant privileges—tenure, promotion, higher salaries, leaves—even though these were not widespread until much later. The journal served as a forum for discussing the lot of composition teaches as well as for encouraging and disseminating theoretical and practical research in the teaching of writing.

During the fifties the pages of *College Composition and Communication* shed considerable light on the concerns of college writing teachers. (*College English* continued to publish essays on composition, but these were until the next decade curtailed in number and length as the new composition journal grew in size and readership.) In addition to publishing scholarly articles, the journal reported on the recommendations of the workshop sessions that were a part of the two-day annual meeting until 1970. Each workshop involved twenty to twenty-five teachers who had registered in advance to meet and discuss a particular topic; the topics selected reveal a great deal about the abiding interests of the profession. The journal's second number is especially interesting because it included sessions entitled "The Function of the Communications Course in General Education" and "Objectives and Organization of the Composition Course." What is immediately apparent from these and similar discussions that followed is the emphasis the communications course placed on the social basis of rhetoric and its importance in a democratic society. Against this is seen the composition course's commitment to "effective communication," meaning by this the current-traditionalist's shuttling of meaning from the mind of the writer to the mind of the reader—"the power of clearly communicating facts or ideas in writing to a specified reader or group of readers." This is the rhetoric of the meritocratic professional, instruction designed to enable students to meet the "requirements of writing without embarrassment to the institution granting them degrees" ("Objectives and Organization" 9). These early workshops also included sessions on grammar and semantics in the freshman course, reading and grading themes, objective tests, the writing laboratory, the reading clinic, freshman English for engineers, high school and college articulation, and administration of the composition and communications courses. All were to remain pressing concerns of the CCCC during the fifties and after. I would now like to turn to three other areas of interest to composition teachers at this time, areas that were to have lasting consequences for the discipline. These are the relation of writing instruction to literature, to linguistics, and to rhetoric.

Literature and Composition

As noted earlier, the sense of professional identity among members of the English department blossomed just before World War II and was further encouraged by the growth in enrollments afterward. And even as enrollments declined during the fifties, the anticipation of the growth in student population projected for the sixties kept spirits high. The New Criticism, furthermore, was providing an approach to literature and its teaching that could serve as the basis for the discipline of literary studies. This critical method promised a common professional purpose to unify the diverse factions within the English department. It was especially appealing because it was politically safe at a time when academics were becoming the objects of witch hunts led by the most powerful political figures in the country. Armed with this new sense of professional resolve, English department members began to protest any method of teaching writing that was not based on the study of literature. If the department was to be saddled with the service course in writing, went this reasoning, it should at least organize the course around what it knew best—the literary text.

This argument took a number of forms. Randall Stewart of Brown adopted the old view of liberal culture, arguing that students have difficulty in composition because they have nothing to write about. He rejected the notion that students should write about themselves since this would require "a flair amounting to genius," and most students "are not geniuses." He dismissed providing rhetorical contexts for discussion since these are commonly trivial (and of course he selected a trivial example to demonstrate his point), and he did not like writing about social or political essays because he felt this resulted in superficiality. But his final objection was that all these "require the teacher to enter areas where he has no particular competence" (16). Literature ought to be the subject of the writing course, and it "should be selected with reference not only to its intrinsic greatness, but the opportunity which it offers for the continuous, cumulative discussion of the deepest things in man" (17). Stewart's aim was to create Arnold's "current of ideas" (18) in the place of "a miscellaneous affair in 'communication skills'" (17). This view was seconded in a letter of 1956 by Kenneth Eble, who advocated replacing the communications course with a course in writing about literature, both for the student's sake and the teacher's: "Nowadays, full professors teach freshman composition, and while this may be a waste of talent (oftentimes I suspect it is), it does keep a teacher anchored for brief periods between his voyages to strange and distant intellectual lands" (477). Great literature, he added, provides the "knowledge and stimulation" that the teacher needs to keep his career alive and vital—both as teacher and as scholar.

This liberal culturist perspective is seen in a number of other essays. In a 1955 piece, Robert M. Estrich of Ohio State argued that people who teach only composition become "composition slaves" whose minds are destroyed by the experience. His opinion was that composition is a remedial course that ought to be handled in high school. If it is to be offered in college at all, those who teach it should also be assigned to teach courses in literature, lest they become "slaves" or "hacks" (87). Harrison Hayford of Northwestern pretended to look at both the communications course and the literature-based composition course in a spirit of fairness. He concluded that the communications course was better adapted to democratic colleges, "tax-supported institutions which because of their admissions policy must cope with a large number of students poorly prepared in skills of basic communications" (44). Composition courses in "great literature," on the other hand, had "proved their value in institutions with a selective admissions policy, usually liberal arts colleges with a relatively homogenous student-group" (45). Northwestern was clearly closer to the latter and so it made a bow to communications skills while emphasizing writing about literature. For both Estrich and Hayford, literature provided salvation for students and teachers in the composition course and maintained the latter's professional standing.

Finally, literature was offered as the subject matter for the composition course because it was seen as preserving the integrity of the individual against the tyranny of the mob. For example, Kenneth Oliver of Occidental College in Los Angeles maintained that the communications course was dangerous because it denied the value of literature in the development of the individual and failed to provide for self-expression: "It is the Homers, Dantes, Cervantes, Shakespeares, Thomas Manns, and the etceteras in their classification who have done most to give us a historical-cultural perspective of human aspirations and the dangers that beset us." Literature is necessary to preserve democracy; to refuse literature to all because the few cannot understand it "is as dangerous to democracy as is the traditionalist's failure to teach competently evaluative response to slanted reports and the persuasive propaganda of special-interest writers and speakers." Similarly, to fail to teach self-expressive writing in favor of persuasive writing in public discourse is "perhaps the greatest danger to democracy that can be conceived." Self-expressive writing "is what has given us the best perspective of man in his process-civilization. Persuasion, inevitably geared down to the masses, can never give as full a perspective" (5). Since it is the individual genius who makes for salutary developments in society, Oliver's view went, it is the individual genius who should be encouraged in the composition class through literature and expressive writing.

This call for literature in the writing class was, at least in part, an obvious response to the political climate of the Cold War period, a time when those who called for collective solutions to social

problems could be charged with a softness on communism. Furthermore, the position favoring literature was encouraged by the
MLA in a 1939 document entitled "Statement of the Committee of
Twenty-Four," finally formulated by Louise Rosenblatt, Howard
Mumford Jones, and Oscar James Campbell. Put together by twenty-
four college English teachers at the annual MLA conference, it attempted "to clarify for the members of the profession and for others
the important service which the study of literature can render individuals in a democratic state." This individualistic stance held that
literature's first business is to warn against the pitfalls of the emphasis on social values as found in the social sciences, the dangerous
consequences of which are clear: "The individual, thus submerged
in the social mass, is merely a cipher, a helpless unit whose thought,
feeling, and action are determined by impersonal forces over which
he has little or no control" (262). Democracy, however, depends
upon "richly endowed and self-reliant individuals, sensitive to the
individual lives of their fellow-men and to their personal potentialities." Literature provides the one thing needed here: "Whatever the errors of rugged individualism in the economic sphere [the
Depression was not yet over], the concept of political democracy assumes the efficacy of rugged individualism on the plane of the
spirit." Literature makes for "self-reliant and well-rounded person-
alities," providing alternatives in "modes of conduct" and teaching a
wide repertoire of choices among values and "among different emotions, temperaments, and achievements." The student thereby
learns "to clarify his personal problems and at once to liberate and
to control his personality." And all of this makes the individual a
better social being since "literature makes him cognizant of the significance of personal and social relations in an immediate and even
dramatic fashion" (263).

This program for literary education was considered to have important political benefits as well. The committee felt that the student could be made a good citizen through literature: "His feelings
are purged and disciplined by an application of the familiar psychological doctrine of empathy. He feels his impulses toward unruly
and subversive emotions to be at once released and controlled by
adopting for the moment the career of fictional characters swayed by
the same emotions. In this way his brute instincts are transmitted
into civilized values." Literature thus rids the individual of any im-

pulses which might be counter to existing political arrangements, defusing them through vicarious experience. Literature also provides the student with "ideals charged with life [that] are thrust into his inmost consciousness." Echoing Arnold, the committee described literature as "one of the formative experiences of civilized life" since it offers "the best and noblest thoughts of the best and noblest men" (265). The committee expected teachers to carry out the program it had outlined by presenting "wisely selected books," one criteria of selection being "that socially subversive emotions find safe release through literature" (266).

In the forties and fifties, then, literature was seen as serving the individual and acting as a safeguard against collectivist notions that might threaten the ideal of "rugged individualism on the plane of the spirit" and, finally, on the plane of politics. When writing teachers attacked the communications course for its neglect of literature, they were thus not exclusively defending the autonomy of the English department—although this certainly was a strong motive. They were also resisting political ideas that opposed their conceptions of the primacy of the individual in the political process. And as Richard Ohmann and others have pointed out, this same tendency is found in the New Criticism, the dominating force in English departments in the fifties.

Linguistics and Composition

The appearance of structural linguistics in the fifties created a stir in English departments that affected teachers of literature as well as writing teachers. Here I will focus on the latter. The claims made for the possibilities of structural linguistics in the composition class were nothing short of extravagant. Structural linguistics, many argued, provided a new way of looking at language that was more accurately explanatory than any that had preceded it. This theory of language, moreover, promised to provide the writing course with its own subject matter, offering a new grammar that was to be the counterpart to literature's New Criticism.

As Wayne State's Donald J. Lloyd explained in 1953, structural linguistics had come to rescue "a course which has sought its subject-matter in the past from anthropology to Marxism and Psychoanalysis, and on through vertebrate and invertebrate zoology, and hence is frequently charged with having no subject-matter of its own at all" (40). *College Composition and Communication* accordingly published in 1953 and 1954 three articles by George Faust of the University of Kentucky that surveyed the new theory. In 1954, the journal sponsored a panel at the annual CCCC gathering entitled "Freshman Texts in the Light of Linguistics," featuring Harold B. Allen of Minnesota, Paul Roberts of San Jose State, Villier Matthes of UCLA, and L. M. Meyers of Arizona State. The recorder for the session was Francis Christensen of the University of Southern California. In a separate essay in the same year, Allen called for empirical research into the application of structural linguistics to the composition course, research that might determine the value of this theory for writing instruction. By 1958, two new textbooks in composition based on structural linguistics had appeared: Lloyd and Harry R. Warfel's *American English and Its Cultural Setting* (1956) and Roberts's *Understanding English* (1958). (It is worth noting, however, that in the same year an article by Ralph B. Long entitled "Grammarians Still Have Funerals" was critical of these textbooks, mentioning in passing the work of Noam Chomsky.)

A lucid statement of the application of structural inguistics in the composition classroom is seen in a 1959 essay by Warfel, of the University of Florida. He described structural linguistics as having "unlocked the secrets of language," so that the "teaching of composition must undergo a revolutionary change" (205). He went on to identify the key propositions of this new discipline. Language is a social activity arising out of the interaction of human beings. It is also a signaling system that can be described in mathematical terms. Speech is primary and writing is derivative of speech, but the differences between the two are as important as the similarities. Speech "is a stream of significant oral sounds uttered into the air in homogenous time relationships in such a way as to give the distinct impression that a tune or melody accompanies the rhythm of production" (206). Gestures and "vocal qualifiers, like whispering, rasping, wheezing" may accompany speech, but sounds and intonation patterns are the most important. Writing, on the other hand, "is a set of significant graphic marks inscribed on a physical substance in homogenous space relationships whose total effect is usually that of geometric design" (207). The effects of the two are markedly different. Writing "poorly represents time, melody, gesture, and vocal qualifiers," whereas speech "has difficulty in conveying the effect of written scrolls and serifs and degrees of darkness on type" (206). The two systems do, however, have similiarities, being made of significant units in contrastive relationship to each other.

All of this points to a new way of teaching composition, a method demonstrated in the textbook Warfel authored with Lloyd. Accordingly, in his essay Warfel went on to assert that composition teachers need to understand the system of English, a system characterized by "the algebraic theory of functions, variables, and constraints" (207). They must come to see the sentence as a sequence of functions that form predictable patterns, not as a sequence of words, and they must then teach "the sentence patterns and the way they are built up" (208). Teachers should let students know that English is marked by stability in the functions of sentences and in the word order within these functions. Recognizing the limits to the number of words within a sentence and within the structures of a sentence involves knowing "the laws of substitution, modification, apposition, compounding, and word order." These limits—the permissible lengths for sentences and structures within sentences—can, furthermore, be studied empirically. They should not be left to the lore of the "rhetorical or logical," as in most composition textbooks. A writer's style grows out of the choices she makes in these matters— out of syntactical choices—and thus "rhetoricians should state these rules in terms of syntactical operations." The composition teacher must finally know "the mathematical laws of language . . . and formulate his didactic procedures upon them" (209).

Warfel pointed out other implications for using the lessons of structural linguistics in the composition classroom. Since speech in children is a "social inheritance" (209) mastered by the age of six, the language system is always more important than individual vocabulary items. The child learns the system and ways of using it more effectively in a social setting. As a result, the composition teacher should duplicate this social process in the classroom so that the student can learn to manipulate the resources of the system: "Expertness in writing the simple sentence patterns must be achieved first, and then the many ways of saying anything can be added as occasion warrants. Imitative pattern practice is essential whenever a student is allegedly 'at a loss for words.' No student lacks words; he lacks experience in putting the words he knows into patterns" (210). And this practice in filling patterns can be applied to all the structures of the sentence. Its primary purpose is "imitation for establishing habits" (211), with a view to inculcating a knowledge of patterns—syntactical devices—before pushing for originality or stylistic variety. The most inappropriate response a teacher can make to these pattern drills is to use the red correction pen. Students should be guided gently and slowly through the various syntactical patterns: the noun function as subject, the verb function, apposition, compounding, the verbals, the noun-function clauses, and the adverb as word-clause and word-group.

In his essay's closing comment, Warfel revealed the revolutionry role he saw for structural linguistics in the writing class. He intended his method to replace three common approaches. First, he wanted to get rid of semantics, "an almost useless and distracting appendage to composition instruction." Second, he recommended abandoning the use of reading selections, the "pre-occupation with ideas as opposed to the student's mastery of the language system." For Warfel, the "business of a composition class is to achieve fluency in writing; it is not to give a general education program—the liberal arts college exists to do that job" (212). The sole activity of the composition class must henceforth be "those aspects of language which provide insight into the student's lifetime task of increasing his skill in writing and reading." And this will have profound professional consequences for the writing teacher: "I dare say that a teacher's self-respect will increase as he senses that his profession has its own subject-matter and its own technology in which he can be an expert. Like a physician or an engineer, he has specialized in a limited field of knowledge; his value to society results wholly from the competence with which he ministers to his clientele. That ministry involves language, its systematic operation in the mouths and ears of all people and the possibility of lifting every student's knowledge, experience, and production in writing to the highest level of competence" (213). At last writing teachers would have a clearly defined intellectual discipline on which they could build a profession. Finally, Warfel advocated replacing the workbooks based on traditional grammar—at the time enjoying great popularity—with the "new structural grammar which relates language operation to composition." In this new scheme, writing instruction would still focus on grammar, but the grammar would be that of structural linguistics. Writing teachers would thereby offer to students "scientific insight into their most important set of social habits" (213)—into language—and could in this way help society achieve unity.

Warfel's optimistic forecast of the place of structural linguistics in writing instruction was not unusual for the fifties and on into the sixties. It led to the work of Christensen and the considerable research built on his foundation during the seventies. The enthusiasm seen in Warfel was rarely afterwards as high, however. The theoretical disagreements among linguists themselves, especially after the emergence of transformational grammar, diminished the confidence of writing teachers in linguistics. Still, the impact of structural linguistics on the development of rhetoric—both theory and practice—ought not to be underestimated and will be considered in the next chapter.

The Revival of Rhetoric

A renewed interest in rhetoric as a discipline of profound historical importance and of considerable contemporary relevance arose in English departments during the fifties. This was especially encouraged by the revival of Aristotelian humanism at the University of Chicago, a part of the move toward general education in response to the Depression and World War II. Indeed, one of the earliest articles to attempt to reintroduce the classical conception of rhetoric to the writing class came from a group of teachers at this university. In 1952, a *College English* article by Manuel Bilsky, McCrea Hazlett, Robert E. Streeter, and Richard M. Weaver stressed the importance in argument of "what the traditional rhetoricians called *invention*," meaning by the term "the discovery of content—of relevant supporting material." Significantly, they emphasized the primacy of invention over logic because it alone would "assist in the process of creation." The essay went on to discuss "what the classical writers called *topoi* or 'regions,' and what have come to be translated as the 'topics'" (211), focusing on genus, consequence, similarity, and authority. While the essay itself introduced little that was new, it displayed a use of rhetorical categories that had been given only passing attention since the lectures of John Quincy Adams were published in

1810. The essay was the first of many in the fifties to propose historical alternatives to current-traditional notions of rhetoric, offering other paradigms for the discipline.

An even more comprehensive attempt to restore the formal study of rhetoric to the English department was described in a 1954 essay by Henry W. Sams, also of the University of Chicago. Sams was interested in identifying the "fields of research in rhetoric"—that is, locating the areas of the discipline that merited study in the academy. He began by identifying "the fundamental conditions of rhetoric which channel and contain research" (60), relying for guidance on Richard McKeon's "Rhetoric in the Middle Ages," a 1942 *Speculum* essay that was reproduced in R. S. Crane's *Critics and Criticism, Ancient and Modern*. Sams considered rhetoric to be a situational art more dependent on history than other kinds of discourse, a systematic discipline based on organized theory, and a practical discipline, meaning that it is "assimilated and shaped by the philosophies which it serves" (61). Given these characteristics, Sams felt that a number of research projects in the field were clamoring for attention. The first of these was the provision of reliable editions of the major texts, including translations. Sams listed those already available from the ancient, the medieval, and the modern periods, and offered suggestions for projects still in need of undertaking. A second area of investigation suggested was the study of "sources, influences, and interrelationships" (63).

Sams went on to discuss briefly the historical influence of the rhetoric classroom in the shaping of thought and literature, pointing to the work of Donald Lemen Clark on Milton and of T. W. Baldwin on Shakespeare. He also considered the areas in which research in rhetoric and literature overlap, citing M. W. Croll, George Williamson, Sister Miriam Joseph, and Rosemund Tuve. Sams closed with a plea for a general history of rhetoric and a list of four contemporary areas of rhetorical activity worth considering: practical research in communications using quantitative procedures; studies of international relations; studies of mass media; and, finally, studies in contemporary rhetorical theory.

Sams's article is especially significant because it provides evidence of a renaissance in rhetoric in the fifties that extended across the curriculum—in English and speech, in social studies and history. The role of rhetoric as the basis of education in the past and as a major concern of a number of key academic disciplines in the present was made clear. Rhetoric was being elevated to a new level of academic respectability—or at least being restored to something like its previous status. And a number of articles that appeared in *College Composition and Communication* shortly after Sams's essay support this notion.

J. E. Congleton's "Historical Developments of the Concept of Rhetorical Proprieties" offered a thumbnail sketch of the history of rhetoric, dividing rhetoricians into those concerned with truth and those concerned with effectiveness. Congleton began his discussion with Aristotle, Cicero, and Quintilian, omitted the medievalists, moved on to Ramus, and then covered Hugh Blair and George Campbell. He next devoted an extensive section to elocution and to American rhetoric, including in the latter a consideration of the role of invention, claiming it to be an abiding concern of the nineteenth century. A significant feature of Congleton's history was that he offered it in the hope that it would contribute to building a better freshman composition course. He wished to recommend concern for "the truth of the message" over "effectiveness of expression" (144), and he was convinced that a knowledge of the history of rhetoric would further this end.

Three related essays appeared alongside Congleton's, each attempting to place rhetoric in its relation to language studies in general, carving out for it a spot in the modern English curriculum. James B. McMillan of the University of Alabama distinguished the concepts of language, linguistics, philology, and rhetoric. He defined rhetoric as "the art of speaking or writing effectively" (146) and divided it into practical and aesthetic studies—the former using experimentation. Rhetoric uses linguistic statements, he explained, but is a separate discipline. Sumner Ives of Tulane focused on grammar in the composition class, but he first asserted that teaching composition involves two other concerns as well: "It should also include study of the relationship between the natural world and the language code which represents it, or semantics; and it should include training in the use of language to inform, to convince, and to move, or rhetoric" (150). It was important to Ives—as to McMillan—that grammar, semantics, and rhetoric all "be based on the same premises about language" (150).

Finally, W. Nelson Francis of Franklin and Marshall College attempted a more ambitious project, a survey of the relation between modern rhetorical theory and developments in linguistics. He concluded that the two come together in style, "the actual selection and disposition of words and sentences" (157). What is of special interest in his article, however, is his estimate of the current state of rhetoric. Francis asserted unequivocally "the return to respectability of the term *rhetoric* itself, as well as of the formal discipline which it denotes" (156). His concept of rhetoric was a broad one, including both eighteenth-century and classical categories. Thus, he saw rhetoric as being concerned with the discussion of virtually all discursive prose, "a method, backed by a long and vigorous tradition, for systematically discussing all forms of discourse that lie between scientific demonstration (which is the domain of logic) on the one hand, and artistic or creative literature (which is the domain of poetic) on the other" (157). This eighteenth-century conception of rhetoric was paired with a classical conception of its function, making rhetoric the discipline used to discover knowledge, not merely to present it: "In the court of law, the legislative assembly, the committee meeting, and the press conference—anywhere, in fact, where issues must be found and decisions reached under circumstances that do not permit the objective thoroughness of science or the imaginative impracticality of art—rhetoric is the tool that must be used to reach an approximation of truth upon which action can be based" (157). Consistent with this notion of discovery is rhetoric's division into invention, disposition, and style. As Francis's treatment makes clear, rhetoric in all its comprehensiveness was being returned to the writing teacher, opening up areas of discussion that had long been abandoned and thereby enriching the composition classroom.

There were still other indications of the restoration of alternative conceptions of rhetoric in the study of writing. Weaver's *Composition: A Course in Writing and Rhetoric*, a textbook influenced by classical rhetoric, was published in 1957. One of the first of Edward P. J. Corbett's contributions to our knowledge of the history of rhetoric appeared in 1958, entitled "Hugh Blair as an Analyzer of English Prose Style." And one of the workshops listed for the 1958 CCCC was "Rhetorical Invention: Good Subject Matter for Composition." Rhetoric as a discipline had clearly arrived, with consequences that would become apparent in the next two decades.

Before closing this chapter, I would like to mention an additional development that had lasting consequences for composition instruction. The previous chapter noted the use of process models of composing by certain proponents of expressionistic rhetoric. This concern for "process" also appeared among a few expressionists in the fifties. For example, a 1954 CCCC workshop report entitled "The Freshman English Teacher as Counselor" explained that if "a teacher is interested in the *process* of writing and insists that his students be aware of the process, he will find that students' personal problems sometimes appear as an integral part of the writing problems" (96). This position was seconded in a 1958 essay by Ronald Cutler, "The Autobiography as Creative Writing." An emphasis on process was also found in discussions of socially based rhetorics. In 1952 Frederick Sorensen recommended an instructional approach that emphasized the democratic social context of composing while insisting that writing be taught as a three-stage process consisting of invention, arrangement, and style. And in 1953 Barriss Mills of Purdue argued in "Writing as Process" against the current-traditional version of the composing act, with its emphasis on assigning subjects, outlining, and superficial correctness. He wanted to base the writing course on a process of composing that emphasized a rhetorical purpose, a rhetorical context, writing, and revision. Accordingly, he recommended using a laboratory method in which the teacher worked with the student at each stage of the process.

Economic, political, and social developments between 1940 and 1960 had placed in motion a current of ideas that would profoundly affect the teaching of writing. These ideas would also be involved in the sweeping economic, political, and social changes that were about to take place in the nation—dialectically acting as both agent and product of historical developments. And this is the subject of the next chapter.

6

The Renaissance of Rhetoric:
1960–1975

THE MOST CRUCIAL EVENTS FOR THE FATE OF WRITING INSTRUC-
tion during the sixties and seventies were the intensification of the
Cold War and changes in economic, social, and political arrangements that resulted in a dramatic increase in the number of students
attending college. The space race signaled by the launching of Sputnik in 1957 eventually led to federal funds being invested in the
teaching of literature and composition for the first time in American
history. This in turn brought about a reintegration of the efforts of
the NCTE and the MLA after a separation of nearly fifty years. The
product of this mutual effort was new activities to improve the
teaching of writing in both high schools and colleges. The growth in
the number of students attending college was as much an effect of
the expansion of the corporate and state sectors of the economy as it
was a result of the growing size of the student-age population. As
colleges during the sixties became the training centers for the new
specialists needed in business and government, their power, prestige, size, and numbers increased. And, as in the 1890s with the appearance of the new university, the research ideal again proved to
be the dominant influence in higher education (Veysey, "Stability and
Experiment" 17). While this development worked against writing
courses because of their position in the undergraduate curriculum, it
also encouraged the professionalization of composition teachers, an
effort that had been underway since the formation of the CCCC in
the fifties. The larger student population necessitated more writing
teachers, and these teachers began to promote graduate training for

their discipline. By 1975, graduate programs in rhetoric and composition were forming, and rhetoric was becoming a respectable academic specialty.

This chapter and the next will consider the developments in the discipline that led to the return of rhetoric to the English department, restoring it to a status nearly equal to that of literature instruction in many departments. The professionalization of composition instruction was accompanied by the corresponding professionalization of literature teaching. As Richard Ohmann has indicated, it was not until the sixties that literature faculties began to enjoy all the perquisites of the profession, earlier accorded only to members of science departments. The growing interest of writing teachers in rhetoric as a discipline had its counterpart in rhetorical approaches to literary criticism appearing in scholarly literature journals. Both developments contributed to a proliferation of articles advocating new methods of writing instruction—some of which, as we shall see, really were not particularly new. This chapter will investigate the historical events attending the revival of interest in rhetoric. The next will examine the theoretical and practical results for the classroom.

As Arthur N. Applebee has demonstrated, the public schools had begun to experience harsh criticism during the forties and fifties. This came from a variety of sources: from Robert M. Hutchins and Mortimer Adler of the University of Chicago, from two Harvard committees appointed by James B. Conant, and from such critics as Mark Van Doren, Arthur Bestor, Paul Woodring, and Vice-Admiral Hyman G. Rickover. The launching of Sputnik in 1957 gave credence to the criticism of the quality of American education and led to the passage of the National Defense Education Act in 1958. This measure was at first designed to improve school instruction in math and the sciences, but by 1964 also included the study of literature, language, and composition—especially the latter two. Meanwhile, the Ford Foundation funded a series of "Basic Issues" conferences in 1958, designed to examine the teaching of high school English. These conferences were undertaken by the MLA, but, after an NCTE protest, included representatives from the American Studies Association and the College English Association as well as from the MLA and the NCTE. A third development that focused on the improvement of high school English instruction was the appearance of the Commission on English founded by the College Entrance Examination Board in 1959. This group extended the work of the Basic Issues conferences, publishing *Freedom and Discipline in English* in 1965. These three developments were important because they signaled a reunion of the efforts of the MLA and the NCTE for the first time since 1910. They are also worth noting because they each encouraged an application of the work of Jerome Bruner to the teaching of literature and, especially, composition, with consequences that are still being felt.

Jerome Bruner, a Harvard psychologist, was an important but largely unacknowledged source of the process models of composing that are now a commonplace of our intellectual environment. He provided the ruling concepts and much of the language on which these models are based, and what he did not supply was developed by those who called upon him—D. Gordon Rohman and Albert O. Wlecke and, later, Robert Zoellner and Janet Emig, for example. Bruner was the author of *The Process of Education*, published in 1960 as the final report of the ten-day Woods Hole Conference sponsored by the National Academy of Sciences. While this meeting was intended to examine the teaching of science in the schools, Bruner included in the final report frequent mentions of literature instruction. More importantly, his thought as found in *The Process of Education* as well as in other works—"The Act of Discovery" and "The Conditions of Creativity" in *On Knowing: Essays for the Left Hand*, for example—was influential in other ways. For example, the Commission on English report mentioned above was strongly influenced by Bruner's notion of learning. When, moreover, the federal funds for research projects, curriculum studies, and teachers institutes in English began to flow, the importance of Bruner's ideas was again marked. These funds first came from the U.S. Office of Education in 1962 under the terms of a program that came to be called Project English. By 1964, the National Defense Education Act had been expanded to include funds for English. Bruner's influence in the programs funded by both agencies was inescapable.

Bruner introduced the language of cognitive psychology, including the influence of Piaget, to education circles. His emphasis was on learning as "process," a concept that had been an important part of progressive education (and, as indicated earlier, an emphasis of some writing teachers in the twenties and after). Bruner differed from his predecessors in that he conceived the learning process in terms of the cognitive level of the student and its relation to the structure of the academic discipline under consideration. Bruner was not interested in relating knowledge to society. He argued that each academic discipline had a structure determined by the experts within its confines, and that students should learn this structure at a level of complexity appropriate to their age. Bruner relied on Piaget's scheme in determining levels of cognitive development. The crucial element was the method to be used. Bruner emphasized the role of discovery in learning, arguing that students should use an inductive approach in order to discover on their own the structure of the discipline under consideration. This did not mean merely pursuing the scientific method in a slavish and mechanical fashion. Instead, Bruner placed a premium on intuitive methods, approaches that enabled the student to go from creative guesses to verification in the more orthodox manner. The student was to engage in the act of *doing* physics or math or literary criticism, and was not simply to rely on the reports of experts. Bruner believed that the student learned the structure of a discipline through engaging in research as a practitioner of the discipline, and this involved "the development of an attitude toward learning and inquiry, toward guessing and hunches, toward the possibility of solving problems on one's own" (*Process of Education* 20).

The implications of Bruner's thought for writing instruction are clear: Students should engage in the process of composing, not in the study of someone else's process of composing. Teachers may supply information about writing or direct students in its structural stages, but their main job is to create an environment in which students can learn for themselves the behavior appropriate to successful writing. The product of student writing, moreover, is not as important as the process of writing. (The emphasis in *The Process of Education* is on intrinsic as opposed to extrinsic rewards—not grades or honors as a motivator, but the sheer joy of discovery.) Writing involves discovery, a process requiring intuition and pursuing hunches—in short, acting in the way that mature writers do. The emphasis in the classroom should be on individuals coming to terms with the nature of composing—its inherent structure—on their own, without regard for social processes. (This approach is seen, for example, in the application of Bruner's ideas in a federally funded study conducted by Rohman and Wlecke.) The individual must arrive at a unique, personal sense of the knowledge of the discipline concerned; only through this private perception is learning and composing possible.

As Applebee has indicated, federal funds for research in the learning of English were at first used almost exclusively for reading skills and composition, literature being a later consideration (201–2). The major reason for this, of course, was the practical orientation of legislators, but the phenomenon also indicated the difficulty of developing student-oriented research projects in literary studies. At any rate, this emphasis on research in writing instruction, coupled with the great increase in the need for writing teachers due to expanding enrollments, contributed to the renaissance in rhetoric in college English departments. As mentioned in the previous chapter, rhetoric as a discipline had already begun its return to academic respectability in the forties and fifties, encouraged by the efforts of the CCCC and such developments as the revival of Aristotelian humanism. The resurgence of rhetoric continued with great vigor in the sixties, with numerous efforts aimed at making sense of the studies being undertaken and at making recommendations for future directions of study. I would now like to turn to these efforts.

One of the most significant documents of the period was a pamphlet entitled *The Basic Issues in the Teaching of English*, based on the 1958 Ford Foundation conferences mentioned earlier and published as a supplement to *College English* in 1959. This document consisted largely of questions that sought to identify the basic issues in the discipline of English, focusing on public high schools as well as colleges. In discussing writing, the report attempted to identify potential research questions, with the influence of Bruner again apparent: "Of what skills is the practical art of writing composed? Which of these can be taught most easily and most effectively at what levels? Can the teaching of these skills be distributed among the various levels?" (9). The report went on to ask whether writing should be taught as expression or as communication and to inquire about the relation of writing to grammar, to thinking, and to literary study. A section on the training of college teachers acknowledged the failure of graduate schools to prepare students for their careers: "It appears that our teaching-assistant graduate students and young Ph.D.'s may expect ninety percent of their first six years of teaching to be in freshman courses and composition. Yet the typical Ph.D. program is almost completely void of courses dealing primarily with language and rhetoric" (12). The report closed this section by asking, "Can the teaching of composition be raised to the same level of academic respectability as the teaching of literature?" The discussion of the issues implicated in this query—the hard work, the low pay, the denial of advancement—did not encourage an affirmative answer. Still, the mere fact that the question could be entertained by a group of scholars representing the MLA signaled a new attitude toward freshman composition—and one that encouraged hope for the discipline of rhetoric.

One of the most perceptive of the observers of developments in college composition teaching at this time was also an integral part of the changes being made. Albert R. Kitzhaber was involved in writing programs at Kansas, Dartmouth, and Oregon, and he served as chair of the CCCC meeting in 1959 and as NCTE president in 1964. When in 1959 the College Section meeting of the annual NCTE conference selected as its topic the elimination of freshman English, as it was then being taught, from the curriculum, Kitzhaber was chosen to respond to Warner G. Rice's affirmative response to the proposition. Kitzhaber's statement was one of the earliest of a succession of enlightened comments he and others were to offer on the issue.

Rice's presentation consisted of the usual recitation of English department commonplaces, all of which had been shown to be questionable during the seventy-five-year history of the subject: Students should learn to write in high schools, and not much could be done in college for those who had not. Students could spend their time in college more profitably by enrolling in an elective course rather than freshman English. While freshman English was inexpensive in terms of cost per credit hour, it constituted a large portion of the English department's budget. Abolishing the course would therefore save money and would (somehow) force high schools to assume responsibility for improving writing instruction. Finally, getting rid of freshman composition would improve the lot of college teachers, enabling them to turn to "different, and more attractive, channels" (362). This, in turn, would improve morale since few teachers wanted to teach the course as their principal concern.

Kitzhaber's response to these charges was based on a historical understanding of the subject that few educators of the time displayed. (After all, his doctoral dissertation had been an analysis of the changes college rhetoric instruction had undergone in the nineteenth century.) Kitzhaber admitted that the course as it then existed was inadequate in content, methods, and materials. The solution, however, was not to abolish it, but to improve it, and no one could do this better than the English department. First of all, changes in high school writing instruction had to be made. This could not be done by mere mandate; English departments needed to become cooperatively involved with high school teachers in developing better methods for teaching writing. Even after this was accomplished, however, the college writing course could not be abolished. The course was, finally, an integral part of the humanistic training of students, and its proper subject matter was language, rhetoric, and literature. Unfortunately, only the last—literature as interpreted by the New Criticism—was currently a strong part of the English teacher's repertoire, even though all three fell within her province. Kitzhaber acknowledged the importance of the "New Grammar" of structural linguistics, seeing it as a counterpart of the New Criticism. What was needed, he asserted, was a "New Rhetoric" to complete the triad.

Kitzhaber's notions of the way writing should be taught and the means for improving it continued to appear in essays published in *College English*, in *College Composition and Communication*, and, most completely, in his book-length treatment of the field entitled *Themes, Theories, and Therapy: Teaching of Writing in College*, published in 1963. It should be noted that although Kitzhaber was among the most conspicuous of the spokespersons arguing for new approaches to writing instruction, he was not alone in this effort. His views will, however, be treated at length here because they so strongly represent the calls for a New Rhetoric that appeared during the sixties.

In "New Perspectives on Teaching Composition" (1962), Kitzhaber reported on the kinds of summer workshops in composition for high school teachers that had been devised by the College Entrance Examination Board's Commission on English. These workshops were extremely important because the premises on which they were based soon became commonplaces of writing instruction in many high schools and colleges. In keeping with the guiding influence of Bruner, the emphasis in the composition class was to be on the writing process. The first premise of these workshops was that the best way to familiarize teachers with the process was to make them writers, enabling them to learn "at first hand the nature of the problems faced by any writer." The second premise was that composition is not merely a mechanical and practical skill, "but instead an important way to order experience, to discover ideas and render them more precise, and to give them effective utterance" (441). Composition, Kitzhaber maintained, "is intimately related to thought itself" (442). Since writing is involved in the very structure and discovery of knowledge, it is at the heart of education, one of its most liberating and humanizing agencies.

Kitzhaber went on to describe the two courses in writing that were designed to prepare high school teachers for writing instruction. It is worth noting that these roughly corresponded to the two approaches to writing instruction that have constituted major forces of innovation in the subject for a considerable period—up to and including the present. The first course, based on a reading of Plato's *Phaedrus*, fell into the category of expressionistic rhetoric, emphasizing the limits of language and the importance of the unique point of view manifested in voice. The second demonstrated an approach closer to that of Aristotle (although he is not named), emphasizing writing as a set of choices growing out of the complete rhetorical context: "the writer's own identity, his subject, his purpose, and his audience" (442). Kitzhaber closed the essay with a plea for more courses in writing instruction at the college level and, significantly, with a call for research into the nature of the writing process—acknowledging, however, that writing is an art and not a science. The call for research, it should be mentioned, made specific reference to the availability of funds through Project English.

Kitzhaber's plea for research in the composing process, his emphasis on writing as an art, and his assertion of the central place of composition in the total curriculum were repeated in "4C, Freshman English, and the Future," an address to the CCCC that was published in its journal in 1963. Here he also called on the CCCC to take up the three recommendations as permanent features of its professional platform, and finally asserted that the freshman composition course should become the focal point of the organization's efforts. Kitzhaber's proposals had come out of a study of the freshman composition course nationwide that he had undertaken at Dartmouth with the financing of a large Carnegie Corporation grant. The results of this study, based on an examination of nearly one hundred syllabi and on visits to eighteen four-year colleges, appeared in two places: "Freshman English: A Prognosis" in *College English* in 1962, and *Themes, Theories, and Therapy* in 1963. Since the first was a capsule statement of the second, it will be considered in detail.

In "Freshman English: A Prognosis," Kitzhaber reported on the changes taking place in the freshman writing course. He found an accelerating decline in the number of remedial courses being offered on college campuses. Writing laboratories and clinics, rather than class time, were being used for students in need of help in grammar and usage. At some schools, even the labs and clinics were being abandoned. Textbooks for the course were becoming "more difficult and more scholarly" (477). Proficiency exams in English for sophomores and juniors were being eliminated because so few students were failing them. As provisions for less able students were decreasing, those for the best students were increasing—for example, waiving of the freshman composition requirement (and sometimes replacing it with a literature requirement), accelerated courses covering the work of two semesters in one, and enriched courses requiring more writing and more reading (especially in literature). Freshman students at four-year colleges were better prepared than in the past, explained Kitzhaber, but this was not the result of an overall improvement in the students entering college. Since the number of college-age students was expanding at a rate greater than enrollments at four-year schools, colleges could select better students. Furthermore, the increase in the establishment of junior colleges meant that the less able students were more often attending two-year schools. High schools were also doing a better job of preparing students for college work. There had been, Kitzhaber explained, "a swing away from 'whole child,' 'life adjustment' education toward a philosophy of greater intellectual rigor in the teaching of academic subjects" (479). Students were writing more in high school English classes, and major efforts had been undertaken to improve the instruction at that level, including teachers institutes, research in writing instruction, and curriculum study centers.

Unfortunately, while high schools had begun to improve their instruction in writing, Kitzhaber discovered no corresponding effort in colleges. In his estimate, the colleges were continuing to rely on high schools for the real work of composition teaching, with the result that the former simply had not in any way been influenced by the new studies in rhetoric and linguistics. The majority of college courses continued to fall into the current-traditional camp (as Kitzhaber would soon demonstrate in the first chapter of *Themes, Theories, and Therapy*), emphasizing grammar, superficial correctness, modes of discourse, and the discussion of "things in general." Kitzhaber went on in his essay to point out that college composition continued to be conceived of as a "service" course: "It has existed only to remedy deficiencies of earlier instruction, to help students write well enough so that they can pursue their other college studies without making gross errors in usage and expression" (481). The changes that had been made in the college course had been designed to make it a class in writing about literature. Unfortunately, this had shifted the emphasis from rhetoric to poetic, and the principles of composing had been lost in the transition.

Kitzhaber proposed in place of the "service" concept and the belletristic method an approach based on the rhetorical tradition, a heritage extending back over twenty-five-hundred years to ancient Greece. As he explained, the subject matter of such a course is rhetoric: "It is a discipline that performs the invaluable function of helping the writer or speaker to find subject-matter for a discourse, to evaluate and select and order it, and to give it fitting expression." Rhetoric and logic, not simply correct usage, are needed, and they will provide the basis for college composition, a course now to be regarded as "a liberal subject, a cultural subject, for it helps to discipline thought and give form and point to its utterance" (481). This course should be provided for all college students—and for a very good reason: "It will be the only course a student takes in which the quality of his thinking and of his written expression, together with the principles that underlie both, is the central and constant concern" (482). Finally, rhetoric courses and courses in teaching students to write should be a part of the program offered by the college

English department to all prospective high school and college teachers. English departments must likewise encourage research in these areas, Kitzhaber noted, so that along with the New Criticism and the New Grammar we would have a New Rhetoric, not a warmed-over nineteenth-century version of this important discipline.

One of the most significant statements supporting Kitzhaber's proposal to return rhetoric to a place of prominence in the English department was Wayne C. Booth's "The Revival of Rhetoric," a lecture delivered at the MLA meeting in 1964 and published in 1965. Admitting that rhetoric had taken on pejorative implications—and not without reason—Booth argued that there was nevertheless a need for what rhetoric at its best had historically trained its students to do: "to engage with one's fellow men in acts of mutual persuasion, that is, of mutual inquiry." English departments were providing nonmajors a composition course "as shameful as any of the ills they purport to cure." Majors and graduate students were being treated in a manner even more deplorable: "At most universities still a student cannot undertake serious rhetorical study even if he wants to, for lack of teachers, courses, or library facilities." Booth charged that members of the English department were neglecting their duty to provide the student with "guidance in the true art of transferring ideas, motives, intentions from his mind to other men's minds" (10). Like Kitzhaber, he called for a new rhetoric to complement the "new grammar and new stylistics" (11). This would not simply be a revival of Aristotle, Quintilian, Campbell, or Whately—although their ideas needed to be made available for study. Booth felt that the age was a rhetorical one with unique demands: "We believe in mutual persuasion as a way of life; we live from conference to conference." Moreover, he felt that English studies as a discipline is inherently rhetorical in that it is concerned first and foremost with persuasion among its members. Consequently, his recommendations to the English department were simple and pointed: "first, that in a rhetorical age rhetorical studies should have a major, respected place in the training of all teachers at all levels; and secondly, that in such an age, specialization in rhetorical studies of all kinds, narrow and broad, should carry at least as much professional respectability as literary history or literary criticism in non-rhetorical modes." Booth closed by asserting that literary scholars could safely turn "from *belles lettres* to rhetoric" (12) with confidence that their new work would be both serious intellectually and relevant to society.

A number of others contributed to the effort to redefine rhetoric and writing in the college classroom. The most effective and least conspicuous of these were the editors of the NCTE publications on writing instruction during this period. Ken Macrorie from 1962 to 1964 and William F. Irmscher from 1965 to 1973 made *College Composition and Communication* the kind of leader in writing instruction that Kitzhaber hoped it would be. And *College English* editors James E. Miller, Jr. (1960–66), and Richard Ohmann (1966–78) continued to keep rhetoric and writing at the center of the concern of English departments. These four figures, along with *Research in the Teaching of English* editors Richard Braddock (1967–72) and Alan Purves (1973–78), were immensely influential in, by and large, salutary ways. Through making available a wide variety of research studies, they contributed to the creation of a discipline.

A host of scholars used these journals to respond to the calls for a new rhetoric. Virginia M. Burke, in a 1965 essay entitled "The Composition-Rhetoric Pyramid," made a plea for "connected and scholarly efforts to restore rhetoric as the informing discipline in the practice of composition at all levels" (3). Displaying her knowledge of the rich history of rhetoric with a brief summary, Burke argued that a "new rhetoric" was nevertheless needed—one that would replace the emphasis on superficial correctness, the four modes of discourse, and the objective method. Hans P. Guth argued in "Two Cheers for Linguistics" against making linguistics the center of the composition class. He insisted that rhetoric must be the subject matter of the writing course—occupying the place between literature and linguistics, encompassing "the potentialities and dangers of language as the powerful medium in which most of the concerns of [the student's] private, practical, and political life find their expression or reflection" (492). In "Rhetoric and the Quest for Certainty," Guth again took up the argument, asserting that rhetoric must combine features of linguistics and literature. The composition teacher deals with public discourse, aiding the student in the discipline of self-expression, the responsible interpretation of experience, and the articulation of policy in public dialogue. Similarly, in "What Are

Colleges and Universities Doing in Written Composition?" Glenn Leggett disputed the notion that freshman composition should be a service course. Instead, he said, its subject should be rhetoric, "the way the raw materials of language get to be communication" (42). Like Guth, he felt that rhetoric combines linguistics and literature, occupying a place between the two.

A number of essays were more ambitious in their attempts to define the scope of modern rhetorical study. In "Rhetorical Research," Martin Steinmann, Jr., called for research in rhetoric, promising to "try to define 'rhetoric,' to outline the sorts of rhetorical research most needed and least needed, and, finally, to briefly describe the present state of rhetorical research" (278). He defined rhetoric as "the effective choice of synonymous expression" involving six variables, variables that recall the Aristotelian triangle: "the speaker or writer, his utterance, his context (occasion or medium), his audience (listener or reader), his purpose (the effect that he intends his utterance to have upon his audience), and the effect of his utterance upon his audience" (280). Steinmann's emphasis on choosing between synonymous expressions—a curious choice since he argued that language and thought are one—led him to fly in the face of most observers of the time by excluding invention—"the choosing between non-synonymous expressions" (281). It also led him to exclude moral and ethical choices—another curiosity—restricting rhetoric to "effective expression," consisting of arrangement and style.

Steinmann went on to define the five kinds of rhetorical research currently needed. In his classification, the first is basic rhetorical research, work that moves from effective expression to theories about what makes for effective expression. Here rhetorical rules are formulated by examining successful rhetorical products. The next is metarhetorical research, the investigation of theories of rhetoric to produce metatheories—description and prescription of what makes for an adequate theory. The third type, pedagogical research, is concerned with studying effective ways of cultivating writing or speaking ability in order to develop theories about how best to teach rhetoric. The fourth, rhetorical criticism, applies theories of rhetorical effectiveness to specific rhetorical texts, demonstrating the features that make the texts successes or failures. Finally, historical or comparative rhetorical research is concerned with studying rhetorical theories and their relation to each other. Steinmann closed his article by reviewing some of the relevant research in rhetoric, emphasizing the interdisciplinary and cross-disciplinary nature of the effort. He acknowledged, however, that little had been done and that the need for such research was just being recognized.

Three related studies are worth mentioning. In "Very Like a Whale—A Report on Rhetoric," Robert Gorrell presented a response to a seminar on rhetoric sponsored by the CCCC at Denver in 1964. He discussed the field of new rhetorics beginning to appear, looked at the history of rhetoric as it applied to the present, and considered the interdisciplinary nature of rhetoric in calling for new research. He closed with a view of the relationship of rhetoric to the teaching of English, warning that any teaching rhetoric must be comprehensive because it must not only deal with the entire composing process but also consider the contextual nature of choices. In "The Four Faces of Rhetoric: A Progress Report," James Murphy responded to the MLA-sponsored Conference on Rhetoric and Literature held at the 1964 and 1965 MLA meetings. These sessions were trying to establish order in the study of rhetoric, defining the term so that it could serve as a useful guide to research and discussion. Murphy argued that the term has four senses. The first is rhetoric as a historical subject—the rhetoric of Cicero or Quintilian. The second is rhetoric as theory, without regard to time—abstract statements about rhetoric in general. The third is rhetoric as a set of formulated precepts—advice about composing the text. And the fourth is rhetoric as recognizable structures in literary works— tropes, for example, or more broadly considered, the analysis of literary works in terms of rhetorical effects on audiences. As Murphy explained, however, the members of the conference sessions arrived at no consensus on the issue, considering only the difficulties of the term as it was then used. Finally, this overview would not be complete without mention of Francis Lee Utley's 1968 essay "The Boundaries of Language and Rhetoric: The English Curriculum." This article offers the most comprehensive overview of the notions of rhetorical theory and research prevalent at the time, identifying the major forces at work in the discipline. It is the best guide to rhetoric and composition in the mid-sixties, and it has been consulted with care in preparing this chapter and the next.

A significant impact on the emerging field of rhetorical studies was also made by a number of essay collections and book-length treatments. Edward P. J. Corbett's *Classical Rhetoric for the Modern Student* (1965) offered an application of Aristotelian rhetoric to the writing class and also provided a useful history of rhetoric as a discipline. Gorrell's *Rhetoric: Theories for Application* (1967) and Gary Tate and Corbett's *Teaching Freshman Composition* (1967) provided classroom applications of new rhetorical approaches. Steinmann's *New Rhetorics* (1967) collected essays on some of the most promising directions that rhetoric was taking, including tagmemics, Francis Christensen's generative approach, and sociolinguistics. Steinmann was following the lead of Daniel Fogarty's *Roots for a New Rhetoric* (1959), an attempt to suggest a theoretical base for a modern rhetoric in the work of S. I. Hayakawa, I. A. Richards, and Kenneth Burke. Fogarty, unfortunately, found no audience until the seventies. Steinmann's effort was treated more favorably in its own day, as were the works of W. Ross Winterowd and James L. Kinneavy, both of which merit separate attention.

Winterowd's *Rhetoric: A Synthesis* (1968) attempted to make sense out of recent developments in rhetoric. Strongly influenced by Aristotle, Burke, and recent linguistic theory, the volume begins with a general introduction and chapters on Aristotle and neoclassic rhetoric. It then considers the theoretical base of the emerging new rhetoric, acknowledging the influence of Burke in general and Chomsky, Christensen, and Bruner in particular. Winterowd's contribution, however, is original in its synthesis of these materials and its application of them to the classroom. Finally, the book includes a section on rhetoric and poetic, showing how the two inform each other. Despite the fact that *Rhetoric: A Synthesis* fails to consider invention except in passing, the work shows a commendable attempt to come to terms with the forces in the sixties that were mapping out new directions for rhetoric.

Kinneavy's *A Theory of Discourse* (1971) was a monumental attempt to make sense out of the new interest in rhetoric, providing a historical, philosophical, and linguistic basis for discussions of rhetorical discourse. Kinneavy took all rhetorical utterances as his province, attempting to create both a taxonomy of the components of rhetoric and a language for discussing it. The book is learned, relating the aims of discourse to their sources in the history of thought. The chapter on expressive discourse, for example, analyzes the history of the form, tracing it through Epicurus, Lucretius, Vico, Rousseau, Herder, von Humboldt, Schelling, Freud, Jung, Croce, Spingarn, and Dewey, among others. The discussion culminates in a lengthy and engaging treatment of Sartre and an application of the expressive theory now demonstrated to a discussion of the Declaration of Independence. A *Theory of Discourse* remains the best theoretical treatment of discourse theory and continues to provide a rich store of materials for informed research in the area. It also has served as an example of the successful use of the historical method in rhetorical research.

Finally, special mention must be made of *Research in Written Composition*, an overview of empirical studies in the field up to 1961. Put together by Richard Braddock, Richard Lloyd-Jones, and Lowel Schoer—all of the University of Iowa—the work took a hard look at the kind of empirical research composition had encouraged. Its findings were highly critical of the efforts undertaken in the area, offering a detailed litany of shortcomings in the research, and posing questions about writing and its teaching that needed answering. The report, however, represented a major step in the development of composition studies. Only a discipline confident of its value and its future could allow this kind of harsh scrutiny. The work signaled a new rigor in empirical research in rhetoric, making specific methodological recommendations for future studies and reporting on studies considered exemplary. This volume led to the establishment in 1967 of the journal *Research in the Teaching of English*, with Braddock as its first editor.

Before closing this chapter, I would like to consider the role of linguistics in shaping the discipline during this fifteen-year period. It is no exaggeration to say that the study of linguistics in the English department during the twentieth century has been one of the most formative influences in the study of both literature and rhetoric—so much so that today language itself has become, in one guise or another, the central focus of nearly all scholars in the English department, regardless of their specialty. As was repeatedly noted in earlier chapters, linguistics research has also been crucial in reminding teachers of the social basis of language and of the class structure on which it is based. This effort, begun early in the century with the likes of Fred Newton Scott and two of his students, Sterling Andrus Leonard and Charles Fries, has been carried on more recently in the work of James Sledd, and bore conspicuous fruit in the CCCC's position statement entitled "Students' Right to Their Own Language" in 1974.

For a number of reasons, however, linguistics did not provide the panacea for composition studies that was predicted by many in the fifties. The theoretical shift from structural linguistics to transformational grammar created considerable confusion among nonspecialists, as discussed, for example, in the exchange between Sledd and Harold B. Allen in volume 23 of *College English*. Arguing from a totally different perspective, current-traditionalists—such as A. M. Tibbetts—feared the relativism in language introduced by the new linguistics and preferred the security of traditional grammar. There were also doubts, as already indicated, about the ability of linguistics to provide all that was needed to learn and teach writing. Guth in "Two Cheers for Linguistics" and Gorrell in "Structure in Thought," for example, both expressed reservations about the ability of modern linguistics to aid students in discovering relevant and meaningful discourse.

Nevertheless, the influence of linguistics in rhetoric has been formidable and, on the whole, salutary. The most influential spokesperson for the value of linguistics in composition instruction has been Francis Christensen. In "A Generative Rhetoric of the Sentence" (1963), "Notes toward a New Rhetoric: I. Sentence Openers; II. A Lesson from Hemingway" (1963), and "A Generative Rhetoric of the Paragraph" (1965), Christensen taught composition teachers a new way to look at sentence and paragraph formation. Combining an empirical approach that considered the way writers actually compose sentences with lessons from the new linguistics, he provided a fresh method for research, as well as a pedagogy for the sentence and paragraph. The claims that Christensen had at last developed *the* new rhetoric were exaggerated, for rhetoric is much more than sentence and paragraph formation. He had, however, taught writing teachers something about the relation of form to meaning, especially the ways in which linguistic forms can themselves generate meaning.

A number of other applications of linguistics were destined to be immensely influential. In 1964, Donald R. Bateman and Frank J. Zidonis published the results of their experience with teaching transformational grammar to high school students. Beginning in 1965, Kellogg W. Hunt and R. C. O'Donnell (early recipients of

Project English funds) used transformational grammar in a number of studies of syntactical maturity among students at various grade levels, as well as among adults. John C. Mellon (1969) and Frank O'Hare (1973) each used sentence-combining techniques—activities suggested by transformational grammar—to improve the syntactical maturity of elementary school children. Eventually, these techniques had an impact on the teaching of writing at the college level, even though their basic premises were at times questioned.

The effect of linguistics on writing instruction has not been monolithic or simple. While the empirical studies of syntactical maturity have led to the use of sentence-combining activities in the writing class, Christensen's use of transformational grammar has encouraged a new approach to teaching paragraph construction as well—moving from style to arrangement without inconsistency. It is true that both teaching techniques could serve the current-traditionalist's emphasis on superficial correctness and patterns of arrangement. That this is not inevitable, however, can be seen in some of the uses of sentence combining reported in the recently published *Sentence Combining: A Rhetorical Perspective* (1985), edited by Donald A. Daiker, Andrew Kerek, and Max Morenberg. It should also be recalled that the tagmemic linguistics of Kenneth Pike has given rise to a rhetoric that is anything but current-traditional in its orientation—a development to be considered in the next chapter. And the diversity of linguistics theory—sociolinguistics, psycholinguistics, speech-act theory, semiotics—has in the late seventies and eighties been called upon in the formation of a variety of rhetorical speculation, some of which will be indicated in the last chapter.

This chapter has examined the historical events surrounding the emergence of rhetoric as a discipline in the English department and has simultaneously considered the complementary professionalization of writing instruction. I have repeatedly mentioned the calls in the sixties and early seventies for a "new rhetoric"—voiced by the likes of Kitzhaber and Booth, for example. As this discussion has begun to demonstrate, no dominant body of rhetorical theory emerged then or has emerged since to satisfy this request. Instead there has appeared a multiplicity of rhetorics, each attempting to describe in its unique way the elements of the rhetorical act and the manner of conducting it. This pluralism has troubled some—a recent *College English* essay by Jim Corder, for example, provocatively raising the specter of the one true way. As this history has attempted to demonstrate, however, rhetoric—like poetic—is always marked by multiplicity. While one system may emerge as dominant—the one preferred by the powerful, for example—it will simultaneously be challenged by other systems, these challenges proliferating in proportion to the freedom tolerated in the society involved. I would now like to consider the intellectually rich and varied rhetorics that arose during this renaissance period of 1960–75—a treatment that will celebrate rather than suspect the variety displayed.

7

Major Rhetorical Approaches:
1960–1975

THE CALLS FOR A NEW RHETORIC IN THE SIXTIES AND EARLY
seventies encouraged a wealth of research and speculation on composing theory. I would now like to consider the major approaches to
writing instruction that appeared at this time, classifying them according to the epistemology that underlies the rhetorical assumptions of each. The first group to be examined will be approaches
based on an objective rhetoric—positivistic theories that locate reality in the material world. The most prominent of these—aside
from current-traditional rhetoric, of course—are the behavioral approaches found in the work of Lynn and Martin Bloom and of
Robert Zoellner. The second category, subjective rhetoric, locates
reality within the individual, the lone agent acting apart from the
material or social realms. Subjective rhetoric, which was especially
prominent during the late sixties and early seventies, is employed in
expressionistic approaches. The third rhetorical class, the transactional, argues that reality is the product of both the observer and
the observed—the private and the public—and is located in the interaction of the two. The most obvious of the transactional approaches is the classical, found especially in the work of Edward P. J.
Corbett and Richard Hughes and Albert Duhamel. Those basing
their approach on cognitive psychology also fall into this category
and include Janet Emig, Janice Lauer, Richard Larson, and Frank
D'Angelo. A third variety of transactionalists will be called the epis-
temics. This group is an especially problematic one because the
term *epistemic* is currently being used in the English department to

refer to two different varieties of rhetoric. The source of this confusion will be considered in discussing this group. Finally, the rhetorics of this period were responding to widespread protests against the Vietnam War, racism, sexism, and related issues, and considering these responses—including the attempts to resist the protests or to ignore them altogether—will be a concern of this chapter.

Objective Rhetoric

The rhetoric most obviously based on a positivistic epistemology during this period arose out of the influence of behaviorist psychology. In 1962, an essay by Douglas Porter, a behaviorist in the Graduate School of Education at Harvard, appeared in *College Composition and Communication.* Entitled "The Behavioral Repertoire of Writing," the article argued that the covert nature of writing behavior does not preclude the application of behavioral learning principles to it. The technique recommended was to "infer and describe covert behavior by observing palpable antecedents and consequents to the behavior" (14). In other words, the successful writing act should be analyzed in terms of its sequence of observable behavior, and students should be directed to engage in this sequence, with rewards attending successful performance. In the same journal in the same year, John F. Huntley of the University of Iowa discussed the principles of programmed learning in writing instruction, basing his comments on B. F. Skinner's behaviorist psychology. He explained that this method would be available to teachers as "soon as someone has the patience to work out the 10,000 steps" (64) in the writing process through experimentation. An article in the same issue by Charles Simon described the unsuccessful use of a programmed learning aid, Joseph C. Blumenthal's *English 2600.* This isolated experiment had little impact, however, as behaviorist principles continued to influence the publication of workbooks on grammar in the sixties and seventies.

Behaviorism in the composition class seemed to be restricted to workbooks on grammar and usage until Lynn and Martin Bloom in 1967 and Zoellner in 1968 began to publish articles on their two different behavioristic approaches. Enthusiasm for their respective methods was never great, and Zoellner attracted outraged replies from colleagues throughout the country. Still, the techniques received considerable attention and became involved in a number of other developments in writing instruction at the time.

The clearest and most complete statement of the position of Lynn and Martin Bloom is seen in "The Teaching and Learning of Argumentative Writing" (1967). Their method is based on psychological learning theory (Martin Bloom was a social psychologist)—more specifically, reinforcement theory: "Rewarded behaviors tend to persist while punished behaviors tend to be dropped." The problem for the teacher "is to identify what stimuli and what responses are present in the writing process in order to reward and to punish appropriately." Difficulties in teaching writing are inevitable because "the stimuli and the responses take place largely at the symbolic level in the student's mind." The traditional approach to teaching writing falls into all the traps implied in this description. Using the language put into currency by D. Gordon Rohman and Albert O. Wlecke, although applying it to a different epistemology, Bloom and Bloom argue that the teacher usually does little in the prewriting stages of composing, focusing instead on the "post-writing critique." The student is largely left to her own devices in discovering meaning. The teacher's critique, meanwhile, is most often ineffective or even harmful because "we don't really know whether we are rewarding the right thing for the right reason from the perspective of the student's learning process—the dynamic process that occurs while the writing is being created" (129). In other words, teachers cannot be sure their comments are reinforcing the desired kinds of behavior because they do not know what kinds of behavior are desirable: they simply do not know how good writers write.

Bloom and Bloom describe three activities they attempted in improving their composition instruction. The first, conducted by Martin Bloom, was a careful and systematic observation of a student as he wrote a number of themes; it involved recording "each discrete sentence or fragment he wrote," and noting "the errors and corrections, pauses, interruptions, 'environmental events,' and timing." Bloom discussed each theme with the student afterward, considering how the parts fit into the whole, stylistic choices, and the larger context of the paper. He discovered that the student followed the current-traditionalist's description of the process: "a theme idea gets introduced, developed, and summarized." He also found, however, that

the process was not neat and orderly, with "discontinuities and interruptions" (130) being a normal part of it. The second activity involved
the application of reinforcement principles. Since the teacher cannot
be present throughout the composing process, she must become a
symbolic presence. Both in-class comments by the teacher and the
instruction   offered   by   rhetoric   texts   may   be   helpful but are usually ineffective because there is no guarantee that
they will be continually in the writer's mind while composing. Programmed learning devices are useful, but they cannot help in matters
of content. Bloom and Bloom propose that the solution to writing
problems can be found "in making the thinking process visible to
both student and teacher." This is done by "having the student make
successive approximations toward preferred goals of writing" in a
number of ways: making the student aware of a given writing problem, getting him to generate several possible solutions to it and then
to select the best one, and, in a conference, giving the student advice
about his choices so that he "creates a set of standards and operating
principles for himself which he can use the next time he writes a
theme" (131). Bloom and Bloom eventually developed a set of work-
book exercises to bring about this kind of behavior, the exercises
being divided into three areas: generating ideas, construction of the
paper, and self-evaluation. These, it should be noted, included such
traditional rhetorical categories as audience and purpose.

The last activity involved the teacher's evaluation of student work.
In this regard Bloom and Bloom advocate that students be made
aware of the standards of evaluation used and how they are to be
applied. The student as well as the teacher should then apply these
standards in evaluating the student's product. The purpose is to
make the student self-sufficient and responsible for his own work
rather than reliant on the teacher for approval and judgment.

Zoellner's "Talk-Write: A Behavioral Pedagogy for Composition"
took up all of the January 1969 issue of College English. Like the
approach of Bloom and Bloom before it, it relies on the language of
Rohman and Wlecke—this time, however, in the service of a rhetoric that is even more explicitly based on the behavioral psychology
of B. F. Skinner. The great mistake of the current approach to writing, Zoellner explains, is that it is grounded in an instrumental metaphor that is flawed. We have defined writing as thought on paper,
formulating "a one-to-one relationship between the thinking pro-

cess on the one hand and the printed word on the other." This has led to a "product-oriented rather than [a] process-oriented" approach (270), in which we assume that we have actually said something meaningful when we have told a student that her essay is unclear or disorganized because of faulty thinking. The problem is not with faulty thinking but with faulty or maladaptive behavior— the "concrete, discriminable, and empirically accessible behavioral dimension to the *act* of writing to which we have insufficiently attended" (271). We must look at the "scribal act" that produced the writing, the process involved in it, rather than the product itself. The important consideration is not the scribal artifact but the student's behavior in producing it.

Zoellner is convinced that many and perhaps most of the students who experience difficulties in writing have these problems because our ruling metaphor for dealing with the process has created a dissociation between what a student thinks and what she writes. He argues that "there exists an intervening behavioral term which, in the phrasing of the information theorists, constitutes a quantifiable and manipulatively accessible amount of 'noise in the channel'" (273). Zoellner proposes that we replace our think-write metaphor with a talk-write metaphor. In order to bring about learning, we must shift our attention from thought, a phenomenon beyond perception, to talk, a phenomenon which can be observed and manipulated. The answer to our difficulty can be found in the learning theory of behavioral scientists, who see learning not as an internal event—as do most writing teachers—but as a "replicable and measurable *external* event, specifically the frequency or rate at which an organism 'emits' a discernable 'bit' in the behavioral continuum" (274). We must isolate these external events in order to reinforce the desirable ones.

Zoellner's proposal for the new composition pedagogy includes, he asserts, much of what is done in the classroom now—for example, the emphasis on rhetorical principles, long themes, model essays, and even outlines. But in each case he would provide a behavioral element. According to Zoellner, teachers must offer students instruction that involves the stages of the writing process and not simply the specifications of the final product. This instruction must be "visible rather than invisible" (284), meaning that it must involve observable behavior rather than thought. It must be directed to the student's unique writing difficulties. And it must always involve engaging in particular acts rather than striving for particular qualities or emulating particular models.

Zoellner spells out the characteristics of the classroom in which this behavioral pedagogy could take place. He advocates that the student talk out her ideas and immediately record them as the teacher provides an instantaneous response. The nature of this response is crucial: it must always be couched in terms that ask the student to talk, not to think. Thinking, Zoellner explains, is in our culture dissociated from talking and invites no immediate response. To accommodate this method, the classroom would have to be redesigned to contain wraparound blackboards or large pads of newsprint on which students could write visibly enough for all to see. The vocal-to-scribal dialogue in the class would involve a number of possible permutations: teacher to student or students, student to student or students, or students to student or students. Such a classroom would resemble an art studio rather than a lecture hall. Revision here would be a simple matter since the student could quickly erase or rip out and throw away what she has rejected. She would also be learning the difference between vocal and scribal conventions as she devised ways to deal with them. Finally, the student would always receive immediate reinforcement, knowing at the moment rather than one or two weeks after the fact about the effectiveness of her performance.

The behavioral approach offers a number of other benefits. It promises to correct the tendency of English teachers to create through their emphasis on "higher things" and superficial correctness a split between words-for-teacher and "words-for-me." It also encourages the expression of the self and the development of a unique voice—or at least does not prevent the voice from developing, as does the correction chart. The behavioral approach also emphasizes the social nature of writing by teaching composing within a social environment. And it shows the writing teacher engaging in the composing act in the classroom, just as the pianist plays for his students.

Zoellner's monograph evoked immediate response, with *College English* presenting some twenty-three pages of letters on it in the May 1969 issue. Not all were disparaging, but the tone of those that were was sometimes irrationally harsh. Zoellner also engaged in a follow-up interchange with Bloom and Bloom in *College English* in November 1969. This response is especially noteworthy because in it Zoellner includes an extensive discussion of Thomas Kuhn's *The Structure of Scientific Revolutions*, a discussion defending the proposition that, as Zoellner explains, "my opponents and I are arguing from two totally different paradigms of human behavior, the differences of which are not susceptible to resolution by rational argument and discussion" ("Response" 215). Finally, in 1972 he criticized narrowly conceived and antihumanistic behavioral objectives in an essay entitled "Behavioral Objectives for English."

While the behavioral rhetorics of Bloom and Bloom and of Zoellner did not attract a large following or inspire many textbooks, they did—as this chapter should make evident—strongly affect the ways in which writing teachers think and talk about the writing process. The distinction between process and product, for example, while not original with the behaviorists, was encouraged by them, as was the notion that the teacher could intervene in the student's writing process to improve it. Indeed, stripped of their behaviorist rationale, many of the techniques recommended by Zoellner and Bloom and Bloom are commonplace today—for example, the focus on the activities of writing rather than on thinking skills or reading.

Subjective Rhetoric

The most pervasive form of subjective rhetoric during the sixties and seventies was found in a group of diverse approaches commonly called expressionistic. These share a common epistemology: the conviction that reality is a personal and private construct. For the expressionist, truth is always discovered within, through an internal glimpse, an examination of the private inner world. In this view the material world is only lifeless matter. The social world is even more suspect because it attempts to coerce individuals into engaging in thoughtless conformity. For the expressionist, solitary activity is always promising, group activity always dangerous.

It is important, however, to distinguish the varieties of expressionistic rhetoric. At one extreme can be found the anarchists, arguing for complete and uninhibited freedom in writing, including the intentional flouting of all convention. At the other extreme are the few that are close to the transactional category—especially to epistemic rhetoric. These rhetoricians see reality as arising out of the interaction of the private vision of the individual and the language used to express this vision. In other words, in this view language does not simply record the private vision, but becomes involved in shaping it. The unique inner glimpse of the individual is still primary, but language becomes an element in its nurturing. This brand of expressionistic rhetoric finally falls short of being epistemic—as the term has been defined in discussions of rhetoric over the past eighteen years, a definition to be considered later—because it denies the place of intersubjective, social processes in shaping reality. Instead, it always describes groups as sources of distortion of the individual's true vision, and the behavior it recommends in the political and social realms is atomistic, the solitary individual acting alone. But this will become clearer in discussing epistemic rhetoric later in this chapter. The important expressionists who fall into this latitudinarian camp are Ken Macrorie, Donald Murray, Walker Gibson, William Coles, Jr., and Peter Elbow.

The earliest and most theoretically complete statement of an expressionistic rhetoric found in this period is Rohman and Wlecke's *Pre-Writing: The Construction and Application of Models for Concept Formation in Writing,* a federally funded research study published in 1964. The two tested a method in which students were required to keep a journal, practice certain meditation techniques, and use analogy. More important for this history is that the study probably did more than any other to establish the language of process in discussions of writing—considering the stages of prewriting, writing, and rewriting in composing, and especially emphasizing the value of the first. This study also set forth the major elements that were to characterize expressionistic writing instruction in the years to come and articulated the sources of these elements. As mentioned earlier, Rohman and Wlecke relied upon Bruner's cognitive psychology. Their purpose in doing so, however, was not to consider stages of cognitive development in the student or even the inherent structure of the discipline, although they make passing mention of the latter. Instead, they were interested in emphasizing writing as discovery—specifically, discovery of the self. In keeping with this commitment, they also called upon M. H. Abrams's discussion of romantic expressionistic theories of poetry in his *The Mirror and the*

Lamp, doing so to underscore the organic, creative features of composing. From this perspective writing is seen as art, an art that arises from within the writer. Rohman and Wlecke further relied on the "self-actualizing" psychology of Rollo May, Abraham Maslow, and Carl Rogers, seeing writing as an act that authenticates and affirms the self. Finally, although these features can be seen in most expressionistic rhetorics of the period—Donald C. Stewart's *The Authentic Voice: A Pre-Writing Approach to Student Writing* being the most complete and intelligent textbook based on the work of Rohman and Wlecke—it should be noted that a given version may stress one feature over another.

I would like to begin with one of the early statements of an extreme form of expressionistic rhetoric. In a previous chapter, the relation between depth psychology and expressionistic rhetoric was mentioned, writing being seen as the attempt to record the truths discoverable within the inner depths of the psyche, truths that are denied and distorted by society. S. I. Hayakawa, in an unusual stance for him, embraced this position in an essay in *College Composition and Communication* in 1962. The essay asserts that freshman English should be like group psychotherapy: "In both Freshman English and therapy, the aim is to integrate conflicting feelings and purposes . . . to come to terms with challenging realities, to acquire self-insight and therefore to grow in one's capacity to understand and handle problems." Both must provide a relaxed and "permissive" atmosphere so that one can feel free "to try out one's ideas" ("Learning to Think" 7). Students must write regularly, and Hayakawa specifically recommends the free-writing method of surrealist poets (themselves, of course, inheritors of certain notions of depth psychology), involving sessions of fifteen or twenty minutes without attempts at revising or editing. The teacher and student readers are then encouraged to read this free writing in order "to find things to comment favorably on" (8). Hayakawa at the same time does suggest that the free writing be combined with the study of semantics and with abundant reading. Still, the expressionistic base of the course remains intact.

Hayakawa's mention of the practice of surrealist poets points to another feature of expressionistic rhetoric: it considers writing to be an art, the original expression of a unique vision. Indeed, one measure of the success of writing in capturing the unique, individual vision is originality of expression. Thus, Margaret Blanchard in a 1964 essay in *College Composition and Communication* contrasts the rational and creative approaches to writing instruction, preferring the creative because it "calls forth imaginative, intuitive, empathetic responses, which stimulate in the student an appreciation of his own interior powers as well as the values incorporated in literature" (20). Creative writing in the composition class "deepens awareness of self and others" (21). In an accompanying essay entitled "The Essay as Art," Harold P. Simonson argues that the essay is not a matter of rhetorical mechanics, erudition, or instruction: "My case, in short, is for the essay as personality, intimacy, inwardness." Simonson appropriately quotes Leslie Fiedler's assertion that the essay offers "the artist's self, his self-revelation" (36). The student uses original language, avoiding clichés, in order "to discover himself and come forward under his own colors" (37). And Simonson closes with a reference to Emerson, who along with Thoreau is most frequently cited by expressionists as an intellectual forebear. Finally, in the issue in which these two essays appeared—entitled "Composition as Art"—Ken Macrorie explains that his interest as editor in assembling the essays was to offer an alternative to linguistic and rhetorical approaches to teaching writing. These approaches, after all, "may become too analytical and mechanical to tap all the human powers of freshman students" ("Composition as Art," back cover).

A later but compatible assertion of the expressionistic notion of writing as art is found in Lou Kelly's "Toward Competence and Creativity in an Open Class" (1973). For Kelly, "the content of composition is the writer—as he reveals his *self*, thoughtfully and feelingly, in his own language, with his own voice" (645). The identification of this kind of classroom with the Rogerian encounter group was by this time so commonplace that Kelly felt compelled to deny that the description fit her classroom. Her objective remained, however, the attempt to provide a free environment in which individuals would creatively discover the self. Similarly, Jean Pumphrey in "Teaching English Composition as a Creative Art" (1973) advocates "a shift in emphasis from teacher-student to student-peer evaluation, and an opening up of the classroom to let in real problems," meaning problems that are of genuine personal concern. Pumphrey uses "write-ins" (five to ten minutes of free writing) and fiction writing, with students arriving at generalizations about writing by examining their own process. Revision then follows but is never allowed to be a part of free writing. The students are creating their own worlds, not recording someone else's—engaging in "a process of scattering, the bringing together of various parts into a new whole" (667) that results in fresh discovery.

Throughout the sixties, essays arguing for writing as self-expression continued to appear, moving, as might be expected, in increasingly original directions. This method of writing instruction was encouraged by the Dartmouth Conference, a meeting in 1966 of teachers and scholars from the United States and Great Britain at Dartmouth College to discuss the teaching of English in the public schools. The emphasis in John Dixon's report on the conference, *Growth through English*, is on language and personal growth, the use of English studies for building an "inner world." Ann Berthoff has offered a telling criticism of this stance, arguing that the Dartmouth Conference supported a bifurcation of language use into the communicative and the expressive, the communicative being identified with the public, rational, and empirical, and the expressive with the private and emotional. The result, she argues, is that expressive writing—including art—has been divorced from the world of practical affairs, becoming powerless and ineffective, a trivial discourse of cathartic but ineffectual emoting. Berthoff's description of the recommendations of the Dartmouth Conference, to be taken up in greater detail later, is compelling. There was also in the late sixties and early seventies, however, a branch of expressionistic rhetoric that attempted to identify explicitly the personal and private with the political.

The connections between the expressive elements of composition as depth psychology, composition as art, and composition as political act are seen in H. R. Wolf's "Composition and Group Dynamics: The Paradox of Freedom," an essay appearing in *College English* in 1969. Using a "psycho-sexual analysis" calling on R. D. Laing and Bruno Bettelheim, Wolf argues that all writing ought to be "the unique expression of one's unique experience" (441). After noting that his best writing section had been made up primarily of activists and creative writers, Wolf concludes that these two groups shared "the free assertion of their own selves and their world views" (442). He further insists that, because of the creative nature of the composing act, only such self-assertive behavior can lead to success. For Wolf, this premise resulted in a course in which small student groups worked independently of the teacher. For others during this time, it gave rise to the "composition as happening" phenomenon, and a number of essays describe this approach.

In a 1967 essay entitled "English Composition as a Happening," Charles Deemer attacks the university, charging that it is opposed to education because it fragments and alienates students. Citing such figures as Norman O. Brown, John Dewey, Paul Goodman, Marshall McLuhan, and Susan Sontag, Deemer calls for the composition course to become "an experience" in which the teacher's authority is removed by having the student become an equal participant in learning. The model for this course is the "happening," an art form distinguished by its making the audience part of its very existence. This aesthetic experience involves shocking and surprising the audience-participant into awareness, and Deemer argues that such experiences should become the basis of the composition class: "Clear writing and clear thought come only after clear experiences, yet the inspiration of such experiences has been virtually neglected by educators." Teachers should shock students into undergoing these clear experiences. They can, for example, speak from the back of the room or from outside the side windows, or they can conduct discussion to Ray Charles records. In this scenario, teachers become actors who reduce the distance between actor and audience, including the audience in the drama. The student will then "participate in the realization of his own awareness of his inadequacy" (124), arriving at his personal version of truth.

Other articles in this vein followed. In a 1971 *College English* essay, Leo Hamalian and James V. Hatch described the use of the happening in the literature class, providing a brief history of the phenomenon and explaining that it "is not concerned with product . . . but with *process*" (325). In 1972, Michael Paull and Jack Kligerman offered a variety of experiences—including the happening—that students could undergo in the classroom in order to overcome their tendency to allow "interpretation of experience embodied in the language of others to order their own experience" (652). The most complete application of the happening in the composition class, however, was reported in an article in the February 1971 issue of *College Composition and Communication*.

In "Making Freshman English a Happening," William D. Lutz describes a variety of forms the happening can take, calling especially on activities that appeared in the freshman English syllabus of the University of North Carolina at Chapel Hill. Lutz explains that since writing is creative it requires "an alteration in the very process by which we attempt to teach writing." This involves breaking down the authoritarian classroom atmosphere and creating unique experiences for students. The happening, of course, provides generously for this, offering "structure in unstructure; a random series of ordered events; order in chaos; the logical illogicality of dreams" (35). This kind of classroom finally "calls for the complete restructuring of the university," including the overthrow of all grading systems and of teacher authority. The happening provides experiences about which the student can write, and the student's writing is completely free, without restrictions of genre or length. The specific happenings used to evoke writing responses were varied and even exotic. In one case each student was given written directions to engage in a specific activity at a given signal. These included such tasks as repeatedly counting to five silently and saying aloud "If I had the wings of an angel" each time five was reached; or hiding one's head in one's hands while standing in the corner of a room; or gently tapping one's forehead against a desk repeatedly; and so on, with each student engaging in a different activity of this kind. After a few minutes, the teacher stopped the students and asked them to write a response to the events they had just witnessed. Other happenings involved listening to the same piece of music in different settings, conducting class discussions in the dark, and making collages and sculpture. Finally, it should be noted that the efforts to use film for writing experiences or to create films in the composition classroom that were recommended in composition journals at this time were closely related to the notion of composition as a "happening" (see, for example, "Staffroom Interchange," 1968; and Baker).

I would now like to examine briefly the works of the leading expressionists of the sixties and seventies: Ken Macrorie, Walker Gibson, William Coles, Jr., Donald Murray, and Peter Elbow. Unlike the behaviorists, who were oblivious to the political and social unrest of the period, these men were attempting to create a comprehensive approach to composition that included the political while avoiding what they considered to be the excesses of certain members of their camp. Consequently, they offered in their essays and textbooks a rhetoric meant to counter the charge of solipsism or anarchy. Sometimes this is explicit. Murray, in a 1969 article entitled "Finding Your Own Voice: Teaching Composition in an Age of Dissent," acknowledges that student power is a fact and that politics enters the writing classroom. This does not mean, however, that the student and teacher do not have responsibilities. Murray maintains that individualism and freedom ought to be encouraged, but that these must be defined within a range of limitations for both teacher and student. Coles similarly takes pains in a 1972 essay to dissociate his approach from approaches that see the composition class as a place for therapy or political confrontation. The self he is concerned with in his composition class, he explains, is "a literary self, a self construable from the way words fall on the page. The other self, the identity of the student, is something with which I as a teacher can have nothing to do" ("Unpetty Pace" 379). These attempts to deny the broader implications of their positions are not always convincing, especially given the individualistic cast of their methods. Still, their emphasis on the place of language in shaping the self does save Murray and Coles, as well as a number of other leaders of their group, from some of the excesses of their contemporaries, and I would like to close this section by commenting on this matter.

Macrorie, Gibson, Coles, Murray, and Elbow all agree that writing is art and, as such, can be learned but not taught. All that the teacher can do is provide an environment in which the student can learn, relying on such activities as free writing, rewriting, journal writing, editorial groups, and the encouragement of the original metaphor. As I have stated elsewhere, the purpose of free writing and journal writing is to capture one's unique, personal response to experience; the purpose of emphasizing metaphor is to learn to capture these preverbal responses in language; and the purpose of editorial groups is to check for the inauthentic in the writer's response (Berlin, "Contemporary Composition"). Such a teaching environment has at its center the cultivation of the singular vision and voice of the student. This cultivation takes place, however, not through the happening or the political confrontation, but through study of the ways in which language is involved in expressing one's perceptions of a private, intuitive version of reality. The writing activities in the classroom are thus designed to teach students to use language in arriving at their own vision of the real—to increase their ability to call on all the resources of language in discovering their personal interpretation of experience. This inner vision finally exists apart from language, but language is necessary in order for the individual to shape an interpretation that constitutes a better approximation of it. Every chapter of Macrorie's *telling writing*, for example, is designed to demonstrate "the way language works in us" (4). Similarly, Murray devotes an entire essay to a word-by-word analysis of his one-sentence definition of the writer: "A writer is an individual who uses language to discover meaning in experience and communicate it" ("Interior View" 21). Here language is emphasized as "a sturdy tool for the exploration of experience" (25). In "Composing the World: The Writer as Map-Maker," Gibson emphasizes that words do not record the world, but construct it. And Coles, like Gibson an admirer of Theodore Baird of Amherst, explains that his sequential writing assignments are designed to get students to the real subject: "language: its relationship to experience and individual identity" ("The Sense of Nonsense" 27). Finally, Elbow similarly asserts that "I don't know what I perceive, feel or think *until* I can get it into language and perhaps even into someone else's head" ("Exploring My Teaching" 751). His emphasis, like that of all the expressionists considered in this section, is on the "I," on defining the self so as to secure an authentic identity and voice.

This type of expressionistic rhetoric focuses on a dialectic between the individual and language as a means of getting in touch with the self. Indeed, even the dialectic between the writer and the editorial group is designed to enable the writer to understand the manifestation of her identity in language through considering the reactions of others—not, for example, to begin to understand how meaning is shaped by discourse communities. And it is this commitment to an epistemology that locates all truth within a personal construct arising from one's unique selfhood that prevents these expressionists from becoming genuinely epistemic in their approach, despite their use of activities—such as the editorial group—that on the surface are social in nature. All of this can be seen in Elbow's *Writing without Teachers*, one of the most articulate and pedagogically resourceful of the expressionistic textbooks.

Elbow's purpose in this text is avowedly to empower students, to enable them "to become less helpless, both personally and politically" (vii). This power, however, is not political in any overt sense; it is instead conceived in personal terms—getting control over one's life through getting control over words. Elbow's authority for his statements is thus appropriately established through his personal experience, "making universal generalizations upon a sample of one" (16). The teacherless classroom gives the student the freedom for self-development, especially crucial in a writing course, a place in which "there is learning but no teaching" (xi). Writing is an organic process of growth and discovery involving words, but it is important to remember that the growth and discovery is always personal: "Only *you* have grown, your words have not" (23). This is always the case because "writing is, in fact, a transaction with words whereby you *free* yourself from what you presently think, feel, and perceive" (15). Writing allows for the attainment of a new and better understanding of the self, a process that involves placing the self in a dialectical relationship with a variety of elements. Thus, Elbow recommends "cooking"—interchanges between people, between ideas, between "words and ideas, between immersion and perspective," between metaphors, between genres and modes, and "between you and the symbols on paper" (xi). All of these interactions are useful heuristics based on a free play of language. This language-play, however, is intended as a method of discovering the nonverbal reality of the self: "Language is the principal medium that allows you to interact with yourself. . . . Putting a thought into symbols means setting it down and letting the mind take a rest from it. . . . A principal value of language, therefore, is that it permits you to *distance* yourself from your own perceptions, feelings, and thoughts" (54). While the distancing does improve communication, the most important benefit is that it leads to self-understanding. The editorial group in Elbow's camp serves the same function; observing the responses of other selves to one's words leads to greater insight into one's identity, a better grasp of how to "fulfill [one's] *own* goals, not their goals" (127). It is not surprising, then, that Elbow's version of the editorial group was influenced by the methods of group therapy and of the encounter group (121). Finally, at the start of this discussion, I said that Elbow's approach is not overtly political. In the last analysis, however, for Elbow as for other expressionists, the personal *is* the political—the underlying assumption being that enabling individuals to arrive at self-understanding and self-expression will inevitably lead to a better social order.

Transactional Rhetoric

Transactional rhetoric does not locate reality in some empirically verifiable external phenomenon (sense impression or the quantifiable) or within some realm apart from the external (ideas or vision). It instead discovers reality in the interaction of the features of the rhetorical process itself—in the interaction of material reality, writer, audience, and language. The differences between the various types of transactional rhetoric lie in the way each of these elements is defined and, more important, in the nature of their relationship. There are three rhetorics in this category: the classical, the cognitive, and the epistemic.

Classical Rhetoric

The distinguishing feature of the version of classical rhetoric that appeared during the sixties and seventies was its commitment to rationality. From this point of view, classical rhetoric as found in Aristotle treated all the elements of the rhetorical situation: interlocutor, audience, reality, and language. Indeed, this version insisted that all are inevitably involved in the rhetorical act and so must be considered in pedagogy. The elements, however, are defined in rational terms, even though slight concessions are made to the emotional and ethical appeals. The main reason for this is that this rhetoric regards reality and the mind of the interlocutor as inherently rational—indeed, as operating according to the strictures of Aristotelian logic. And although recent discussions of classical rhetoric have challenged this interpretation (Grimaldi; Lunsford and Ede), discussions in the sixties and seventies clearly did not.

I have already indicated in some detail the revival after 1950 of interest in rhetoric and its classical origins. The most conspicuous spokesperson for this point of view had been Edward P. J. Corbett, first at Creighton and then at Ohio State. However, before we consider his extensive contribution to the study of classical rhetoric in particular and composition studies in general, we should take note of a few other figures.

Richard Hughes and Albert Duhamel published *Rhetoric: Principles and Usage* in 1962. Their approach is Aristotelian, and the rationale for their method is explained in Hughes's "The Contemporaneity of Classical Rhetoric," published in 1965. For Hughes, Aristotelian rhetoric is "explorative and pedagogic," offering the materials needed for a modern rhetoric. Its three distinguishing characteristics are its vitalism, its concept of argument, and its concept of topics. Vitalism refers to the creative quality of Aristotelian rhetoric, its concern with "moving an idea from embryo to reality" (157); it is an art that deals with a process. The concern of Aristotle for argument grows out of this creativity. Argument holds sway in the area between fact and opinion and is concerned with "the generative power of the rhetorical process producing a judgment from just such an area" (158). Rhetoric for Aristotle is first and foremost concerned with discovery—with locating the material of effective argument. The topics, finally, are at the center of this discovery process, providing the means for arriving at a judgment. Hughes takes the position that Aristotelian rhetoric, flanked on the one side by logic and on the other by stylistics, can provide a corrective to our specialization and a center for a student's education.

In "A Plea for a Modern Set of Topoi" (1964), Dudley Bailey calls for the study of the rhetorical tradition and argues that the new rhetoric will emanate from Coleridge, displaying "the sort of relations which obtain among the details of our thought—obtain successfully, that is, in educated discourse." These relations "are the logical and psychological patterns which listeners and readers of our language understand, and indeed anticipate in our discourse" (114). These are the patterns Bailey proposes as a modern set of *topoi* for the writing class. Similarly, in "Honesty in Freshman Rhetoric" (1971), Margaret B. McDowell explains that the rhetoric course replaced the communications course and the literature-composition course during the late fifties and the sixties. She argues that this new rhetoric course should be based on three Aristotelian premises—premises articulated by Donald C. Bryant. The course should include both persuasive and expository writing, it should emphasize informed opinion rather than merely skillfully expressed opinion, and it should offer instruction in dealing with controversial issues. In other words, the modern composition course ought to apply Aristotelian principles in taking social problems as its subject matter, providing a purpose and an audience for writing, and emphasizing argumentation. Finally, in "The Boundaries of Language and Rhetoric: Some Historical Considerations" (1968), Robert O. Payne presents an excellent survey of the rhetorical thought of Plato, Aristotle, Cicero, Quintilian, and the Sophists. He goes on to argue that historical conceptions of rhetoric should be reexamined in our attempts to educate the whole person.

The most influential of the spokespersons for the return of classical rhetoric to the composition classroom has been Corbett. His *Classical Rhetoric for the Modern Student,* published in 1965, presents both a rhetorical pedagogy and a history of the discipline from ancient to modern times. I have commented on the features of this rhetoric text elsewhere ("Contemporary Composition"; *Writing Instruction*), and here I would like simply to summarize its major features. Corbett's text is comprehensive in every way. Despite its emphasis on the rational, it includes the emotional and ethical appeals, arguing for a holistic response to experience. For Corbett, the aesthetic and the moral must be included in the rhetorical act. Because Corbett understands that rhetoric deals with the probable, he places persuasion at its center. The result is a rhetoric that includes invention, arrangement, and style, guiding the student at every step of the composing act.

Especially relevant to this discussion of classical rhetoric are Corbett's attempts to show the appropriateness of classical rhetoric to the modern political and social context. In "The Usefulness of Classical Rhetoric" (1963), he argues that classical rhetoric addresses the whole person, providing for the rational, emotional, and ethical appeals. This rhetoric is likewise aware of the role of audience in shaping discourse. Classical rhetoric further provides for invention through the Roman system of *status* as well as for arrangement and style, the latter including schemes and tropes. The ancient discipline of imitation can, furthermore, be applied to the lessons of modern linguistics. Corbett closes by offering classical rhetoric as a corrective to "the cult of self-expression," asserting that "what most of our students need, even the bright ones, is careful, systematized guidance at every step in the writing process" (164). In "What Is

Being Revived?" (1967), Corbett offers "a rapid survey of the rhetorical tradition" (166)—perhaps the best of these to appear in any essay of the period. It is significant in that, after pointing to the most promising contemporary developments, he concludes: "What we need now is a rhetoric of the process, rather than of the product" (172). The language of process has found its way into discussions of classical rhetoric, just as it had with behaviorist and expressionistic rhetorics.

In "The Rhetoric of the Open Hand and the Rhetoric of the Closed Fist" (1969), Corbett applies the lessons of his conception of classical rhetoric to the controversies of the day, setting up his key terms at the very start: "The open hand might be said to characterize the kind of persuasive discourse that seeks to carry its point by reasoned, sustained, conciliatory discussion of the issues. The closed fist might signify the kind of persuasive activity that seeks to carry its point by non-rationale [sic], non-sequential, often non-verbal, frequently provocative means. The raised closed fist of the black-power militant may be emblematic of the whole new development in the strategies of persuasion in the 1960's" (288). The essay goes on to discuss the features of the rhetoric of the closed fist and its departure from the rhetoric of the open hand, starting with a discussion of Renaissance rhetoric and calling upon Marshall McLuhan and Walter Ong in interpreting the shift. The rhetoric of the closed fist, Corbett concludes, is nonverbal and relies on demonstration— "marches, boycotts, sit-ins, take-overs, riots" (291). Rather than being geared to the solitary speaker or writer, it is "a group rhetoric, a gregarious rhetoric" (292), based on community and a commitment to community. Still another feature of the rhetoric of the closed fist is that it is coercive rather than persuasive, resting on an irrational base that denies choices. This leads to its being nonconciliatory, with speakers intentionally working "to antagonize or alienate the audience" (295) rather than trying to ingratiate themselves. Corbett admits in closing that he has indicated his preference through his method of presentation. And although he finally tries to be conciliatory, attempting to find commendable elements in the rhetoric of the closed fist and to establish a degree of rapprochement between the two rhetorics, he finally explicitly asserts his preference for the rational rhetoric of the open hand.

Classical rhetoric continued to be a powerful force in the composition classroom through the sixties and seventies. While it was never widely used, its supporters managed to keep it at the center of the discipline, a reminder of the possibilities denied for so long by current-traditional rhetoric. Classical rhetoric was eventually reinterpreted in the eighties, but this is a matter for the next chapter.

The Rhetoric of Cognitive Psychology

The school of rhetoric based on cognitive psychology is distinguished by its assertion that the mind is composed of a set of structures that develop in chronological sequence. The most important of these structures are those that deal with the relationship of language and thought. In attempting to understand the nature of writing, it is necessary to know the nature of these structures, how they unfold in time, and how they are involved in the composing process. Since the intellectual forebears of this rhetorical approach are Bruner and Piaget, this school most legitimately embraces the language of process, seeing both learning and language as parts of development and of cognitive stages. Although the rhetoric of cognitive psychology focuses on the psychology of the individual, it is indeed a transactional approach. While the mind is made up of structures that develop naturally, it is necessary for the individual to have the right experiences at the right moment in order for this development to take place. Without these experiences, or with the wrong sequence of experiences, cognitive structures do not properly mature. Thus, the individual's environment can play as important a role as the inherent makeup of the mind. From this point of view, writing also involves a transaction among the elements of the rhetorical context. The structures of the mind are such that they correspond to the structures of reality, the structures of the minds of the audience, and the structures of language. Learning to write requires the cultivation of the appropriate cognitive structures so that the structures of reality, the audience, and language can be understood. In this connection, it should also be noted that since there is a correspondent harmony among these elements, to learn about any one of them is to learn about all.

Janet Emig's *The Composing Process of Twelfth Graders* (1971) was one of the most notable efforts of this school of rhetoric. While Emig is not ordinarily identified as a proponent of cognitive psychology, especially in her most recent work, this landmark study of

student writers called on some of the basic assumptions of the cognitivists. The case-study approach used, for example, was based in
part on the method of Piaget's *The Language and Thought of the
Child*. Twelfth graders were chosen because "ostensibly they have
experienced the widest range of composition teaching presented by
our schools" (3), and, by implication, are near the upper reaches of
the developmental stages of learning. Emig was specifically concerned in this study with the process of composing rather than the
product, but differed from Rohman and Wlecke in seeing the stages
as recursive rather than linear. Still, the stages were the same for all
the students investigated—or, stated differently, the evidence Emig
found most significant was that which could be found in all of the
student responses. One of her major concerns, furthermore, was information about the language development of twelfth graders. Although her focus was on the process of the twelfth graders, she in-
vited research into the composing process of "persons of all ages"
(5), assuming "there are elements, moments, and stages within the
composing process which can be distinguished and characterized in
some detail" (33). And in pointing to the research implications of her
study, Emig drew a parallel between her study and the work of
those who attempted to identify the developmental stages of linguistic performance—specifically, the efforts of Kellogg W. Hunt
and R. C. O'Donnell. She recommended comparing the process and
practice of her twelfth graders with that of both professional and
nonprofessional adult writers, and she suggested longitudinal studies of students to "make better known the developmental dimensions of the writing process, both for the individual and for members
of various chronological and ability age groups" (95). She was also, it
should be noted, concerned with the effects of intervening in the
developmental process as well as with the ways in which the process
varies among cultures and even personality types. Most important,
Emig assumed that the rhetorical complexities involved in composing—complexities she did not underestimate—can be explained by
studying the cognitive skills discovered in a case-study of twelve
high school students. To understand the way these students perform
cognitively in writing is to understand the role of reality, audience,
purpose, and even language in the rhetorical act.

The effect of Emig's study was widespread and significant. She
provided documented evidence suggesting that the composing pro-

cess described in most composition textbooks did not conform to the behavior of actual writers. She indicated flaws in the way writing instruction is commonly approached, and further indicated the complex and unsystematic nature of composing, encouraging new approaches to teaching it. Her effort resulted in more teachers calling upon the process model of composing—prewriting, writing, and rewriting recursively—as it suggested ways teachers could assist students in all stages of the process. Emig also pointed out the inappropriateness of the criteria commonly used by teachers in evaluating student work. And early on, she urged that teachers be writers. In short, this study contributed greatly to the way we think and talk about writing and, as has been recently pointed out (Faigley et al. 5), the way we conduct research about it.

One of the most engaging applications of cognitive psychology to composition studies was proposed by Janice Lauer in "Heuristics and Composition" (1970). Arguing that writing teachers must "break out of the ghetto," she suggested calling upon research and theoretical work in areas outside of studies in English and rhetoric. The most significant of this research, in her view, had to do with discovery—invention, the heart of a vital rhetoric. Lauer recommended going to the literature in psychology in search of heuristic procedures—inventional techniques—that could enrich the composition classroom, and she accordingly presented an extensive bibliography of the area. Lauer's essay prompted a response from Ann Berthoff entitled "The Problem of Problem Solving," in which she charged Lauer with positivism. While Berthoff's response perhaps shed more light on her own position (of which more later) than on Lauer's, it did enable Lauer to make a helpful response. Lauer explained that rather than proposing that composition be taught as a mechanical art of problem-solving, she was in fact offering a series of articles that examined the act of creation. Thus, she was not proposing that students be taught to find "the right solution, the correct answer, in a finite number of steps governed by explicit rules"; instead, she was proposing problem-solving as creativity, the open-ended quest for reasonable answers: "Problem solving as creativity uses not sets of rules but heuristic procedures, systematic but flexible guides to effective guessing" ("Counterstatement" 209).

This attempt to provide writing teachers with heuristics—flexible guides to effective guessing—that were derived from the work of cognitive psychologists is also found in the work of Richard Larson. We recall that the expressionistic rhetoricians were also concerned with invention, but that their method of addressing it was to provide students with experiences or to get students to write freely about their experiences. Rhetoricians influenced by cognitive psychology, like classical rhetoricians, are more likely to provide a set of procedures for students to follow in generating the matter of discourse. Thus, in "Discovery through Questioning: A Plea for Teaching Rhetorical Invention," Larson offers a set of questions for students designed "to stimulate active inquiry into what is happening around them in place of the indifference or passivity with which they often face other than the most dramatic experiences" (127). These questions, he explains, have grown out of his reading of cognitive and other psychologists—Bruner and Rollo May, for example—on creativity, as well as from the work of the tagmemicists Richard Young, Alton Becker, and Kenneth Pike on perspective. (This is the part of tagmemics, incidentally, most influenced by cognitive psychology, and Lee Odell makes the connection between Piaget, Bruner, and Pike explicit in "Piaget, Problem-Solving, and Freshman Composition.") Similarly, in "Invention Once More: A Role for Rhetorical Analysis," Larson distinguishes between two strategies for invention. The first, like his own, helps "the student to organize and define his observations" (665) and is designed to lead the student to understand data. The other, explained by E. M. Jennings in an essay entitled "A Paradigm for Discovery"—based on Arthur Koestler and Bruner—attempts to get the student to think in the way that creative people think, juxtaposing unrelated ideas in order to develop new concepts. As Larson explains, both "procedures must deal with the sense data of observation or the conceptual data from reading and speaking." The difference, he notes, is that Jennings "looks first at the ways in which the mind works, not at ways of understanding data" (666). For both Larson and Jennings, the structures of the mind parallel the structures of the world—the inside functioning in a way that is identical to the outside when both inside and outside are operating normally.

This view is also seen in "Problem-Solving, Composing, and Liberal Education" (1972), where Larson defines problem-solving as "the process by which one moves from identifying the need to accomplish a particular task (and discovering that the task is difficult), to finding a satisfactory means for accomplishing that task" (629). Citing Dewey, Herbert Simon, and Lauer's "Heuristics and Composition," Larson presents a seven-stage process and applies it to analyzing Swift's "A Modest Proposal." Larson makes explicit that the method "is a mode of thought that assists the identification and resolution of difficulties." It is both a way of thinking, "an activity of the mind" (632), and a description of the structure of the external-world—the world being the place where "a problem appears." The external world presents "a disagreeable condition" or information that "demands explanation" or, alternately, it poses "internal contradictions." The mind is so structured that it can immediately perceive these problematic conditions and "satisfy a need perceived in the data" (633). Once again, the structure of the external world and the structure of the mind are seen as working together in harmonious correspondence. Problems and solutions arise out of the inherently rational nature of both the external world and the mind perceiving it. In this process, historical, social, or economic considerations are irrelevant; the individual responds to problems as objective situations to which objective responses must be made.

There were other forces in the sixties and seventies emphasizing the value of cognitive psychology to writing instruction. As Applebee has indicated, the Dartmouth Conference was influenced by Piaget, L. S. Vygotsky, and the American George Kelly. The diversity of these figures led it to define language as a continuum extending from the purely external, referential, and objective, to the purely internal, expressive, and subjective. Its emphasis on the expressive encouraged expressionistic rhetoric (see Gorrell, "Traditional Course"). On the other hand, its emphasis on learning as a process and on developmental levels encouraged the cognitive approaches of James Britton in England and James Moffett in this country. Britton's influence in America did not come into play until well into the seventies. Moffett's *Teaching the Universe of Discourse*, on the other hand, quickly became a strong influence in public education. As this work makes clear, Moffett sees students as moving in their language development through levels of abstraction: from interior dialogue, to conversation, to correspondence, to public narrative, to published generalization and inference. The distinctions have to do with the distances separating interlocutor, audience, and subject. Moffett thus recommends writing and speaking activities that are appropriate to the stages of the student's development.

One final rhetorical approach displaying the peripheral influence of cognitive psychology ought to be mentioned. In *A Conceptual Theory of Rhetoric* (1975), Frank D'Angelo makes a rigorous and ambitious attempt to create a comprehensive rhetoric that takes into account a generously wide variety of speculation in the field during the previous twenty years. D'Angelo wishes to explain the relation between writing and thinking. His basic assumption is that reality and the mind are identical, corresponding structures that can be studied directly: "The universe is characterized by intelligence, by design, and by interdependence." But this orderly universe is at the same time not merely logical. Approaches to understanding the external world and the mind that perceives it must "combine the scientific views of Aristotle or Tielhard de Chardin with the metaphysical views of Plato, Jung, and Assagioli, to achieve a new synthesis." Unlike most other cognitivists, D'Angelo attempts to include in his synthesis the "anti-rationalistic, counter cultural movement of the sixties." His goal is a rhetoric that focuses "on logical and nonlogical modes of thought, on reason and imagination, on thinking and feeling, on linearity and holism, on personal writing as well as expository and persuasive writing" (vii).

Taking this broad spectrum as his province, D'Angelo proceeds in his investigation along interdisciplinary lines, moving from cognitive psychology to linguistics, to anthropology, to philosophy, to rhetorical theory and history. His guiding principle is the search for structures—in the mind, in the external world, in language, and in discourse—that can be taken as constitutive, as basic units of order. As the title *A Conceptual Theory of Rhetoric* indicates, D'Angelo starts with the mind and works outward: "The study of rhetoric is the study of the nature of human intellectual capacities. What are the innate organizing principles, the deeper underlying mental operations, the abstract mental structures that determine discourse?" (26). D'Angelo moves from the mind to structures of discourse and back again, allowing each to illuminate the other. He follows this method, furthermore, in examining the traditional areas of rhetoric—invention, arrangement, and style—although, as has been indicated, not in a traditional way, especially in the kind of structural relations he finds in and among them.

Epistemic Rhetoric

Epistemic rhetoric has been a topic of discussion in communication departments since 1967, when Robert L. Scott's "On Viewing Rhetoric as Epistemic" appeared in *Central States Speech Journal*. The term has also recently been used in English studies in the work of Kenneth Dowst and of C. H. Knoblauch and Lil Brannon, as well as in my own. The rhetoric this term indicates has, however, been advocated in composition circles for quite some time. In this section I will trace the emergence of epistemic rhetoric in the English department as one important response to the call for a new rhetoric. Before doing so, I would like to sketch a definition of the rhetoric as it has been used in communication departments, relying on the best overview of the subject in print—Michael Leff's "In Search of Ariadne's Thread: A Review of the Recent Literature on Rhetorical Theory."

The distinguishing characteristic of the epistemic view, explains Leff, is "that rhetoric is a serious philosophical subject that involves not only the transmission, but also the generation of knowledge" (75). Rhetoric exists not merely so that truth may be communicated: rhetoric exists so that truth may be discovered. The epistemic position implies that knowledge is not discovered by reason alone, that cognitive and affective processes are not separate, that intersubjectivity is a condition of all knowledge, and that the contact of minds affects knowledge. Leff outlines four different senses in which rhetoric may be regarded as epistemic, but the most extreme is the one at issue here. In this point of view, rhetoric is epistemic because knowledge itself is a rhetorical construct. Having historical precedents in Vico and Marx and a brilliant modern articulation in Kenneth Burke, this stance argues that epistemology is rhetorical, is itself a social and historical construct. As Leff points out, this is the antithesis of the positivistic contention that reality is empirical, with language simply reporting what is determined outside its domain. For the epistemic, the symbolic includes the empirical because all reality, all knowledge, is a linguistic construct. Meaning emerges not from objective, disinterested, empirical investigation, but from individuals engaging in rhetorical discourse in discourse communities—groups organized around the discussion of particular matters in particular ways. Knowledge, then, is a matter of mutual agreement appearing as a product of the rhetorical activity, the discussion, of a given discourse community. In fairness to Leff I should note that, while he presents this view without distorting it, he adds the objections to the position that have been proposed, including his own reservations about it.

I would now like to consider this concept as it has emerged in the literature of composition studies between 1960 and 1975. From the epistemic perspective, knowledge is not a static entity located in the external world, or in subjective states, or even in a correspondence between external and internal structures. Knowledge is dialectical, the result of a relationship involving the interaction of opposing elements. These elements in turn are the very ones that make up the communication process: interlocutor, audience, reality, language. The way they interact to constitute knowledge is not a matter of preexistent relationships waiting to be discovered. The way they interact with each other in forming knowledge emerges instead in acts of communication. Communication is at the center of epistemic rhetoric because knowledge is always knowledge for someone standing in relation to others in a linguistically circumscribed situation. That is to say, all elements of the communication act are linguistically conditioned: interlocutor, audience, and reality are all defined by language and cannot be known apart from the verbal constructs through which we respond to them. Language forms our conceptions of our selves, our audiences, and the very reality in which we exist. Language, moreover, is a social—not a private— phenomenon, and as such embodies a multitude of historically specific conceptions that shape experience, especially ideological conceptions about economic, political and social arrangements. Thus, in studying the way people communicate—rhetoric—we are studying the ways in which language is involved in shaping all the features of our experience. The study of rhetoric is necessary, then, in order that we may intentionally direct this process rather than be unconsciously controlled by it.

Epistemic rhetoric holds that language is the key to understanding the dialectical process involved in the rhetorical act. Knowledge does not exist apart from language. Thus, the task of the interlocutor is not simply to find the appropriate words to communicate—to contain—a nonverbal reality. Language, instead, embodies and generates knowledge, and there is no knowledge without language. For epistemic rhetoric, language is not, however, a single, monolithic entity. Within each society there is a host of languages, each serving as the center of a particular discourse community. Each community—whether made up of biologists, composition teachers, autoworkers, ward members, or baseball fans—is built around a language peculiar to itself so that membership in the group is determined by the ability to use the language according to the prescribed method. This specialized language can serve an inclusionary function because it prescribes and enforces assumptions about external reality and the relationship of its members to this reality. Knowledge of what is "real" to the group can only be displayed by using its language. More important, implicit in this language are rules of evidence—codes restricting what can and cannot be used in establishing truth. Being a member of a community requires knowledge of these rules, knowledge that is often tacit. Thus, for a community of biologists or composition teachers or autoworkers or ward members or baseball fans, establishing truth involves engaging in a dialectical interchange that entails rules of evidence (what is real and not real), the members of the community (the audience), and an individual who wishes to change or affirm the community's truths (the interlocutor). This dialectic, moreover, is a complicated process that is not cumulative or arithmetic in nature; knowledge does not usually result from simply adding or subtracting rhetorical elements. Instead, meaning comes about as the external world, the conceptions the writer or speaker brings to the external world, and the audience the writer or speaker is addressing all simultaneously act on each other during the process of communicating. The result of this dialectic is unpredictable, providing for creativity and accounting for the inevitability of change.

I would now like to trace the manifestations of epistemic rhetoric during this period, showing its theoretical and practical orientation. As mentioned in chapter 5, epistemic rhetoric grew out of the activity surrounding the emphasis on general education and its commitment to the communications course, especially the focus on rhetoric as public discourse for a democracy and the insistence (originating with General Semantics) on the importance of language. This concern for language has been shared by linguistics and composition teachers. In fact, during the sixties, seventies, and eighties language has been the central preoccupation of the English department, a focal point of literary and rhetorical studies as well as studies in linguistics. It should be noted, however, that no single rhetoric I will be discussing under the heading of epistemic has realized all of the elements of the theory as I have just described it. Each instead displays strong epistemic elements, elements sometimes denied by other features of the system proposed. Still, in each case, the epistemic characteristics are the dominant ones, warranting placement in this category.

One of the earliest statements of a type of epistemic rhetoric appeared in Harold Martin's "The Aims of Harvard's General Education A," published in *College Composition and Communication* in 1958. Martin argues that the freshman composition course should be "concerned with language not simply as the medium by which a transmission of information takes place but as a phenomenon of particular interest itself." This does not mean that it should be a course in linguistics or in the history of the language or in theories of communication. Since thought is language, explains Martin, students will learn to write in order to improve their thinking. This reversal of the thinking-writing sequence is important since writing thereby becomes a way of thinking, not simply a way of recording thought. Language, then, is for the student "a tool for discovery, for inquiry about the world and his reaction to it." Finally, Martin distinguishes satisfying the self from communication and in the end sees persuasion as the most important function of rhetoric—convincing "another to view an object or situation in a particular light and, perhaps, to begin action on the basis of that view" (88). According to Martin, language—the focus of rhetoric—constitutes thought, discovery, and persuasion.

In an influential essay entitled "In Lieu of a New Rhetoric" (1964), Richard Ohmann, coauthor with Martin of a composition textbook, presents some of the spadework for an epistemic rhetoric. Rather than attempting a new rhetoric, Ohmann proposes to discuss the ways in which contemporary ideas of rhetoric resemble each other, drawing on the work of I. A. Richards, Kenneth Burke, S. I. Hayakawa, Alfred Korzybski, Daniel Fogarty, Richard Weaver, Marie Hochmuth Nichols, and Northrop Frye. Ohmann in fact creates a synthesis that is uniquely his own, although the spirit of Burke is present throughout.

The old rhetoric emphasized persuasion, Ohmann explains, but modern rhetoric includes other forms: "communication, contemplation, inquiry, self-expression, and so on." The old was more aggressive in its design on the audience, whereas "modern rhetoric . . . lowers the barriers between speaker or writer and audience. It shifts the emphasis toward cooperation, mutuality, social harmony. Its dynamic is one of joint movement toward an end that both writer and audience accept, not one of an insistent force acting upon a stubborn object" (18). The second characteristic of modern rhetoric is that it regards the discipline as "the *pursuit*—and not simply the transmission—of truth and right." Truth becomes "not a lump of matter decorated and disguised, but finally delivered intact; rather it is a web of shifting complexities whose pattern emerges only in the process of writing, and is in fact modified by the writing (form is content)." A corollary of this stance is that the "writer does not begin in secure command of his message, and try to deck it out as beguilingly as possible; he sets his own ideas and feelings in order only as he writes." Rhetoric is also self-discovery, and this involves the writer's style being an expression of the writer's personality. Finally, writing always takes place within a discourse community: "The community that a piece of genuine writing creates is one, not only of ideas and attitudes, but of fundamental modes of perception, thought, and feeling. That is, discourse works within and reflects a conceptual system, or what I shall call (for want of a term both brief and unpretentious) a world view. Experience, subtle shape-changer, is given form only by this or that set of conceptual habits, and each set of habits has its own patterns of linguistic expression, its own community." Thus language communities form, in fact, "a hierarchy of world views and corresponding communities" (19), ranging greatly in size and makeup.

Ohmann then turns his attention to the implications of this position for the classroom. He suggests that the course begin with a study of linguistic structures, including dialects, so students will understand that "to master standard written English is to become capable of participating in a linguistic community of considerable importance in our culture" (21). This should be followed by a study of semantics and syntactical alternatives. The course should then turn to rhetorical considerations in composing the written text, with an emphasis on dialectical relationships. The text-content relationship involves the ways in which the writing process discovers meaning. The text-author relationship has to do with the author's self-discovery and revelation in writing. The text-audience relationship considers the appeal from ethos in the search for a Burkeian identification. Finally, the text in relation to a world view is involved in all three—content, author, and audience—but should be treated separately and in detail in the composition class. The point is to enable students to realize the diversity of world views within our society—the different ways in which language is used to organize experience. The object, ultimately, is training for citizenship in a democracy: the student "becomes a voting citizen of his world, rather than a bound vassal to an inherited ontology" (22).

Ohmann's essay is a major theoretical statement of epistemic rhetoric. Another such appeal was articulated by Kenneth Pike, later joined by Alton Becker and Richard Young. Pike, the founder of tagmemic linguistics, offered two preliminary essays toward a new rhetoric in *College Composition and Communication* in 1964. A year later this statement was systematized by Young and Becker in "Toward a Modern Theory of Rhetoric: A Tagmemic Contribution" (reprinted in W. Ross Winterowd's *Contemporary Rhetoric: A Conceptual Background with Readings* in 1975). The three went on to write a textbook, *Rhetoric: Discovery and Change*, published in 1970. Here I will focus on the latter two works.

"Toward a Modern Theory of Rhetoric" presents the epistemic theoretical base on which the textbook was later built. Young and Becker explain that their point of departure is an application of certain principles of tagmemic theory to rhetoric, arguing that "the procedures a linguist uses in analyzing and describing a language are in some important ways like the procedures a writer uses in planning and writing a composition" (131). They indicate that there are two basic heuristics or discovery procedures: a taxonomy of the sorts of solutions found in the past, and, as in tagmemic theory, an epistemological heuristic. Since modern rhetoric is concerned with discovering the new rather than deductively applying the already established, the epistemological heuristic is the main concern. The first premise of such a heuristic posits "the active role of the observer in discovering pattern, and hence meaning, in the world around him" (132). The second premise is that "a complete analysis of a problem necessitates a trimodal perspective." This means that language phenomena and, indeed, all human acts must be "viewed in terms of particles (discrete contrastive bits), waves (unsegmentable physical continua), or fields (orderly systems of relationships)" (133). This gives rise to the well-known tagmemic grid through which the writer is led to examine the topic and the reader from three perspectives. (The grid was made more complicated in the textbook.) The point of this approach is to develop "a wide range of significant perspectives" (143).

Having introduced the inventional heuristic—the basis of rhetoric being discovery—Young and Becker explain that they look upon rhetoric from a Burkeian point of view, seeing it as the effort of a writer to establish identification with an audience by understanding that audience's perspective and attempting to get it to understand the world through the writer's perspective. This is a "discussion rhetoric" rather than a rhetoric of persuasion; it is based on mutual respect and is dedicated to discovering shared interpretations of experience.

After presenting a discussion of discourse patterns, the essay turns to the matter of style, and here the full implications of Young and Becker's position are made apparent. In their view, form and content are one. This means that discussions of arrangement and style are finally discussions of invention: "A writer's style, we believe, is the characteristic route he takes through all the choices presented in both the writing and prewriting stages. It is the manifestation of his conception of the topic modified by his audience, situation, and intention—what we might call his 'universe of discourse'" (140). The individual writer functions within a discourse community, and the choices made at all levels of composing involve language and are the product of verbal interactions among the topic (reality), the writer, and the audience.

Rhetoric: Discovery and Change reveals a concern with preparing the student for citizenship in a democracy. The book is an attempt to establish a new rhetoric that can address the "conflicting ideologies" (8) of the time. Young, Becker, and Pike explain: "We have sought to develop a rhetoric that implies that we are all citizens of an extraordinarily diverse and disturbed world, that the 'truths' we live by are tentative and subject to change, that we must be discoverers of new truths as well as preservers and transmitters of old, and that enlightened cooperation is the preeminent ethical goal of communication" (9). Their approach conceives of rhetoric as a matter of public discourse defined in terms of ethical deliberation and choice. This is important given the dialectical nature of establishing truth. Knowledge is not outside in the material world or inside in the spiritual world or located in a perfect correspondence of the two. It is the product of a complicated dialectic:

> Constantly changing, bafflingly complex, the external world is not a neat, well-ordered place replete with meaning, but an enigma requiring interpretation. This interpretation is the result of a transaction between events in the external world and the mind of the individual—between the world "out there" and the individual's previous experience, knowledge, values, attitudes, and desires. Thus the mirrored world is not just the sum total of eardrum rattles, retinal excitations, and so on; it is a creation that reflects the peculiarities of the perceiver as well as the peculiarities of what is perceived. (25)

Language is the ground of this dialectical interplay. Rather than simply embodying truth so that it may be communicated, language constitutes experience:

> Language provides a way of writing: a set of symbols that label recurring chunks of experience. . . . Language depends on our seeing certain experiences as constant or repeatable. And seeing the world as repeatable depends, in part at least, on language. A language is, in a sense, a theory of the universe, a way of selecting and grouping experience in a fairly consistent and predictable way. (27).

And the dialectic of language between the writer and the material world is accompanied by a dialectic between the writer and the discourse community in which the writer is taking part:

> The writer must first understand the nature of his own interpretation and how it differs from the interpretation of others. Since each man segments experience into discrete, repeatable units, the writer can begin by asking how his way of segmenting and ordering experience differs from his

reader's. How do units of time, space, the visible world, social organization, and so on differ? . . . Human differences are the raw materials of writing—differences in experiences and the ways of segmenting them, differences in values, purposes, and goals. They are our reason for wishing to communicate. Through communication we create community, the basic value underlying rhetoric. To do so, we must overcome the barriers to communication that are, paradoxically, the motive for communication. (30).

All of this leads to a version of the composing process (and the use of the language of process) that rivals Aristotelian rhetoric in its comprehensiveness. Young, Becker, and Pike provide for heuristics, for patterns of arrangement, and for direction in creating an effective style. Structure and language here are indeed a part of invention since they are at the center of the formation of meaning, of truth, not simply the dress of thought. The way a text is arranged and stated is, after all, inextricable from meaning, so to change the shape or its language is to change meaning.

Although I have placed Young, Becker, and Pike among the epistemic rhetoricians, I must admit there is much in their system that resists this placement. Growing out of a linguistics influenced by structuralism, they are at times more closely aligned with the rhetoric of cognitive psychology. This is especially seen in their emphasis on the tagmemic grid, their primary heuristic procedure. The device seems to indicate that meaning is the product of rational and empirical categories, categories that characterize both the observer (the writer) and the observed (the social and material worlds). Related to this is their seeing the issues that concern writers as reducible to matters of problem-solving, with problems conceived of in rational terms, resolvable through the application of the tagmemic grid. Finally, their reliance on Rogerian strategies tends to underestimate the complexities of disagreement, of conflict, in matters of public debate and, as a result, the notion of the dialectic necessary to resolve it. These elements should not, however, obscure the epistemic basis of their approach, a system that sees knowledge as a rhetorical construct.

In the early seventies, Kenneth Bruffee began presenting a conception of rhetoric meant to be an alternative to both expressionistic and current-traditional rhetoric. His approach was grounded in epistemological concerns, examining the ways in which the classroom behavior of teacher and student defines "human nature, the human mind, the nature of knowledge, and the experience of learning" ("The Way Out" 458). Thus, Bruffee looks especially at pedagogy, particularly the definitions of the roles of teacher and student and the relationship between them that is enforced by classroom procedures. Bruffee's orientation regards knowledge as social and communal in nature, seeing "teaching and learning not just as activities which occur in a social context, but as activities which are themselves social in nature." When he looks at the dominant pattern of behavior in the English class, he finds an "authoritarian-individualist mode" (458), a mode that includes a number of disturbingly familiar features. In such a class, the only social relationships that exist are those between teacher and student: "A student talks to the teacher, writes to the teacher, and determines his fate in relation to the teacher individually" (459). There is no relationship among the students, and any attempt by students to act collaboratively in learning is regarded as suspect. In this class, two teaching conventions are typically followed: either the teacher lectures or the students recite. In the first, the teacher is completely in control of all activities; even when the Socratic method is used the teacher shapes the responses permissible. While recitation seems to place power in the hands of students—taking as it does the form of seminars, laboratory work, writing assignments, team projects, and tutorials—in fact the teacher continues to be in control of the activities since each student is finally responsible for her own work, and then only to the teacher. In all of these conventions and their various forms, the teacher possesses absolute power: the student's duty is to follow course requirements and to absorb knowledge from the teacher; the teacher's duty is "to formulate the requirements of the course, impart knowledge to students, and evaluate students' retention of it." Underlying this power relationship is a mechanistic analogy, the notion that "knowledge is subject *matter*, a kind of substance which is contained in the mind." The teacher's mind holds more of this matter than does the student's, and her responsibility is thus to reduce this inequality—through her teaching to transfer portions of her share into the waiting vacancy of the student's mind. Finally, the most important criteria in deciding on the knowledge to be shared with students are precedent and convention: "The teacher's responsibility is not only to impart knowledge which was imparted to him, but also to impart knowledge *as* it was imparted to him" (460).

Bruffee proposes collaborative learning as an alternative to this traditional arrangement, pointing to the successful efforts in this direction taking place outside the classroom—especially in the women's liberation movement and in certain anti-war activities. His strategy for collaborative learning emulates these efforts by calling for the redistribution of power in the classroom, its "poly-centralization," a scheme consisting of "a number of small groups more or less equal in power contending with one another." This situation results in individuals supporting each other in a collaborative relation within each group, enabling "the power of each individual to equal the power of the group as a whole" (462). The shift is from authoritarian modes of acting to collaborative and nonauthoritarian modes. The teacher's responsibility in this classroom is to be not a philanthropist, munificently bestowing knowledge on his students, "but a *metteur en scene* whose responsibility and privilege is to arrange optimum conditions for other people to learn." Such an environment fosters social relationships "in which students share power and responsibility as well as information not peripherally but in the very process of learning." The teacher must relinquish control, finding "his purpose as a teacher . . . in helping people discover, accept, and develop their own intelligence and talent." This method is designed to serve the individual within a social framework, encouraging "the personal autonomy and wholeness which develops through learning in a context of human values, and with a recognition of human interdependence" (470).

Although Bruffee followed up this theoretical presentation with a practical statement entitled "Collaborative Learning: Some Practical Models" in 1973 and a textbook in 1972, he did not fully work out the epistemic implications of his view for the writing classroom until just recently—especially in the 1985 edition of the textbook and in a 1984 *College English* essay called "Collaborative Learning and the 'Conversation of Mankind.'" Still, as his later work makes clear, Bruffee's critique of writing instruction and the alternative he proposed were from the start based on a conception of knowledge as a social construction—a dialectical interplay of investigator, discourse community, and material world, with language as the agent of mediation. The rhetorical act is thus implicated in the very discovery of knowledge—a way not merely of recording knowledge for transmission but of arriving at it mutually for mutual consideration.

A number of others during the seventies also encouraged an epistemic rhetoric. In "Topics and Levels in the Composing Process" (1973), W. Ross Winterowd argues that theories of form and theories of style are sets of inventional topics. This contention serves to unify the process of composing within the field of invention, regarding it as an act of discovering meaning. Language is thus placed at the center of composing, itself serving as the means and end of writing. And Winterowd again takes up this theme as the organizing principle of *Contemporary Rhetoric: A Conceptual Background with Readings* (1975). Hans Guth in "The Politics of Rhetoric" (1972) tries to demonstrate the relevance of dialectic in teaching writing as discovery, showing how this method is inevitably implicated in political questions. For Guth, truth emerges from the interaction of conflicting views, making writing an integral part of the search for knowledge. I would finally like to consider two essays by an educator who has become a spokesperson for epistemic rhetoric, although she has never used the term in describing her method.

In "The Problem of Problem Solving" Ann Berthoff argues that education, including the teaching of writing, is a political act. The fundamental question for writing teachers, she explains, is clear: "Can we change the social context in which English composition is taught by the way we teach English composition?" (240). Writing must be taught so that it is involved in students' personal and social lives. Furthermore, students must be regarded as shapers of their personal and social environments—language users who find and create forms of experience through language. They must be regarded as active agents who shape the world in which they live, calling on language to structure new social arrangements—not simply personal ones divorced from the larger social context. Berthoff's objection to the Dartmouth Conference is that it divided the use of language into two unrelated areas: communication and expression. According to this view, communication deals with the public world but is limited to the rational and empirical; expression deals with the personal but is exclusively emotional and creative. The flaw is that this conception permanently sunders the two, rendering the second powerless. For Berthoff, language in both realms is creative, the individual user shaping consequences—and doing so, furthermore, as an integrated being who thinks and feels simultaneously. In "From Problem-solving to a Theory of Imagination" Berthoff elaborates on her position. Calling on Ernst Cassirer, she defines humans as symbol-using animals—"that one creature whose world of behavior is built by language and who makes sense of 'reality' by a process of linguistic invention and documentation" (638). She goes on to emphasize "that all language is dialectical; that in the very nature of linguistic predication, dialectic is born" (643). Language is not simply a sign system—is not simply, in Richards's phrase, "a sort of catching a nonverbal butterfly in a verbal butterfly net" (641). In this essay Berthoff again denounces the arbitrary split between thinking and feeling, between the intellectual and the creative. Here she especially emphasizes the dangerous political implications of this division, citing in her behalf Paulo Freire. Reality is not "something out there," but the product of a dialectic involving observer and observed, and the agency of mediation is language—the center of the work of the literature and composition teacher. For Berthoff, "language builds the human world" (646). Rhetoric is especially important in this regard because, rightly considered, it "is a formulation of the laws of imagination, that operation of mind by which experience becomes meaningful. . . . Rhetoric reminds us that the function of language is not only to name but also to *formulate* and to *transform*—to give form to feeling, cogency to argument, shape to memory. Rhetoric leads us again and again to the discovery of that natural capacity for *symbolic transformation*, a capacity which is itself untaught, God-given, universal" (647). Language is a "speculative instrument" that enables us to understand and change the world, and the study of the way language does this is rhetoric.

As indicated earlier, all of the rhetorics considered in this chapter were inevitably a part of the political activism on college campuses during the sixties and seventies. They were in fact involved in a dialectical relationship with these uprisings, both shaped by them and in turn affecting their development. The demand for "relevance" in the college curriculum was commonplace, and these rhetorics—

particularly the classical, expressionistic, and epistemic varieties—were attempting to respond. We have already seen this response made explicit in a number of the essays considered—in those by Corbett, Murray, and Berthoff, for example. Even more pointed responses were seen in numerous articles on teaching writing to particular populations—these approaches subscribing to a variety of rhetorics. The December 1968 issue of *College Composition and Communication*, for example, was entitled "Intergroup Relations in the Teaching of English" and included pieces on special approaches to teaching Black and American Indian students—among them James A. Banks's "A Profile of the Black American: Implications for Teaching" and Lorraine Misiaszek's "A Profile of the American Indian: Implications for Teaching." There were also numerous commentaries on the relationship between writing and the feminist movement. For example, the *College English* issue for October 1972 was entitled "Women Writing and Teaching"—with Elaine Hedges serving as guest editor—and included essays by Tillie Olsen, Adrienne Rich, Ellen Peck Killoh, Elaine Reuben, and others. Related to this attempt to raise consciousness regarding inequities in the political and social system were experiments in teaching undergraduate literature and composition courses. Jerry Farber's "The Student as Nigger," an essay denouncing the disempowering of students in the classroom, was an underground best seller on college campuses in 1969 and 1970. Pedagogical essays by Elbow and Bruffee offering new classroom approaches also appeared. In addition, the December 1971 issue of *College English* was given over to the topic "How can we shift responsibility and authority in the classroom? Is it right to do so?" The essays presented—both affirmative and negative—dealt with teaching experiments designed to give students more freedom and responsibility. (The best evaluation of these experiments is Bruffee's "The Way Out.")

Finally, numerous essays in *College English* and *College Composition and Communication* discussed the preparation of college English teachers, encouraging graduate schools to make course offerings more closely aligned with the undergraduate teaching responsibilities most graduates would face upon entering the profession. For example, *College English* devoted its April 1972 issue to the topic "Our discipline and its professional degrees: do they need reconstruction?" This question had been put forth frequently in the preceding decades, but, as the next chapter will demonstrate, not until the late seventies and the eighties was it addressed by the profession as a whole. In this it fared better, I might add, than the programs of most of the campus political activities of the period.

8

Conclusion and Postscript on the Present

BY THE BEGINNING OF THE SEVENTIES, THE BOOM IN STUDENT enrollment was subsiding, and freshman composition—always the object of close scrutiny—was being considered in a new light. Throughout the sixties there had been the customary occasional essay charging that freshman composition should be abolished. Warner Rice's appeal of 1960 has already been discussed; it was followed by a piece by William Steinhoff, also of Michigan, in 1961, by Leonard Greenbaum's "The Tradition of Complaint" in 1969, and by D. G. Kehl's satiric "An Argument against Abolishing Freshman Composition" and Louis Kampf's "Must We Have a Cultural Revolution?" in 1970. The thrust of these arguments—growing out of the sixties experience—included the old allegations that the course was high school material, did not achieve its goals, and was outside the domain of a literature department. To these were occasionally added the charge that students were better prepared than in the past and no longer needed the course, or that to continue the course was to violate the students' rights. The calls for abolishing the course in the seventies, on the other hand, were related to harsh economic realities. Thomas W. Wilcox in his generally unfriendly chapter on freshman English in *The Anatomy of College English* (1973) reported that a comparison of the surveys he made in 1967 and 1972 indicated "about 10 percent of all departments have recently reduced the amount of English freshmen are required to take." He also argued that more department would follow suit, especially among "institutions of highest prestige" (99). In 1970, Michael F.

Shugrue, English secretary of the MLA, predicted that some universities would abandon the required freshman English course "because of budgetary cutbacks, fear of organized teaching assistants, conviction that the course is ineffective in improving the syntactic versatility of freshmen, belief that students no longer need a freshman composition course, and edicts from state boards assigning students in the first two years to junior and community colleges" (251). He admitted, however, that not many colleges had as yet abolished the course, and that only a few would eventually do so. In 1972 Wayne C. Booth pointed to cuts in government funding and the clamor for accountability in education as being behind the calls for getting rid of freshman English, the course most likely to be demonstrated a failure "by the crude tests of the accountability folk" ("Meeting of Minds" 242). Booth lamented that the English department was prepared to make this sacrificial offering in the hope that it would leave literature teachers unscathed, free to pursue their special areas of interest in the classroom.

The value of these predictions was tested in Ron Smith's essay "The Composition Requirement Today: A Report on a Nationwide Survey of Four-Year Colleges and Universities," published in 1973—interestingly enough, the year that marked the one-hundredth anniversary of the first appearance of freshman English at Harvard. Smith contrasted his findings with those of Wilcox's earlier study. Wilcox had reported that in 1967, 93.2% of the freshmen at the schools surveyed were required to take at least one term of English and 77.8% were required to take two terms. In 1973, however, only 76% of the schools surveyed had at least a one-course composition requirement, only 45% had a requirement of two or more courses, and 24% had no requirement at all. It is important to note that there was a marked contrast between private and state schools: Smith found that although 31% of private schools had no composition requirement at all, only 11% of state schools fell into this category; furthermore, at many of the schools that had no required course, students chose the freshman writing class as an elective. Still, there was no denying that fewer students than in 1967 were required to enroll in freshman writing courses. In addition, Smith discovered that 41% of the state schools in his survey were experiencing pressures to reduce the requirement, and that over half of these (56%) required two or more courses. (He also found that 2% of the state schools were under pressure to reinstate or increase the requirement.) The major alternative method of satisfying the freshman requirement was through exemption credit, with 68% of all schools exempting at least some students (leaving only 8% of the total sample that did not, it should be noted). Smith concluded, "More and more students are being exempted at the fewer and fewer schools where there are composition requirements" (143). On the other hand, "the higher the percentage of students exempted at schools, the likelier it is that the entrance requirements at those schools are high" (144). Exemption criteria included Advanced Placement scores, SAT and ACT scores, College Level Examination Program (CLEP) scores, and the results of departmentally administered exams.

Smith concluded his report with a look at the future. He predicted a continuing decline of the freshman composition course: "All signs point to more schools dropping the composition requirement, more diminishing the one that exists, and more taking advantage of what will probably soon be better equivalency examinations" (148). He pointed to tighter budgets, the difficulty of proving the worth of the course with hard figures, the example of schools that had reduced the requirement without adverse effects (especially appealing to schools that had to compete for money and/or students), and the rigidity of required courses in a curriculum that was becoming more student-centered.

Smith's prognosis, like all other predictions of the demise of the freshman writing course, proved to be inaccurate. In the December 8, 1975, issue of *Newsweek*, one of the earliest of the "Why Johnny Can't Write" articles deplored the writing deficiencies of high school graduates and questioned the response of colleges to this problem. Shortly thereafter, colleges that had recently abolished or diminished the freshman writing requirement began to reinstate it. And this was not simply a response to the heavily publicized declines in SAT and ACT scores among entering students. As Lester Faigley and Thomas P. Miller have recently pointed out, changes in the economy during the seventies served to increase the amount of writing required of college graduates, so that the "literacy crisis" that *Newsweek* and other popular periodicals were discussing was inevitable. "It is no coincidence," they explain, "that the 'literacy crisis' occurred at a time when many colleges and universities were reducing or abolishing their writing programs while the jobs that their graduates were entering increasingly required more writing" (569). Since the mid-seventies, English departments everywhere have responded to the call for more and better writing instruction. Moreover, specialists to teach these courses and to train prospective college teachers in conducting them are now available—the growth in graduate departments in rhetoric having been one of the responses to the demand for better writing. Today the freshman writing course remains an essential element in the education of the majority of college students, and the graduate training and research effort given to rhetoric—history, theory, and practice—is greater than ever before.

Rhetoric underwent a renaissance after World War II that has reached full flower in the years since 1975. Signs of this are everywhere. Graduate programs in rhetoric, as already mentioned, began to appear in the seventies and continue to proliferate, with some of the most prestigious English departments in the country providing a place for them. New scholarly journals have emerged to deal with the growing interest in the history and theory of rhetoric as well as in classroom activities—pedagogy having been since the time of ancient Greece an essential feature of rhetorical considerations. These journals include the highly theoretical *PRE/TEXT* as well as the highly practical *Journal of Basic Writing*, both of which have found a ready audience among writing teachers as well as among many literature teachers. (For an overview of these journals, see Connors, "Review: Journals in Composition"). Most important, the mushrooming of research in rhetoric has continued, and I would like to close this study with a brief overview of this work.

I should at the start mention that the taxonomy I have used in discussing rhetoric and writing up to 1975 does not prove as descriptive after this date. The most important reason for this has been the tendency of certain rhetorics within the subjective and transactional categories to move in the direction of the epistemic, regarding rhetoric as principally a method of discovering and even creating knowledge, frequently within socially defined discourse communities. Behind this has been what Fredric Jameson has characterized as "the discovery of the primacy of Language or the Symbolic" (186). Rhetoricians of all stripes have become involved in the discussions encouraged by poststructuralist literary and cultural criticism, by Marxist and other sociologistic speculations on culture, and, especially, by the reawakening of philosophical pragmatism as led by Richard Rorty. All of these share to some extent an emphasis on the social nature of knowledge, locating language at the center of the formation of discourse communities which in turn define the self, the other, the material world, and the possible relations among these. As I have suggested elsewhere, thinkers as diverse as Alfred North Whitehead, Susanne Langer, Michael Polanyi, Thomas Kuhn, Hayden White, Michel Foucault, and Rorty have put forth the notion that the elements traditionally considered the central concerns of rhetoric—reality, interlocutor, audience, and language—are the very elements that are involved in the formation of knowledge (Berlin, "Contemporary Composition"). To these theorists I would add the names of Jameson, Roland Barthes, Raymond Williams, Terry Eagleton, Edward Said, and Frank Lentricchia. Rhetoricians operating from a variety of perspectives have appropriately turned to these figures and others like them in discussing their enterprise, and in so doing have underscored the epistemic nature of rhetoric.

In considering the developments in the various categories of subjective and transactional rhetoric since 1975, I will mention both those that fall within the boundaries that I earlier established for each group and those that have passed beyond these boundaries. I should emphasize that I am not suggesting that these new developments have led to an inevitable collapse of all schools into the epistemic camp. I am simply saying that certain rhetorics, in the way they have begun to consider the symbolic and social context of discourse, have introduced elements ordinarily associated with epistemic rhetoric.

Expressionistic rhetoric continues to be a vital force in English departments, although its more extreme manifestations have vanished. The work of Peter Elbow, Ken Macrorie, Donald Murray, William Coles, and Walker Gibson still attracts a wide hearing. And as I indicated in the previous chapter, there have also been efforts to characterize certain branches of this rhetoric as epistemic. Kenneth Dowst uses the term *epistemic* in aligning himself with Coles, Gibson, Theodore Baird, and David Bartholomae. Calling on such figures as Langer, Wittgenstein, I. A. Richards, L. S. Vygotsky, A. R. Luria and Jerome Bruner (who recently has himself begun to see language as constitutive of reality), Dowst looks upon certain uses of language as epistemic, forming as well as expressing knowledge. However, these uses are still primarily involved in shaping private rather than social versions of knowledge, and are distinct from a rhetoric that serves nonepistemic functions—in persuasive or expository writing, for example. Bartholomae—whose earlier work (on error analysis, for example) seemed more closely related to cognitivist approaches but can as easily be treated here—has recently moved firmly into the ranks of the epistemic category, calling on the discussions of discourse communities in Foucault and on the cultural analysis of Said, as well as on the rhetorical speculations of Kenneth Burke and Patricia Bizzell. C. H. Knoblauch and Lil Brannon have also used the term *epistemic* in describing the rhetoric they are constructing, a rhetoric that invokes Jacques Derrida as well as Foucault, Langer, and Cassirer. However, their position, in both theory and practice, conceives composing in personal terms, as the expression of an isolated self attempting to come to grips with an alien and recalcitrant world. This view accordingly denies the social nature of language and experience and has students respond to external conflicts through such activities as keeping a journal and writing personal essays, rather than by engaging in public discourse to affect the social and political context of their behavior.

Classical rhetoric is also still alive and well in the English department and has recently taken a number of new directions. S. Michael Halloran has called for a rhetoric of public discourse based on a Ciceronian model—a rhetoric of citizenship like the one dominant in American colleges just prior to the Revolutionary War. Still another revival of classical rhetoric has appeared in response to the reinterpretation of Aristotle found in William Grimaldi's *Studies in the Philosophy of Aristotle's Rhetoric*. The approach is seen in a number of pieces appearing in *Essays on Classical Rhetoric and Modern Discourse*, edited by Robert Connors, Lise Ede, and Andrea Lunsford. The selections by Ede and Lunsford, by James Kinneavy, and by John Gage are avowedly concerned with epistemological issues, and each in its own way argues for the centrality of invention in Aristotle—taking positions which move in the direction of considering his rhetoric to be, in a certain limited sense, epistemic. From these points of view, Aristotelian rhetoric is not primarily rational and deductive—as it had been interpreted in the fifties, for example—but is a system that provides heuristics encouraging the discovery of knowledge in the probabilistic realm of law, politics, and public occasions, discoveries that include the emotional, the ethical, and the aesthetic as well as the rational. In this scheme, while knowledge may not be a social construct, it is discovered through social behavior.

Cognitive approaches have perhaps been the most prolific during the past ten years. These include the work of several people already mentioned—Janice Lauer, Richard Larson, James Moffett, and James Britton, for example—as well as a number of new investigators. The examination of the behavior of writers while composing has been one recent development, appearing in the research of Linda Flower and John Hayes, Sondra Perl, Nancy Sommers, Sharon Pianko, Lillian Bridwell, and Ann Matsuhashi. Another has been the examination of texts that writers produce in order to locate in them demonstrations of the cognitive processes that were involved in their generation—as in work by Lester Faigley and Stephen Witte, Joseph Williams, E. D. Hirsch, Anne Ruggles Gere, Robin Bell Markels, Lee Odell, Charles Cooper, Glenn Broadhead, and the team of Donald Daiker, Andrew Kerek, and Max Morenberg. Theories of cognitive development have also been used in describing composing in the efforts of Lunsford, Mina Shaughnessy, Loren Barritt and Barry Kroll, and Mike Rose. The considerable work in computers and composing also belongs in this category, with contributors too numerous to mention here, although the 1984 monograph on the subject by Jeanne W. Halpern and Sarah Liggett is a good initial overview of these developments.

Those applying cognitive strategies to writing behavior have also broadened the theoretical base of their study, some including a new interest in the social influence of learning and others expanding the range of psychological premises on which they rely. Ede and Lunsford have collaborated in presenting essays on the role of audience in composing as well as on the nature of collaborative writing, the latter invoking Foucault and Barthes in some of its claims, and both emphasizing the social nature of knowledge. Kroll and Joseph Williams have also expanded their cognitive approaches to provide for the social. Faigley has recently presented an essay entitled "Nonacademic Writing: The Social Perspective" that includes references to Barthes, Stanley Fish, Clifford Geertz, and Raymond Williams. Faigley has also collaborated with Roger Cherry, David Jolliffe, and Anna Skinner in *Assessing Writers' Knowledge and Processes of*

Composing, a work that considers three conceptions of the composing process—the literary-expressionist, the cognitive, and the social, the last emphasizing the role of language and discourse communities in forming knowledge. Broadhead and Richard Freed have combined cognitivist approaches and a concern for the constraints imposed by the discourse community in a study of writing within a business setting. Frank D'Angelo, who continues to break new ground with his phenomenological—rather than empirical—approach to the field, recently presented one essay on a Freudian semiological analysis of advertising and another on the relation of Freudian and Piagetian cognitive structures to the master tropes. Finally, the "process approach" to writing instruction has been most influenced by cognitive psychology, and its expansion to allow a place for the social in shaping knowledge and learning can be seen in Maxine Hairston's "The Winds of Change: Thomas Kuhn and the Revolution in the Teaching of Writing."

Rhetorics displaying the epistemic features described in chapter 7 continue to attract proponents. Berthoff and Winterowd have offered sustained leadership in this area, and a number of other studies have expanded the discussion of this rhetoric. Booth's *Modern Dogma and the Rhetoric of Assent*, a theoretical statement of this position, is strongly indebted to American pragmatism as well as to Kenneth Burke and Richard McKeon. Chaim Perelman and L. Olbrechts-Tyteca—whom Michael Leff has described as displaying epistemic features—have, on the other hand, called for a reinterpretation of Aristotle in positing a rhetoric of discovery. Further applications of their method, showing argumentative strategies in the process of structuring knowledge, are found in Charles Kneupper, Jeanne Fahnestock, and Marie Secor. Richard Lanham calls for the sophistic tradition to be placed in dialectical relation to the Platonic, proposing a rhetoric in which at least part of the time "words determine thought" (140). Donald Stewart also calls upon Plato, as well as Fred Newton Scott's interpretation of Plato, to make a plea for ethical considerations at a time when language is regarded as shaping reality. Kinneavy in two recent essays traces the hermeneutic tradition that regards meaning as dependent upon situation and context from the sophists through Socrates, Plato, Aristotle, Cicero, and Quintilian, and on up to more recent hermeneutic speculation. Kinneavy's argument is that rhetoric is involved in discovering and shaping knowledge because of its role in assessing the relevant situational context of meaning.

Janet Emig's recent efforts, especially on research paradigms and on writing as a way of knowing, further demonstrate the role of discourse communities in forming meaning. Robert Scholes has also discussed the effects of discursive formations in determining knowledge, calling upon Foucault for his ruling concepts, an effort in which he was preceded by James Porter. Kenneth Bruffee has recently offered a theoretical statement of his collaborative rhetoric, which is grounded in the pragmatism of Richard Rorty. Patricia Bizzell has likewise offered numerous statements on the role of rhetoric in structuring knowledge, calling on Rorty as well as such diverse figures as Thomas Kuhn and Terry Eagleton, probing—as I have here and elsewhere—into the ideological as well as the epistemological implications of rhetoric. The best work in writing across the disciplines has also investigated the ways in which the rhetorical behavior of academic disciplines shapes the nature of knowledge within the separate provinces. Carolyn Miller, Charles Bazerman, and Greg Myers have each in different ways examined the social nature of discourse in science—Myers calling upon Marxist conceptions in his analysis. In another area, George Dillon in *Constructing Texts: Elements of a Theory of Composition and Style* invokes psycholinguistic, deconstructionist, and reader-response theories to show how reading and writing conventions are influenced by discourse communities, and Sharon Crowley has in a similar fashion dealt with the uses of deconstruction in the writing classroom. Joseph Comprone has recently applied the thinking of Barthes in considering the art of composing, asking for a process "poised between lock-step exercise and uncontextualized free writing" (231)—a range of activities based on the complex "array of structural codes" (230) that constitutes language. Finally, Richard Ohmann has continued to explain the implications of his epistemic rhetoric for the writing course; and Ira Shor in *Critical Teaching and Everyday Life*, calling in part on Paulo Freire, has proceeded along the same lines as Ohmann—creating, however, his own theoretical and practical statement.

Writing instruction has been dramatically transformed in the past twenty-five years—a transformation that is salutary and ongoing. We have begun to see that writing courses are not designed exclusively to prepare students for the workplace, although they certainly must do that. Writing courses prepare students for citizenship in a democracy, for assuming their political responsibilities, whether as leaders or simply as active participants. Writing courses also enable students to learn something about themselves, about the often-unstated assumptions on which their lives are built. In short, the writing course empowers students as it advises in ways to experience themselves, others, and the material conditions of their existence—in methods of ordering and making sense of these relationships. It is encouraging to report that it is once again receiving the attention it deserves.

Works Cited

Alden, Raymond Macdonald. "Preparation for College English Teaching." *EJ* 2 (1913):344–56.

Allen, Harold B. "Linguistic Research Needed in Composition and Communication." *CCC* 5 (1954):55–60.

———. "A Reply on Pluralism." *CE* 23 (1962):20–22.

Allport, Floyd H., Lynette Walker, and Eleanor Lathers. *Written Composition and Characteristics of Personality.* No. 173, *Archives of Psychology.* New York: Columbia U, n.d.

Applebee, Arthur N. *Tradition and Reform in the Teaching of English: A History.* Urbana: NCTE, 1974.

Armstrong, Edward C. "Taking Counsel with Candide." Proceedings for 1919. *PMLA* 35 (1920):xxiv–xliii.

Arnold, Aerol. "The Limits of Communication." *CCC* 11 (1960):12–16.

Aydelotte, Frank. "The Correlation of English Literature and Composition in the College Course." *EJ* 3 (1914):568–74.

Babbitt, Irving. *Literature and the American College: Essays in Defense of the Humanities.* Boston: Houghton, 1908.

———. *Rousseau and Romanticism.* Boston: Houghton, 1919.

Bailey, Dudley. "A Plea for a Modern Set of Topoi." *CE* 26 (1964):111–17.

Baker, William D. "Film as Sharpener of Perception." *CCC* 15 (1964): 44–45.

Baldwin, Charles Sears. *Ancient Rhetoric and Poetic.* New York: Macmillan, 1924.

———. *College Composition.* New York: Longmans, Green, 1917.

Banks, James A. "A Profile of the Black American: Implications for Teaching." *CCC* 19 (1968):288–96.

Barnes, Walter. "American Youth and Their Language." *EJ* coll. ed. 26 (1937):283–90.

Barritt, Loren, and Barry Kroll. "Some Implications of Cognitive-Developmental Psychology for Research in Composing." *Research on Composing: Points of Departure.* Ed. Charles R. Cooper and Lee Odell. Urbana: NCTE, 1978.

Bartholomae, David. "Inventing the University." *When a Writer Can't Write: Research on Writer's Block and Other Writing Process Problems.* Ed. Mike Rose. New York: Guilford, 1986.

———. "The Study of Error." *CCC* 31 (1980):253–69.

The Basic Issues in the Teaching of English. Supplement to *CE* 21 (1959).

Bateman, Donald R., and Frank J. Zidonis. *The Effect of a Study of Transformational Grammar on the Writing of Ninth and Tenth Graders.* Research Report no. 6. Champaign: NCTE, 1966.

Baugh, Albert C., Paul Kitchen, and Matthew W. Black. *Writing by Types: A Manual of Composition for College Students.* New York: Century, 1924.

Bazerman, Charles. "Scientific Writing as a Social Act: A Review of the Literature of the Sociology of Science." *New Essays in Technical Writing and Communication: Research, Theory, and Practice.* Ed. P. V. Anderson, R. J. Brockman, and C. Miller. Farmingdale: Baywood, 1983.

———. "What Written Knowledge Does: Three Examples of Academic Discourse." *Philosophy of the Social Sciences* 11 (1981):361–87.

Beck, E. C. "Composition-Teaching in a State Teachers College." *EJ* coll. ed. 18 (1929):593–97.

Bennett, C. Ralph. "Where There Is Life." *EJ* 15 (1926):758–64.

Bercovitch, Sacvan. "The Rites of Assent: Rhetoric, Ritual, and the Ideology of American Consensus." *The American Self: Myth, Ideology, and Popular Culture.* Ed. Sam Girgus. Albuquerque: U of New Mexico P, 1981.

Berlin, James A. "Contemporary Composition: The Major Pedagogical Theories." *CE* 44 (1982):765–77.

———. "Rhetoric and Literacy in American Colleges." *Oldspeak/Newspeak: Rhetorical Transformations.* Ed. Charles W. Kneupper. Arlington: Rhetoric Society of America, 1985.

———. "Rhetoric and Poetics in the English Department: Our Nineteenth-Century Inheritance." *CE* 47 (1985):521–33.

———. *Writing Instruction in Nineteenth-Century American Colleges.* Carbondale: Southern Illinois UP, 1984.

Berlin, James A., and Robert P. Inkster. "Current-Traditional Rhetoric: Paradigm and Practice." *Freshman English News* 8 (1980):1–4, 13–14.

Berthoff, Ann E. "From Problem-solving to a Theory of Imagination." *CE* 33 (1972):636–49.

———. *The Making of Meaning*. Upper Montclair: Boynton/Cook, 1981.

———. "The Problem of Problem Solving." *CCC* 22 (1971):237–42.

Bildersee, Adele. *Imaginative Writing*. Boston: Heath, 1927.

Bilsky, Manuel, McCrea Hazlett, Robert E. Streeter, and Richard M. Weaver. "Looking for an Argument." *CE* 14 (1952):210–16.

Bird, Nancy Kenney. "The Conference on College Composition and Communication: A Historical Study of Its Continuing Education and Professionalization." Diss. Virginia Polytechnic Institute and State U, 1977.

Bizzell, Patricia. "Cognition, Convention, and Certainty: What We Need to Know about Writing." *PRE/TEXT* 3 (1982):213–43.

———. "College Composition: Initiation into the Academic Discourse Community." *Curriculum Inquiry* 12 (1982):191–207.

———. "The Ethos of Academic Discourse." *CCC* 29 (1978):351–55.

———. "Thomas Kuhn, Scientism, and English Studies." *CE* 40 (1979):764–71.

———. "William Perry and Liberal Education." *CE* 46 (1984):447–54.

Bizzell, Patricia, and B. Herzberg. "'Inherent' Ideology, 'Universal' History, 'Empirical' Evidence in 'Context Free' Writing: Some Problems with E. D. Hirsch's *The Philosophy of Composition*." *Modern Language Notes* 95 (1980):1181–1202.

Blair, Hugh. *Lectures on Rhetoric and Belles Lettres*. Ed. Harold F. Harding. Carbondale: Southern Illinois UP, 1965.

Blanchard, Margaret. "Composition, Literature, and Interior Power." *CCC* 15 (1964):20–23.

Bledstein, Burton J. *The Culture of Professionalism: The Middle Class and the Development of Higher Education in America*. New York: Norton, 1976.

Bloom, Lynn Z., and Martin Bloom. "The Teaching and Learning of Argumentative Writing." *CE* 29 (1967):128–35.

Blumenthal, Joseph C. *English 2600*. New York: Harcourt, 1960.

Booth, Wayne C. "The Meeting of Minds." *CCC* 23 (1972):242–50.

———. *Modern Dogma and the Rhetoric of Assent*. Notre Dame: U of Notre Dame P, 1974.

————. "The Revival of Rhetoric." *PMLA* 80, pt. 2 (1965):8–12.

Bower, Warren. "All Aboard the Omnibus." *EJ* coll. ed. 27 (1938):841–51.

Bowersox, Herman C. "The Idea of the Freshman Composition Course—A Polemical Discussion." *CCC* 6 (1955):38–44.

Bowles, Samuel, and Herbert Gintis. *Schooling in Capitalist America.* New York: Basic, 1976.

Boynton, Percy H. "Sorting College Freshmen." *EJ* 2 (1913):73–80.

Braddock, Richard, Richard Lloyd-Jones, and Lowel Schoer. *Research in Written Composition.* Urbana: NCTE, 1963.

Brereton, John C. "Sterling Andrus Leonard." *Traditions of Inquiry.* Ed. John C. Brereton. New York: Oxford UP, 1985.

Bridwell, Lillian S. "Revising Strategies in Twelfth Grade Students' Transactional Writing." *Research in the Teaching of English* 14 (1980): 197–222.

Britton, James. *Language and Learning.* Coral Gables: U of Miami P, 1970.

Britton, James, et al. *The Development of Writing Abilities (11–18).* London: Macmillan, 1975.

Broadhead, Glenn, James A. Berlin, and Marlis M. Broadhead. "Sentence Structure in Academic Prose and Its Implications for College Writing Teachers." *Research in the Teaching of English* 16 (1982):225–40.

Broadhead, Glenn, and Richard Freed. *The Variables of Composition: Process and Product in a Business Setting.* Carbondale: Southern Illinois UP, 1986.

Brooks, Cleanth, and Robert Penn Warren. *Modern Rhetoric.* New York: Harcourt, 1949.

————. *Understanding Poetry: An Anthology for College Students.* New York: Holt, 1938.

Bruffee, Kenneth A. "Collaborative Learning and the 'Conversation of Mankind.'" *CE* 46 (1984):635–52.

————. "Collaborative Learning: Some Practical Models." *CE* 34 (1973): 634–43.

————. *A Short Course in Writing.* Boston: Little, Brown, 1985.

————. "The Way Out." *CE* 33 (1972):457–70.

Bruner, Jerome S. *On Knowing: Essays for the Left Hand.* Cambridge: Belknap-Harvard UP, 1962.

————. *The Process of Education.* Cambridge: Harvard UP, 1960.

———. *Toward a Theory of Instruction*. Cambridge: Belknap-Harvard UP, 1966.

Bruner, Jerome S., Jacqueline L. Goodnow, and George A. Austin. *A Study of Thinking*. New York: Wiley, 1956.

Buckley, Jerome H., and Paul L. Wiley. "The Technique of the Round Table in College Composition." *CE* 6 (1945): 411–12.

Burke, Kenneth. *Language as Symbolic Action*. Berkeley: U of California P, 1966.

———. "Rhetoric, Poetics, and Philosophy." *Rhetoric, Philosophy, and Literature: An Exploration*. Ed. Don M. Burks. West Lafayette: Purdue UP, 1978.

Burke, Rebecca. *Gertrude Buck's Rhetorical Theory*. Occasional Papers in Composition History and Theory, no. 1. Ed. Donald C. Stewart. Manhattan: Dept. of English, Kansas State U, n.d.

Burke, Virginia M. "The Composition-Rhetoric Pyramid." *CCC* 16 (1965): 3–6.

Cairns, William B. *A History of American Literature*. New York: Oxford UP, 1912.

Callahan, Raymond E. *Education and the Cult of Efficiency*. Chicago: U of Chicago P, 1962.

Campbell, George. *The Philosophy of Rhetoric*. Ed. Lloyd F. Bitzer. Carbondale: Southern Illinois UP, 1963.

Campbell, Oscar James. "The Failure of Freshman English." *EJ* coll. ed. 28 (1939): 177–85.

Chalfant, James M. "The Investigative Theme—A Project for Freshman Composition." *EJ* coll. ed. 19 (1930): 41–46.

Childs, Herbert Ellsworth. "Motivating Freshman Composition." *EJ* coll. ed. 26 (1937): 232–37.

Christensen, Francis. "A Generative Rhetoric of the Paragraph." *CCC* 16 (1965): 144–56.

———. "A Generative Rhetoric of the Sentence." *CCC* 14 (1963): 155–61.

———. "Notes toward a New Rhetoric: I. Sentence Openers; II. A Lesson from Hemingway." *CE* 25 (1963): 7–18.

Clark, J. D. "A Four-Year Study of Freshman English." *EJ* coll. ed. 24 (1935): 403–10.

Coles, William E., Jr. "The Sense of Nonsense as a Design for Sequential Writing Assignments." *CCC* 21 (1970): 27–34.

———. "An Unpetty Pace." *CCC* 23 (1972):378–82.

Commission on English. *Freedom and Discipline in English*. New York: College Entrance Examination Board, 1965.

Comprone, Joseph J. "Syntactic Play and Composing Theory: What Sentence Combining Has Done for Teachers of Writing." *Sentence Combining: A Rhetorical Perspective*. Ed. Donald A. Daiker, Andrew Kerek, and Max Morenberg. Carbondale: Southern Illinois UP, 1985.

Congleton, J. E. "Historical Development of the Concept of Rhetorical Proprieties." *CCC* 5 (1954):140–49.

Connors, Robert J. "Review: Journals in Composition Studies." *CE* 46 (1984):348–65.

———. Rev. of *Writing Instruction in Nineteenth-Century American Colleges*, by James A. Berlin. *CCC* 37 (1986):247–49.

———. "The Rhetoric of Explanation: Explanatory Rhetoric from 1850 to the Present." *Written Communication* 2 (1985):49–72.

———. "The Rise of Technical Writing Instruction in America." *Journal of Technical Writing and Communication* 12 (1982):329–52.

Connors, Robert J., Lisa S. Ede, and Andrea Lunsford, eds. *Essays on Classical Rhetoric and Modern Discourse*. Carbondale: Southern Illinois UP, 1984.

Coon, Arthur M. "An Economic X Marks the Spot." *CE* 9 (1947):25–31.

———. "The Freshman English Situation at Utopia College." *CE* 5 (1943): 282–84.

Cooper, Charles R. "Holistic Evaluation of Writing." *Evaluating Writing: Describing, Measuring, Judging*. Ed. Charles R. Cooper and Lee Odell. Urbana: NCTE, 1977.

Cooper, Charles R., et al. "Studying the Writing Abilities of a University Freshman Class: Strategies from a Case Study." *New Directions in Composition Research*. Ed. Richard Beach and Lillian S. Bridwell. New York: Guilford, 1984.

Cooper, Lane. "The Correction of Papers." *EJ* 3 (1914):290–98.

Corbett, Edward P. J. *Classical Rhetoric for the Modern Student*. New York: Oxford UP, 1965.

———. "Hugh Blair as an Analyzer of English Prose Style." *CCC* 9 (1958): 98–103.

———. "The Rhetoric of the Open Hand and the Rhetoric of the Closed Fist." *CCC* 20 (1969):288–96.

———. "The Usefulness of Classical Rhetoric." *CCC* 14 (1963): 162–64.

———. "What Is Being Revived?" *CCC* 18 (1967): 166–72.

Corder, Jim W. "On the Way, Perhaps, to a New Rhetoric, but Not There Yet, and If We Do Get There, There Won't Be There Anymore." *CE* 47 (1985): 162–70.

Corson, Hiram. *The Aims of Literary Study.* New York: Macmillan, 1895.

Crane, R. S., ed. *Critics and Criticism, Ancient and Modern.* Chicago: U of Chicago P, 1952.

———. "Criticism as Inquiry; or, The Perils of the High Priori Road." *The Idea of the Humanities and Other Essays.* Chicago: U of Chicago P, 1967.

Creek, Herbert L. "Forty Years of Composition Teaching." *CCC* 6 (1955): 4–10.

Cremin, Lawrence. *The Transformation of the School: Progressivism in American Education, 1876–1957.* New York: Vintage, 1961.

Crowley, Sharon. "On Post-Structuralism and Compositionists." *PRE/TEXT* 5 (1984): 185–95.

Currier, Raymond P. "Facts or Attitudes? A Survey of the English Courses in 109 Colleges." *EJ* coll. ed. 18 (1929): 841–49.

Cushman, Robert Earl. *Therapeia: Plato's Conception of Philosophy.* Chapel Hill: U of North Carolina P, 1958.

Cutler, Ronald. "The Autobiography as Creative Writing." *CCC* 9 (1958): 38–42.

Dabbs, J. McBride. "Freshman Special." *EJ* coll. ed. 21 (1932): 743–50.

Daiker, Donald A., Andrew Kerek, and Max Morenberg, eds. *Sentence Combining: A Rhetorical Perspective.* Carbondale: Southern Illinois UP, 1985.

———. "Sentence Combining and Syntactic Maturity in Freshman English." *CCC* 29 (1978): 36–41.

D'Angelo, Frank J. *A Conceptual Theory of Rhetoric.* Cambridge: Winthrop, 1975.

———. "Rhetoric and Cognition: Toward a Metatheory of Discourse." *PRE/TEXT* 3 (1982): 105–19.

———. "Subliminal Seduction: An Essay on the Rhetoric of the Unconscious." *Rhetoric Review* 4 (1986): 160–72.

Davidson, Levette J., and Frederick Sorensen. "The Basic Communications Course." *CE* 8 (1946): 83–86.

Davis, H. W. "Mastering Principles of Composition." *EJ* coll. ed. 19 (1930): 795–803.

Deemer, Charles. "English Composition as a Happening." *CE* 29 (1967): 121–26.

Denney, Joseph Villiers. "Preparation of College Teachers of English." *EJ* 7 (1918): 322–26.

————. *Two Problems in Composition-Teaching.* Contributions to Rhetorical Theory 3. Ed. Fred Newton Scott. Ann Arbor: n.p., n.d.

Dillon, George L. *Constructing Texts: Elements of a Theory of Composition and Style.* Bloomington: Indiana UP, 1981.

Dixon, John. *Growth through English: A Report Based on the Dartmouth Seminar 1966.* Reading, England: National Association for the Teaching of English. 1967.

Dowst, Kenneth. "Cognition and Composition." *Freshman English News* 11 (1983): 1–4, 11–14.

————. "The Epistemic Approach: Writing, Knowing, and Learning." *Eight Approaches to Teaching Composition.* Ed. Timothy Donovan and Ben W. McClelland. Urbana: NCTE, 1980.

————. "An Epistemic View of Sentence Combining: Practice and Theories." *Sentence Combining: A Rhetorical Perspective.* Ed. Donald A. Daiker, Andrew Kerek, and Max Morenberg. Carbondale: Southern Illinois UP, 1985.

Dykema, Karl W. "An Experiment in Freshman English." *EJ* coll. ed. 25. (1936): 762–64.

Earle, Samuel Chandler. "The Organization of Instruction in English Composition." *EJ* 2 (1913): 477–87.

Eble, Kenneth. "The Freshman Composition Course Should Teach Writing." *CE* 17 (1955): 475–77.

Ede, Lisa, and Andrea Lunsford. "Audience Addressed/Audience Invoked: The Role of Audience in Composition Theory and Pedagogy." *CCC* 35 (1984): 155–71.

————. "Why Write . . . Together?" *Rhetoric Review* 1 (1983): 150–57.

Ehninger, Douglas. "On Systems of Rhetoric." *The Rhetoric of Western Thought.* Ed. James L. Golden, Goodwin F. Berquist, and William E. Coleman. Dubuque: Kendall/Hunt, 1976.

Elbow, Peter. "Exploring My Teaching." *CE* 32 (1971): 743–53.

————. "A Method for Teaching Writing." *CE* 30 (1968): 115—25.

————. *Writing without Teachers.* New York: Oxford UP, 1973.

Emig, Janet. *The Composing Process of Twelfth Graders.* Research Report no. 13. Urbana: NCTE, 1971.

———. *The Web of Meaning: Essays on Writing, Teaching, Learning, and Thinking.* Ed. Dixie Goswami and Maureen Butler. Upper Montclair: Boynton/Cook, 1983.

"English A-1 at Harvard." *EJ* coll. ed. 21 (1932):388–90.

Estrich, Robert M. "And Now the Tailor: Trimming Ideals to Fit the Situation." *CCC* 6 (1955):85–88.

Eurich, Alvin C. "Should English Composition Be Abolished?" *EJ* coll. ed. 21 (1932):211–19.

An Experience Curriculum in English. A Report of the Curriculum Commission of the National Council of Teachers of English. W. Wilbur Hatfield, Chairman. New York: Appleton, 1935.

Fahnestock, Jeanne, and Marie Secor. "Teaching Argument: A Theory of Types." *CCC* 34 (1983):20–30.

———. "Toward a Modern Theory of Stasis." *Oldspeak/Newspeak: Rhetorical Transformations.* Ed. Charles W. Kneupper. Arlington: Rhetoric Society of America, 1985.

Faigley, Lester. "Nonacademic Writing: The Social Perspective." *Writing in Nonacademic Settings.* Ed. Lee Odell and Dixie Goswami. New York: Guilford, 1986.

Faigley, Lester, et al. *Assessing Writers' Knowledge and Processes of Composing.* Norwood: Ablex, 1985.

Faigley, Lester, and Thomas P. Miller. "What We Learn from Writing on the Job." *CE* 44 (1982):557–69.

Faigley, Lester, and Stephen R. Witte. "Analyzing Revision." *CCC* 32 (1981):400–414.

Farber, Jerry. *The Student as Nigger: Essays and Stories.* North Hollywood: Contact Books, 1969.

Faust, George. "Basic Tenets of Structural Linguistics." *CCC* 4 (1953):122–26.

———. "Something of Morphemics." *CCC* 5 (1954):65–70.

———. "Terms in Phonemics." *CCC* 5 (1954):30–34.

Fisher, John H. "Remembrance and Reflection: *PMLA* 1884–1982." *PMLA* 99 (1984):398–407.

Florescu, Vasile. "Rhetoric and Its Rehabilitation in Contemporary Philosophy." *Philosophy and Rhetoric* 3 (1970):193–224.

Flower, Linda S., and John R. Hayes. "The Cognition of Discovery: Defining a Rhetorical Problem." *CCC* 31 (1980):21–32.

———. "A Cognitive Process Theory of Writing." *CCC* 32 (1981):365–87.

———. "The Pregnant Pause: An Inquiry into the Nature of Planning." *Research in the Teaching of English* 15 (1981):229–44.

———. "Problem-Solving Strategies and the Writing Process." *CE* 39 (1977):449–61.

Foerster, Norman. "The 'Idea Course' for Freshmen." *EJ* 5 (1916):458–66.

Fogarty, Daniel. *Roots for a New Rhetoric.* New York: Columbia U, 1959.

Foucault, Michel. *The Archaeology of Knowledge and The Discourse on Language.* Trans. A. M. Sheridan Smith. New York: Pantheon, 1972.

———. "Nietzsche, Genealogy, History." *Language, Counter-Memory, Practice: Selected Essays and Interviews.* Ed. Donald F. Bouchard. Trans. Donald F. Bouchard and Sherry Simon. Ithaca: Cornell UP, 1977.

Francis, W. Nelson. "Modern Rhetorical Doctrine and Recent Developments in Linguistics." *CCC* 5 (1954):155–61.

French, J. Milton. "The New Curriculum of Harvard, Yale, and Princeton." *CE* 8 (1946):73–82.

"The Freshman English Teacher as Counselor." *CCC* 5 (1954):96–98.

Fries, Charles Carpenter. *American English Grammar: The Grammatical Structure of Present-Day American English with Especial Reference to Social Differences or Class Dialects.* New York: Appleton, 1940.

Gage, John T. "An Adequate Epistemology for Composition: Classical and Modern Perspectives." *Essays on Classical Rhetoric and Modern Discourse.* Ed. Robert J. Connors, Lisa S. Ede, and Andrea A. Lunsford. Carbondale: Southern Illinois UP, 1984.

Geertz, Clifford. *The Interpretation of Cultures.* New York: Basic, 1973.

Genung, John F. *A Study of Rhetoric in the College Course.* Boston: Heath, 1887.

Gerber, John C., ed. *The College Teaching of English.* New York: Appleton, 1965.

Gere, Anne Ruggles. "Insights from the Blind: Composing without Revising." *Revising: New Essays for Teachers of Writing.* Ed. R. A. Sudol. Urbana: NCTE, 1982.

———. "Written Composition: Toward a Theory of Evaluation." *CE* 42 (1980):44–58.

Gibson, Walker. "Composing the World: The Writer as Map-Maker." *CCC* 21 (1970):255–60.

Gilbert, Allan H. "What Shall We Do with Freshman Themes?" *EJ* 11 (1922):392–403.

Gilman, Wilbur E. "The English Language in Its Relation to the Teaching of Composition." *EJ* 16 (1927):15–24.

Glicksburg, Charles I. "In Defense of College Composition." *CE* 12 (1950): 90–98.

Gorrell, Robert M., ed. *Rhetoric: Theories for Application.* Champaign: NCTE, 1967.

———. "Structure in Thought." *CE* 24 (1963):591–98.

———. "The Traditional Course: When Is Old Hat New." *CCC* 23 (1972): 264–70.

———. "Very Like a Whale—A Report on Rhetoric." *CCC* 16 (1965): 138–43.

Graff, Gerald. *Literature against Itself: Literary Ideas in Modern Society.* Chicago: U of Chicago P, 1979.

Greenbaum, Leonard. "The Tradition of Complaint." *CE* 31 (1969): 174–87.

Greenough, Chester Noyes. "An Experiment in the Training of Teachers of Composition for Work with College Freshmen." *EJ* 2 (1913):109–21.

Grimaldi, William M. A. *Studies in the Philosophy of Aristotle's Rhetoric.* Wiesbaden, W. Ger.: Franz Steiner Verlag, 1972.

Guth, Hans P. "The Politics of Rhetoric." *CCC* 23 (1972):30–43.

———. "Rhetoric and the Quest for Certainty." *CE* 24 (1962):131–36.

———. "Two Cheers for Linguistics." *CE* 22 (1961):489–97.

Hackett, Herbert. "Language as Communication: A Frame of Reference." *Etc.: A Review of General Semantics* 11 (1954):290–98.

Hairston, Maxine. "The Winds of Change: Thomas Kuhn and the Revolution in the Teaching of Writing." *CCC* 33 (1982):76–86.

Halloran, S. Michael. "Rhetoric in the American College Curriculum: The Decline of Public Discourse." *PRE/TEXT* 3 (1982):245–69.

Halpern, Jeanne W., and Sarah Liggett. *Computers and Composing.* Carbondale: Southern Illinois UP, 1984.

Hamalian, Leo, and James V. Hatch. "How to Turn the Hip Generation on to Shelley and Keats." *CE* 33 (1971):324–32.

Hanford, James H. "The Future of English Teaching." *EJ* coll. ed. 28 (1939):268–75.

Hart, James Morgan. "The College Course in English Literature: How It

May Be Improved." *Transactions of the Modern Language Association*. 1 (1884–85):44–49.

Hayakawa, S. I. *Language in Action*. New York: Harcourt, 1941.

———. *Language in Thought and Action*. New York: Harcourt, 1949.

———. "Learning to Think and to Write: Semantics in Freshman English." *CCC* 13.1 (1962):5–8.

Hayford, Harrison. "Literature in English A at Northwestern." *CCC* 7 (1956):42–45.

Henry, Ralph L. "Models for Freshman English." *EJ* coll. ed. 20 (1931): 394–99.

Heyda, John. "Captive Audiences: Composition Pedagogy, the Liberal Arts Curriculum, and the Rise of Mass Higher Education." Diss. U of Pittsburgh, 1979.

Hicks, Granville. *The Great Tradition: An Interpretation of American Literature since the Civil War*. New York: Macmillan, 1933.

Hicks, Phillip. "Honors Course in English." *EJ* coll. ed. 18 (1929):230–37.

Hirsch, E. D. *The Philosophy of Composition*. Chicago: U of Chicago P, 1977.

Hoffman, Frederick. *Freudianism and the Literary Mind*. Baton Rouge: Louisiana State UP, 1957.

Hook, J. N. *A Long Way Together: A Personal View of NCTE's First Sixty-seven Years*. Urbana: NCTE, 1979.

Hopkins, Edwin M. "Can Good Composition Teaching Be Done under Present Conditions?" *EJ* 1 (1912):1–8.

Housh, Snow Longley. "Report on Creative Writing in Colleges." *EJ* coll. ed. 20 (1931):672–76.

Hubbell, George Shelton. "A Hireling Prefers to Lecture." *EJ* coll. ed. 19 (1930):820–26.

Hudson, Arthur Palmer. "The Perennial Problem of the Ill-Prepared." *EJ* coll. ed. 27 (1938):723–33.

Hughes, Merritt Y. "Freshman English at the University of Wisconsin." *EJ* coll. ed. 27 (1938):809–17.

Hughes, Richard. "The Contemporaneity of Classical Rhetoric." *CCC* 16 (1965):157–59.

Hughes, Richard, and P. Albert Duhamel. *Rhetoric: Principles and Usage*. Englewood Cliffs: Prentice, 1962.

Hunt, Kellogg W. *Grammatical Structures Written at Three Grade Levels*. Research Report no. 3. Champaign: NCTE, 1965.

———. "Syntactic Maturity in Schoolchildren and Adults." *Monograph of the Society for Research in Child Development.* Serial no. 134, vol. 35, no. 3. 1970.

Huntley, John F. "Programmed Teaching Involves Patience and Love." *CCC* 13.4 (1962):7–15.

Ives, Sumner. "Grammatical Assumptions." *CCC* 5 (1954):149–55.

Jameson, Fredric. "Periodizing the 60s." *The 60s without Apology.* Ed. Sohnya Sayres, Anders Stephonson, Stanley Aronowitz, and Fredric Jameson. Minneapolis: U of Minnesota P, 1984.

Jefferson, Bernard L. "English Literature for the Pre-Professional Student." *EJ* coll. ed. 20 (1931):331–37.

———. "Our First Semester." *EJ* coll. ed. 19 (1930):543–53.

Jefferson, Bernard L., S. E. Glenn, and Royal Gettman. "Freshman Writing: September to February." *EJ* coll. ed. 24 (1935):28–38.

Jennings, E. M. "A Paradigm for Discovery." *CCC* 19 (1968):192–200.

Johnson, Burges, and Helene Hartley. *Written Composition in American Colleges.* Schenectady: Union College, 1936.

Johnson, Edith Christina. "Teaching Values in the Essay." *EJ* coll. ed. 27 (1938):761–66.

Johnson, Oakley Calvin. "Higher Aims for Rhetoric." *EJ* coll. ed. 17 (1928):410–14.

Jones, Llewellyn. "Aesthetics and Contemporary Literature II." *EJ* 14 (1925):665–75.

Kampf, Louis. "Must We Have a Cultural Revolution?" *CCC* 21 (1970):245–49.

Karier, Clarence J. *Man, Society, and Education: A History of American Educational Ideas.* Glenview: Scott, 1967.

Kehl, D. G. "An Argument against Abolishing Freshman English." *CE* 32 (1970):60–65.

Kelly, Lou. "Toward Competence and Creativity in an Open Class." *CE* 34 (1973):644–60.

Kennedy, George A. *Classical Rhetoric and Its Christian and Secular Tradition from Ancient to Modern Times.* Chapel Hill: U of North Carolina P, 1980.

Kinneavy, James L. "The Relation of the Whole to the Part in Interpretation Theory and in the Composing Process." *Visible Language* 17 (1983):120–45.

———. *A Theory of Discourse*. New York: Norton, 1971.

———. "Translating Theory into Practice in Teaching Composition: A Historical View and a Contemporary View." *Essays on Classical Rhetoric and Modern Discourse*. Ed. Robert J. Connors, Lisa S. Ede, and Andrea A. Lunsford. Carbondale: Southern Illinois UP, 1984.

Kitzhaber, Albert R. "Death or Transfiguration?" *CE* 21 (1960):367–73.

———. "4C, Freshman English, and the Future." *CCC* 14 (1963):129–38.

———. "Freshman English: A Prognosis." *CE* 23 (1962):476–83.

———. "New Perspectives on Teaching Composition." *CE* 23 (1962): 440–44.

———. "Rhetoric in American Colleges, 1850–1900." Diss. U of Washington, 1953.

———. *Themes, Theories, and Therapy: Teaching of Writing in College*. New York: McGraw, 1963.

Kneupper, Charles W. "The Tyranny of Logic and the Freedom of Argumentation." *PRE/TEXT* 5 (1984):113–21.

Knoblauch, C. H., and Lil Brannon. *Rhetorical Traditions and the Teaching of Writing*. Upper Montclair: Boynton/Cook, 1984.

Koller, Katherine. "Broadening the Horizon: Cultural Value in Freshman English." *CCC* 6 (1955):82–85.

Kroll, Barry M. "Social-Cognitive Ability and Writing Performance: How Are They Related?" *Written Communication* 2 (1985):293–305.

———. "Writing for Readers: Three Perspectives on Audience." *CCC* 35 (1984):172–85.

Lanham, Richard A. *Literacy and the Survival of Humanism*. New Haven: Yale UP, 1983.

Larson, Richard. "Discovery through Questioning: A Plan for Teaching Rhetorical Invention." *CE* 30 (1968):126–34.

———. "Invention Once More: A Role for Rhetorical Analysis." *CE* 32 (1971):665–72.

———. "Problem-Solving, Composing, and Liberal Education." *CE* 33 (1972):628–35.

Lauer, Janice. "Counterstatement: Response to Ann E. Berthoff." *CCC* 23 (1972):208–10.

———. "Heuristics and Composition." *CCC* 21 (1970):396–404.

Leff, Michael. "In Search of Ariadne's Thread: A Review of the Recent Literature on Rhetorical Theory." *Central States Speech Journal* 29 (1978):73–91.

Leggett, Glenn. "The Large State University." *CCC* 7 (1956):18–21.

———. "What Are Colleges and Universities Doing in Written Composition?" *CE* 23 (1962):40–42.

Leonard, Sterling Andrus. "As to the Forms of Discourse." *EJ* 3 (1914): 201–11.

———. *Current English Usage*. Chicago: Inland, 1932.

———. *The Doctrine of Correctness in English Usage, 1700–1800*. U of Wisconsin Studies in Language and Literature 25. 1929.

———. *English Composition as a Social Problem*. Boston: Houghton, 1917.

———. "Old Purist Junk." *EJ* 7 (1918):295–302.

Lloyd, Donald J. "An English Composition Course Built around Linguistics." *CCC* 4 (1953):40–43.

Long, Ralph. "Grammarians Still Have Funerals." *CCC* 9 (1958):211–16.

Lounsbury, Thomas. "Compulsory Composition in Colleges." *Harper's Monthly Magazine* 123 (1911):866–80.

Lunsford, Andrea A. "Cognitive Development and the Basic Writer." *CE* 41 (1979):38–47.

———. "What We Know—and Don't Know—about Remedial Writing." *CCC* 29 (1978):47–52.

Lunsford, Andrea A., and Lisa S. Ede. "On Distinctions between Classical and Modern Discourse." *Essays on Classical Rhetoric and Modern Discourse*. Ed. Robert J. Connors, Lisa S. Ede, and Andrea A. Lunsford. Carbondale: Southern Illinois UP, 1984.

Lutz, William D. "Making Freshman English a Happening." *CCC* 22 (1971):35–38.

McCloskey, John C. "The Breakdown of Tradition." *EJ* coll. ed. 24 (1935): 116–25.

McDowell, Margaret B. "Honesty in Freshman Rhetoric." *CE* 32 (1971): 673–78.

McGrath, Earl James, ed. *Communications in General Education*. Dubuque: Brown, 1949.

McKee, J. H. "A New Spelling List." *EJ* coll. ed. 19 (1930):652–61.

———. "Portrait of a Department." *EJ* coll. ed. 25 (1936):752–59.

———. "Wherein They Improve: And Who, and When, and Where, and—Perhaps—Why." *EJ* coll. ed. 21 (1932):473–86.

McKeon, Richard. "Rhetoric in the Middle Ages." *Critics and Criticism, Ancient and Modern*. Ed. R. S. Crane. Chicago: U of Chicago P, 1952.

McMillan, James B. "Summary of Nineteenth Century Historical and Comparative Linguistics." *CCC* 5 (1954):145–49.

Macrorie, Ken. "Composition as Art." *CCC* 15 (1964):back cover.

———. *telling writing*. 3d ed. Hasbrouck Heights: Hayden, 1980.

Malmstrom, Jean. "The Communication Course." *CCC* 7 (1956):21–24.

Manly, John M. "New Bottles." Proceedings for 1920. *PMLA* 36 (1921): xlvi–lxx.

Marckwardt, A. H., and Fred G. Walcott. *Facts about Current English Usage*. New York: Appleton, 1938.

Markels, Robin Bell. "Cohesion Paradigms in Paragraphs." *CE* 45 (1983): 450–64.

Martin, Harold. "The Aims of Harvard's General Education A." *CCC* 9 (1958):87–90.

Matsuhashi, Ann. "Pausing and Planning: The Tempo of Written Discourse Production." *Research in the Teaching of English* 15 (1981):113–34.

Mead, W. E. "Report of the Pedagogical Section: Conflicting Ideals in the Teaching of English." Proceedings for 1902. *PMLA* 18 (1903):viii–xxiii.

———. "Report of the Pedagogical Section: The Graduate Study of Rhetoric." Proceedings for 1900. *PMLA* 16 (1901):xix–xxxii.

———. "Report of the Pedagogical Section: The Undergraduate Study of English Composition." Proceedings for 1901. *PMLA* 17 (1902):x–xxiv.

Mellon, John C. *Transformational Sentence-Combining: A Method for Enhancing the Development of Syntactic Fluency in English Composition*. Research Report no. 10. Urbana: NCTE, 1969.

Merriam, Harold G. "Inhibitions, Habits, and the Student's Right of Way." *EJ* 7 (1918):419–27.

Middlebrook, Samuel. "English I in Cellophane." *CE* 9 (1947):140–43.

Miller, Carolyn R. "Genre as Social Action." *Quarterly Journal of Speech* 70 (1984):157–78.

———. "A Humanistic Rationale for Technical Writing." *CE* 40 (1979): 610–17.

Mills, Barriss. "Writing as Process." *CE* 15 (1953):19–26.

Misiaszek, Lorraine. "A Profile of the American Indian: Implications for Teaching." *CCC* 19 (1968):297–99.

Moffett, James. *Teaching the Universe of Discourse*. Boston: Houghton, 1968.

Montgomery, Margaret L. "Communications Work for Freshmen at Talladega College." *CE* 9 (1947):99–103.

Morison, Samuel Eliot. *Three Centuries of Harvard, 1636–1936*. Cambridge: Harvard UP, 1936.

Mulderig, Gerald P. "Gertrude Buck's Rhetorical Theory and Modern Composition Teaching." *Rhetoric Society Quarterly* 14 (1984): 95–104.

Murphy, James J. "The Four Faces of Rhetoric: A Progress Report." *CCC* 17 (1966): 55–59.

———. *Rhetoric in the Middle Ages: A History of Rhetorical Theory from Saint Augustine to the Renaissance*. Berkeley: U of California P, 1974.

Murray, Donald. "Finding Your Own Voice: Teaching Composition in an Age of Dissent." *CCC* 20 (1969): 118–23.

———. "The Interior View: One Writer's Philosophy of Composition." *CCC* 21 (1970): 21–26.

Myers, Greg. "Reality, Consensus, and Reform in the Rhetoric of Composition Teaching." *CE* 48 (1986): 154–74.

———. "The Social Construction of Two Biologists' Proposals." *Written Communication* 2 (1985): 219–45.

Myrick, Kenneth. "College Teaching and Creative Scholarship." *EJ* coll. ed. 28 (1939): 296–306.

"National Council of Teachers of English College Section." *CE* 3 (1942): 584–86.

Nystrand, Martin. "Rhetoric's 'Audience' and Linguistics' 'Speech Community': Implications for Understanding Writing, Reading, and Text." *What Writers Know: The Language, Process, and Structure of Written Discourse*. Ed. Martin Nystrand. New York: Academic, 1982.

"Objectives and Organization of the Composition Course." *CCC* 1.2 (1950): 9–11.

O'Connor, William Van. *An Age of Criticism: 1900–1950*. Chicago: U of Chicago P, 1952.

Odell, Lee. "Defining and Assessing Competence in Writing." *The Nature and Measurement of Competency in English*. Ed. Charles R. Cooper. Urbana: NCTE, 1981.

———. "Piaget, Problem-Solving, and Freshman Composition." *CCC* 24 (1973): 36–42.

O'Donnell, R. C., W. J. Griffin, and R. C. Norris. *Syntax of Kindergarten and Elementary School Children: A Transformational Analysis*. Research Report no. 8. Urbana: NCTE, 1967.

O'Hare, Frank. *Sentence Combining: Improving Student Writing without Formal Grammar Instruction*. Urbana: NCTE, 1973.

Ohmann, Richard. *English in America: A Radical View of the Profession.* New York: Oxford UP, 1976.

———. "In Lieu of a New Rhetoric." *CE* 26 (1964): 17–22.

———. "Reflections on Class and Language." *CE* 44 (1982): 1–17.

Oliver, Kenneth. "The One-Legged, Wingless Bird of Freshman English." *CCC* 1.3 (1950): 3–6.

Ong, Walter. *Rhetoric, Romance, and Technology.* Ithaca: Cornell UP, 1971.

Osgood, Charles G. "Humanism and the Teaching of English." *EJ* 11 (1922): 159–66.

———. "No Set Requirement of English Composition in the Freshman Year." *EJ* 4 (1915): 231–35.

Palmer, Glenn E. "Culture and Efficiency through Composition." *EJ* 1 (1912): 488–92.

Parker, William Riley. "Where Do College English Departments Come From?" *CE* 28 (1967): 339–51.

Parrington, Vernon Louis. *Main Currents in American Thought: An Interpretation of American Literature from the Beginnings to 1920.* New York: Harcourt, 1930.

Pattee, Fred Lewis. *The First Century of American Literature, 1770–1870.* New York: Appleton, 1935.

———. *A History of American Literature since 1870.* New York: Century, 1915.

———. *The New American Literature, 1890–1930.* New York: Century, 1930.

Pattee, George K. "An Unusual Course in Composition." *EJ* 5 (1916): 549–55.

Paull, Michael, and Jack Kligerman. "Invention, Composition, and the Urban College." *CE* 33 (1972): 651–59.

Payne, Robert O. "The Boundaries of Language and Rhetoric: Some Historical Considerations." *CCC* 19 (1968): 109–16.

Payne, William Morton. *English in American Universities.* Boston: Heath, 1895.

Perelman, Chaim, and L. Olbrechts-Tyteca. *The New Rhetoric: A Treatise on Argumentation.* Trans. J. Wilkinson and P. Weaver. Notre Dame: U of Notre Dame P, 1969.

Perl, Sondra. "The Composing Process of Unskilled College Writers." *Research in the Teaching of English* 13 (1979): 317–36.

———. "Understanding Composing." *CCC* 31 (1980): 363–69.

Phelps, William Lyon. *Teaching in School and College.* New York: Macmillan, 1912.

Pianko, Sharon. "A Description of the Composing Processes of College Freshmen Writers." *Research in the Teaching of English* 13 (1979):5–22.

———. "Reflection: A Critical Component of the Composing Process." *CCC* 30 (1979):275–78.

Pike, Kenneth L. "Beyond the Sentence." *CCC* 15 (1964):129–35.

———. "A Linguistic Contribution to Composition." *CCC* 15 (1964): 82–88.

Pooley, Robert C. *Grammar and Usage in Textbooks on English.* U of Wisconsin Bureau of Educational Research Bulletin no. 14. 1933.

Popper, Sir Karl Raimund. *The Open Society and Its Enemies.* Princeton: Princeton UP, 1966.

Porter, Douglas. "The Behavioral Repertoire of Writing." *CCC* 13.3 (1962): 14–17.

Porter, James E. "Reading Presences in Texts: Audience as Discourse Communities." *Oldspeak/Newspeak: Rhetorical Transformations.* Ed. Charles W. Kneupper. Arlington: Rhetoric Society of America, 1985.

———. "This Is Not a Review of Foucault's *This Is Not a Pipe.*" *Rhetoric Review* 4 (1986):210–19.

President's Commission on Higher Education. *Higher Education for American Democracy: A Report.* Washington: GPO, 1947.

Priestley, J. B. "The Approach to Literature: A Series of Brief Papers." *EJ* coll. ed. 18 (1929):365–74.

Pumphrey, Jean. "Teaching English Composition as a Creative Art." *CE* 34 (1973):666–73.

Rathbun, John W., and Harry H. Clark. *American Literary Criticism, 1860–1905.* Vol. 2. Boston: Twayne, 1979.

Reeve, Richard. "A Study in Dreams and Freshman Composition." *EJ* coll. ed. 17 (1928):835–44.

"Report of the Committee on Place and Function of English in American Life." *EJ* 15 (1926):110–34.

"Report of the Committee on the Preparation of College Teachers of English." *EJ* 5 (1916):20–32.

Rice, Warner G. "Internships for Teachers of English at the University of Michigan." *CE* 1 (1939):128–34.

———. "A Proposal for the Abolition of Freshman English, As It Is Now Commonly Taught, from the College Curriculum." *CE* 21 (1960): 361–67.

Ringnalda, Margaret B. "One More Opinion." *EJ* coll. ed. 27 (1938): 678–84.

Rohman, D. Gordon. "My Friend Henry." *CCC* 23 (1972):373–77.

———. "Pre-Writing: The Stages of Discovery in the Writing Process." *CCC* 16 (1965):106–12.

Rohman, D. Gordon, and Albert O. Wlecke. *Pre-Writing: The Construction and Application of Models for Concept Formation in Writing.* U.S. Office of Education Cooperative Research Project no. 2174. East Lansing: Michigan State U, 1964.

Rorty, Richard. *Philosophy and the Mirror of Nature.* Princeton: Princeton UP, 1979.

Rose, Mike. *Writer's Block: The Cognitive Dimension.* Carbondale: Southern Illinois UP, 1984.

Rosenblatt, Louise, Howard Mumford Jones, and Oscar James Campbell. "Statement of the Committee of Twenty-four." *EJ* coll. ed. 28 (1939): 261–67.

Rudolph, Frederick. *The American College and University: A History.* New York: Vintage, 1962.

———. *Curriculum: A History of the American Undergraduate Course of Study Since 1636.* San Francisco: Jossey-Bass, 1977.

Sams, Henry W. "Fields of Research in Rhetoric." *CCC* 5 (1954):60–65.

Scholes, Robert. "Is There a Fish in This Text?" *CE* 46 (1984):653–64.

Scott, Fred Newton. "English Composition as a Mode of Behavior." *EJ* 11 (1922):463–73.

———. "Our Problems." *EJ* 2 (1913):1–10.

———. "Rhetoric Rediviva." Reprinted in *CCC* 31 (1980):413–19.

———. "The Standard of American Speech." *EJ* 6 (1917):1–11.

Scott, Fred Newton, and Joseph Villiers Denney. *Elementary English Composition.* Boston: Allyn and Bacon, 1900.

Scott, Robert L. "On Viewing Rhetoric as Epistemic." *Central States Speech Journal* 18 (1967):9—16.

Secor, Marie. "Perelman's Loci in Literary Argument." *PRE/TEXT* 5 (1984): 97–110.

Seeley, Howard Francis. "Composition as a Liberating Activity." *EJ* coll. ed. 19 (1930):107–17.

Self, Robert T. *Barrett Wendell.* Boston: Twayne, 1975.

Shaughnessy, Mina. *Errors and Expectations: A Guide for the Teacher of Basic Writing.* New York: Oxford UP, 1977.

————. "Two Cheers for the Authoritarian." *CE* 25 (1964):370–73.

Tieje, R. E., et al. "Systematizing Grading in Freshman Composition at the Large University." *EJ* 4 (1915):586–97.

Todorov, Tzvetan. *Symbolism and Interpretation.* Trans. Catherine Porter. Ithaca: Cornell UP, 1982.

————. Theories of the Symbol. Trans. Catherine Porter. Ithaca: Cornell UP, 1982.

Towle, Carroll S. "The Awkward Squad at Yale." *EJ* coll. ed. 18 (1929): 672–77.

Tyler, Moses Coit. *A History of American Literature.* New York: Putnam's, 1879.

————. *A History of American Literature during the Colonial Period, 1607–1765.* New York: Putnam's, 1898.

————. *A Literary History of the American Revolution, 1763–1783.* New York: Putnam's, 1897.

Utley, Francis Lee. "The Boundaries of Language and Rhetoric: The English Curriculum." *CCC* 19 (1968):118–27.

Valesio, Paolo. *Novantiqua: Rhetorics as a Contemporary Theory.* Bloomington: Indiana UP, 1980.

Vance, Earl L. "Integrating Freshmen to Composition." *EJ* coll. ed. 26 (1937):318–23.

Veysey, Laurence R. *The Emergence of the American University.* Chicago: U of Chicago P, 1965.

————. "Stability and Experiment in the American Undergraduate Curriculum." *Content and Context: Essays on College Education.* Ed. Carl Kaysen. New York: McGraw, 1973.

Ward, Frank Earl. "Social Ideals in Freshman English." *EJ* coll. ed. 19 (1930):297–307.

Warfel, Harry R. "Structural Linguistics and Composition." *CE* 20 (1958): 205–13.

Watt, Homer A. "The Philosophy of Real Composition." *EJ* 7 (1918): 153–62.

Weaver, Bennett. "The Reading of Literature." *CE* 1 (1939):30–38.

Weaver, Raymond. "What Is Description?" *EJ* 8 (1919):63–80.

Weaver, Richard M. *Composition: A Course in Writing and Rhetoric.* New York: Holt, 1957.

————. "The *Phaedrus* and the Nature of Rhetoric." *The Province of Rhetoric.* Ed. Joseph Schwartz and John A. Rycenga. New York: Ronald, 1965.

Weimann, Robert. *Structure and Society in Literary History.* Expanded ed. Baltimore: Johns Hopkins UP, 1984.

Wendell, Barrett. *A Literary History of America.* New York: Scribner's, 1901.

Wesenberg, Alice Bidwell. "The American Public: Poet." *EJ* 16 (1927): 212–18.

Whately, Richard. *Elements of Rhetoric.* Ed. Douglas Ehninger. Carbondale: Southern Illinois UP, 1963.

White, Hayden. "Interpretation in History." *Tropics of Discourse: Essays in Cultural Criticism.* Baltimore: Johns Hopkins UP, 1978.

Whitney, Norman. "Ability Grouping at Syracuse." *EJ* 13 (1924): 482–89.

———. "Ability Grouping Plus." *EJ* coll. ed. 17 (1928): 559–65.

Wiebe, Robert H. *The Search for Order, 1877–1920.* New York: Hill and Wang, 1967.

Wiksell, Wesley. "The Communications Program at Stephens College." *CE* 9 (1947): 143–48.

Wilcox, Thomas W. *The Anatomy of College English.* San Francisco: Jossey-Bass, 1973.

Williams, Joseph. "On Defining Complexity." *CE* 40 (1979): 595–609.

———. "The Phenomenology of Error." *CCC* 32 (1981): 152–68.

Williams, Raymond. *Marxism and Literature.* Oxford: Oxford UP, 1977.

Winterowd, W. Ross. *Contemporary Rhetoric: A Conceptual Background with Readings.* New York: Harcourt, 1975.

———. *Rhetoric: A Synthesis.* New York: Holt, 1968.

———. "Topics and Levels in the Composing Process." *CE* 34 (1973): 701–9.

Wise, J. Hooper. "The Comprehensive Freshman English Course—Reading, Speaking and Writing—at the University of Florida." *CCC* 4 (1953): 131–35.

Wolf, H. R. "Composition and Group Dynamics: The Paradox of Freedom." *CE* 30 (1969): 441–44.

Woolley, Edwin C. "Admission to Freshman English at the University." *EJ* 3 (1914): 238–44.

———. *Handbook of Composition.* Boston: Heath, 1907.

Worthington, Katherine Stewart. "The Clasical Loss in Modern Democratic Rhetoric." *EJ* 5 (1916): 525–29.

Wozniak, John Michael. *English Composition in Eastern Colleges, 1850–1940.* Washington: UP of America, 1978.

Wright, Robert L. "Creative Writing in Communication Skills." *CCC* 8 (1957):204–7.

Wykoff, George S. "Army English Experiences Applicable to Civilian, Postwar English." *CE* 6 (1945):338–42.

———. "An Open Letter to the Educational Experts on Teaching Composition." *CE* 1 (1939):140–46.

———. "Teaching Composition as a Career." *CE* 1 (1940):426–37.

Young, Richard E., and Alton L. Becker. "Toward a Modern Theory of Rhetoric." *Contemporary Rhetoric: A Conceptual Background with Readings.* Ed. W. Ross Winterowd. New York: Harcourt, 1975.

Young, Richard E., Alton L. Becker, and Kenneth L. Pike. *Rhetoric: Discovery and Change.* New York: Harcourt, 1970.

Zoellner, Robert. "Behavioral Objectives for English." *CE* 33 (1972): 418–32.

———. "Response: Mentalizing S. R. Rodent." *CE* 31 (1969):215–30.

———. "Talk-Write: A Behavioral Pedagogy for Composition." *CE* 30 (1969):267–320.

Index

James A. Berlin, Director of Freshman English at the University of Cincinnati, received his Ph.D. in 1975 from The University of Michigan. He has published widely on rhetoric and on Victorian literature and is the author of *Writing Instruction in Nineteenth-Century American Colleges*.